YOUR LIFE AND SEX ISLAND

Your life, your economy,
your country;
now and in your future

To Lindsay
Best Real Head.
Ted West

By Ted West

What people? Are saying about:

Your Life and Sex Island

Be warned: the next two pages are parody!

"This inferior tome, standing athwart history, is a dilatory attempt to persuade the reader that our current ruthlessly progressive tax system which confiscates the earnings of the producers, the doers and shakers, is inadequate in that regard. His proposals are so far left as to be beyond socialism. Indeed, they are past radical socialism. So much for rationality and reason! The book should not be read but the cover should be red!"

--MAXWELL FLOGISTON, DHR; SENIOR FELLOW OF THE AMERICAN HERETICS INSTITUTE

"Why would anybody listen to him? He says he's an engineer. An engineer doing satire!? That's a contradiction in terms – a whatchamacallit, one of those oxymoron things. Yeah! He ought to just shut up."

--WILLIAM O'MASIBATTER, FUX NEWS COMMENTATOR

"He blames everything on the "rich", except the good things like our fabulously successful wealth producing free enterprise system. He says illegal immigration would stop if it did not benefit the "rich" by providing low income workers. What a farce!"

--WILLIMNOT MINIPOOPER, UNCOMMONTATER

"His little fantasy of the Life and Sex Island is such an oversimplification of how economic systems work that even Karl Marx could understand it. His attempt in that same overworked chapter to rate the Presidents of the United States based upon 'facts' is scornful; no self-respecting historian would consider mere 'facts' to rate Presidents."

--INA MINIT, THE NEW YORK BRUSSELS SPROUT

"Viciously anti-Catholic; I dare him to say about Muslims what he says about Catholics! Then he wouldn't be civilly burned at the stake; then he would be cruelly suicide-bombed! Then, at the final resurrection, let them just try to find all the tiny little bits."
--ARKBISHOP MOST REFEREND FATHER PEPO DE LA MORMOND, MOST HOLY, MOST BENEVOLENT

"Frivolous... wonderful... mischievous... wicked... unassuming... beyond-comprehension... overwhelming... laugh-an-hour... worth-four-bucks-easily... chocked-with-wisdom... reverence-for-laugh. Teddy was always naughty... even his birth was trouble."
--TEDDY'S MOTHER

"His time-line – time-line!-he-calls-it! – for how we got into the Iraq/ Afghanistan/ Pakistan/ Syria/ Iran/ Kuwait/ Saudi Arabian War begins in 1950. It should either begin in 1776 or not until 2001; unless you consider the events of... well we'll leave it there. Exactly when we blundered in is not as important as the fact that we are there and there we shall stay until victory or something is achieved, finalized, and justified."
--GENROLISIMO FRANCO MC MULLEN

"He say he got a fix for all our shit. Oh! Yeah! Real Smartass! Then why ain't he King or something? They goddamn engineers! Why don't no one else ever come up with his "fixes" if they's so damn hot? Huh? Ain't gotta answer, is ya, Smartfart! If it sounds like a turd and it walks like a turd; maybe it just is a duck. Ducks don't come otta nowhere, ya know!"
--JEB B. HOOSIER YAHOO

"He copied this entire manuscript from your humble servant."
--CAPT. LEMUEL GULLIVER

O.K. I warned you that these previous two pages were parody; If you have read them anyway, blame yourself. Take personal responsibility for your life.

Your Life And Sex Island

Your life, your economy,
your country;
now and in your future

Ted West

The Geyer Avenue Publishing House

Published by:
The Geyer Avenue Publishing House
% The Soulard Coffee Garden Café
910 Geyer Avenue
St. Louis, MO 63104

Cover design by Casey Marburger

ISBN 0-982-49660-5

To Rita, most of my life.

Thanks to Travis Hoffmann, the second pair of eyes; Casey Marburger, the third pair of eyes.

Pre-Preface

A navel gazing geezer sees through himself to the rectum of the world; send money, all problems solved! (I am in league with god!) 'I can repair the break of day; I can patch the crack of dawn (if not fill Dawn's crack); I can catch the fall of evening; I can calm a tempest in a teacup; I and Death can cure the common cold; I and Time can mend a broken heart; and I can temporarily relieve a nymphomaniac's stress.'

(I use the half-quote-marks here because sometime ago [I know not when] I read something like what I wrote there. So the thought is not entirely original with me. When I use unexplained quotation-marks or half-quote-marks later you now know why.)

PREFACE

As I begin this book, I know that I, primarily, will be discussing some ways to improve our country; this United States or Ours.

Hold on, you talking about IMPROVING America? Then you must think that there is something wrong with America. Hence, you Egg-Head, must think that America is not perfect. So you must not love my country. If you don't love my country; why in the hell don't you just leave? Love it or leave it, I say. DO YOU LOVE MY COUNTRY?

Do I love my country? What a question! I don't even know if I love my wife (but I can say that I get immense comfort holding her at night); how in the hell can I tell if I love my country; how do you love an inanimate object like a country? I certainly have never MADE love to an inanimate object and, if I did, I wouldn't talk about it, certainly not here. As I might tell my wife if she were foolish enough to ask if I loved her, "I'm still here, ain't I?" Of course, the way things have been going, I can't afford to divorce my wife or to emigrate from here anyway. Besides, who vants to learn Svedish? As some comedian said long ago: 'We didn't get divorced because of the children; she wouldn't take 'em and I sure as hell wasn't going to'. She had more to do with bringing them into the world than I did! She should accept 80% responsibility. One time I said to her, "I forgot, how many kids do we have again?" She said, "I have four, I don't know about you." She said that in public.

Here's a test: If this is the country that Adams and Madison intended (one that I or they could love), then I should be able to write what I want without fear. Can I? As long as I tell the truth or express my opinion; can I? As I have been writing this thing, I have been going back and fourth:

Back: I must disguise any reference to real people or real corporations (legal entities)! Or they will sue my ass. They can break me because they are richer.

Forth: NO! I don't have to! Truth will out. Justice will triumph.

A guy wrote a book recently about his experience working minimum-wage jobs. Someone asked him if he used the names of real companies. "Oh, no!" he said as if it were a stupid question, "A lot of this stuff is highly litigatious!" What? Why? If you told the truth about real companies, real people, real situations, real real, then why the hell should you have to disguise your sources? Why, why, why? Where is Justice when you need her? Do you have to depend upon Lady Luck? Is Lady Luck more faithful than Mistress Justice? In this country?

"There is one rule for the great: to do nothing; and one rule for the lowly: to say nothing. The poor have but one friend, -- silence."

Why? Why, you goddamn idiot! Let me tell ya something, Sonny; traduce G.M. and see your butt melt! Don't you remember Nader, "Unsafe at Any Speed"! Look what they did to him. You think that they'd stop at murder? You nitwit! Look at what DuPont did to the guys who came-up with the evidence for the hole in the ozone layer hurting their Freon sales. Why do you have to disguise your sources? Let me tell you! You fucking idiot! This is the real world. The rich rule. The law protects the rich against the poor. The big dog fucks. Haven't you lived five minutes? Haven't you learned anything? Why, indeed, you stupe? It is not necessary to advertise your ignorance! Keep it under a bushel basket with your light and ego. Good lord, how can you be so stupid!?!?

So one day I am busy scrubbing off any references to reality and the next I am standing there with my nose hanging out saying, "I love my country and will not allow the rich and powerful to thwart honesty!"

What a fool! Aren't you aware that Judges and Lawyers are politicians? Do you not know that politicians and corporate presidents hang out at the same bars; belong to the same country-clubs; lick the same cunts; do you not know that Clarence Darrow said, "Don't look for justice in court or out of court."?

So I have become Diprosopus as I try to look out of both sides of my head at once. What shall I do? Well, I have to trust my country. We shall see! I know that any corrupt corporation or rich asshole can ruin me by suing me even though they know that they cannot win the battle they also know that I cannot win the war (see chapter 'Legal' [next book, sorry]). Any idiotic judge (sorry about that redundancy) who can read at the third-grade level can slap an injunction on the sale and distribution of this book. But I have always been stupid; that's why I have not been appointed Emperor of the Universe. Yet.

So here's the deal; my capitulation: this book is fiction. All of it. I made it all up. Yes, I use some real names. Sure, that's because I'm an idiot. I just wanted to make this thing seem authentic because I am not very smart. But everything is made up. If I were clever, I would have made up funny names too, like Dickens did, instead of cowardly using, occasionally, names of real innocent, good-hearted, god-fearing people and corporations. (I tear my heart out apologizing.)

Also, this book is satire. All satire. Satirical. (Well, there may be some parody.) It's like Aesop without the Hare. It's like Robinson Crusoe without the adventure. It's like Gulliver's Travels without Lilliput or Brobdingnag. It's like Through the Looking Glass without a spoiled prissy missy. It is all un-poetic poetic liberty. It is meant to be humorous, it is meant to be funny. There is nothing factual, actual, or real really here. It is all made-up phantoms, poltergeists, and ghosts. It is NOT meant to be considered seriously by serious minded people. If you are reading this, it is quite possible that you will never amount to anything. If you break into a smile, it may be a sign of poor judgment. Maybe your mother was right after all.

I took advantage of all the good advice that I got for the last three-quarters-of-a-century; now I'm broke. I did everything right; now I'm broke. What a great country! Now I'm going to tell you everything that I learned and how to fix things that ARE broke. Maybe you shouldn't listen to me after all. Listen to Exxon-Mobil or the Heritage Foundation; they always tell the tooth, the hole truth, and anything but the truth.

Protect me and throw the sable cloak of Dark Knight over me; I am about to commit thoughtcrime (crimethink) ["Thoughtcrime does not entail death: thoughtcrime IS death." —Orwell, 1984].

I mean to inquire if, in the civic realm, there can be any sure and legitimate role of government, men being taken as they are and laws as they might be. In this inquiry I shall endeavor always to balance what Justice demands with what is prescribed by Necessity, in order that the ideal and the reality may in no case be divided.

I enter upon my task without proving the importance of the subject. I shall be asked if I am a prince or a legislator, to write on politics. I answer that I am neither, and that is why I do so. If I were a prince or a legislator, I should not waste time in saying what wants doing; I should do it, or hold my peace.

As I was born a citizen of a free State, and have the right to vote, I feel that, however feeble the influence my voice can have on public affairs, the right of voting on them makes it my duty to study them: and I am happy, when I reflect upon governments, to find my inquiries always furnish me with new reasons for loving the governance of my own country.

--------------------Jean Jacques Rousseau, b. 1712 Geneva; d. 1778 France.--------------

Contents:

Chapter One

My Software

In the interest of providing full disclosure and sowing confusion, let me begin by listing my foibles in order of worst first:

I'm over seventy years old and I am not rich. That is a major crime and I apologize profusely. That is actually two major crimes; the first count against me: being old; second count: not being rich. Well, what is rich? I probably couldn't buy enough gold to fill a Midas cup. But all my kids and grandkids are each and all taxpayers. And all are smarter than me. And better looking. But not better looking than my wife. And she's smarter than me too. O.K. that's three crimes.

I can't sing. Sorry, I know that that is un-American. My son, who can't sing, says that he is the second worse singer in the world. My daughter, who can't sing, says that she is the third worse singer in the world. I have two or three other kids who don't bring up the subject. My wife, who can sing, doesn't to avoid embarrassing us. No nightingales nest near us but some mocking birds do but they don't mock us as their ears are plugged.

I believe in objective reality. That statement looks pretty bland and reasonable on paper but the corollaries that necessarily follow from it will make me contemned or hated by something like eighty percent of the earth's human population. That's a lot. About half of that eighty percent would joyfully slay me for believing in objective reality and not believing in what they believe in. Most of the non-human population of earth doesn't give a damn one way or the other what I believe. Bedbugs might,

I don't know for sure, I think that they would bite me whether I slept tight or not, they don't discriminate. I'll have to ask e. e. cummings' cockroach what he thinks. There was one cow in Vermont who cared but she was milked by Ben & Jerry's and when they sold out she stopped caring and became a cynic though I heard that her milk was still good.

I was raised and educated Catholic until the age of about fifteen (although I quit at about eleven years old). Despite or because of this, most folks, not including my mother, would agree that I did not turn out as badly as some other fellers who were likewise raised and educated. Counted among those raised and educated Catholic were the likes of Hitler, Mussolini, Stalin, Kennedy, Franco, Castro, McCarthy, Kennedy, Chang, Diem, Kennedy, Roberts, Scalia, Kennedy, Thomas, Alito, Pol Pot, Kennedy, etc. It is a great tribute to Catholic education that neither George H. W. Bush nor George W. Bush went to Catholic school although they did go to private school.

I never served in the military. Well, sort of. I spent one semester in the army R.O.T.C. and one semester in the air force R.O.T.C. Does that count? They taught me to "about face"; that was their big mistake. I would have spent two semesters in the army R.O.T.C. except that they did not have a 2:00 Wednesday opening. (This was back in the days when we registered for classes by waiting in line for a week.) (To those of you who were born after 1970, there was life before computers; not much life but, hard to believe, some people did eat and some even had sex even without the aid of computers.)

I am a pro-lifer. Not the jingoistic, sloganeering "pro-lifer", but the real "objective reality" pro-lifer which is about the opposite of the slogan's "pro-life" meaning.

I consider myself a Goldwater Conservative. But maybe I'm wrong. I never did read his book "Conscience of a Conservative" but I did go to hear him speak when he was running for President. If he believed in Fiscal

Responsibility; Limited Government; Freedom of Religion (or not); Open Covenants Openly Arrived At; Our Word Is Our Honor; All Men Are Created Equal; and Treat Others as We Would Be Treated; then I'm a Goldwater Conservative – the opposite of Ronnie. As far as I can tell, I am the last Goldwater Conservative remaining alive. But "Conservative" and "Liberal" have lost their meaning due to deliberate misuse. (Some digit actually wrote a book called something like, "Liberal Fascist".) Some people even say that Ronnie Reagan was a Conservative! Oh my! Lions and tigers, oh my! Scarecrows and Tin-men too! The word no longer has meaning. Don't look behind the curtain.

I am an engineer. Forgive me; I was led astray when very young. Once started, it was like quicksand; I just couldn't extricate myself. I sank lower and lower, taking graduate courses in things like Vibration Control, Methods Analysis, Work Simplification, and then doing independent study in the likes of Boolean Algebra; Plant Management; and Ladder, Control, and Wiring Diagrams. Then I took enough economics, finance, and accounting to be CPA. I sinfully piled on enough business courses to be an MBA. It was like a metastasizing cancer, I couldn't stop it. My saving grace is that I never studied Political Science, Law, or Journalism. (Well, a little law; not enough to do serious damage.)

I believe that Professional Liars are highly valuable. This is not my judgment; this is the "considered judgment" of Democracy, Theocracy, and the Free Enterprise System.

Four years ago, I did not know what a "prostate gland" was. Sure, I used it twice a day; just like I used the drive shaft in my car. Though, unlike my drive shaft, I didn't know at all about my prostate gland until it made me prostrate. My prostate gland is somewhat exclusive, less than half the people on earth have one. If you don't know about your prostate, we have a surprise for you. You will learn about it if you are male and if you live long enough; get prepared for an eighteen inch long, quarter inch diameter snake which has no purpose in life other than to crawl up your pecker. On the plus side, it was the only opportunity in my life to lay semi-naked with four women administering to my sex organs. The doctor only looked in occasionally. Voyeur! I also found that I have a much more exclusive organ, it probably has a technical name (diverticulum – I also have one in my intestinal tract that is completely different) but I just call it my Pouch. It protrudes from my bladder; holds about two cups of urine and, well, that's enough about that.

I am pro sex and anti violence and I believe that they should be two different things; not "sex and violence" as is usually stated suggesting that they are one and the same instead of opposites.

I am anti education when it is merely an ego prop and not connected and supported by actual learning. There was a video of one guy who could list all of the Presidents' last names in less than ten seconds. Wonderful. We have octopuses (that's figuratively; they are not as smart as octopi.), highly educated idiots in charge of the major institutions on earth (maybe elsewhere too); that's including the Blue Chip Corps.

I recognize four levels of knowing. 1. First person, palpation. 2. Second person, witness. 3. Third person, theory. 4. Fourth person, rumor. Rumor is by far the most popular; most people prefer hearsay or faith to personal reality experience. My Wife says that everybody loves a good story.

I recognize four levels of doing. 1. First person, goods production. 2. Second person, knowledge production. 3. Third person, passive activity. 4. Fourth person, negative production (destruction). Everyone, it seems, prefers "negative production"; they want to live off other people's work; they want grants or government jobs or to go to military academies or to get contributions or grants, or apply for defense work or congressional earmarks. They want to be Models, Singers, Actors, Journalists, Lawyers, Bankers, Preachers, Priests, Generals, Admirals, Accountants, etc. (Why not? Pay's better than engineering.)

I hate to lord it over everyone and I hate to wear all my brass bars and gold medals on my chest but I really must lay out my credentials. I was the son of the town drunk. I was born in 1935, the second last of thirteen children, for those of you who nodded off in history, that was the depth of the depression. To say the least, I was an unwanted child. All my older siblings were allowed, nay, encouraged, to kick the shit out of me and to belittle me; when I reached eighteen or twenty years of age and could kick the shit out of any and all of them it suddenly became illegal and "not nice". Just my luck. Americans believe that 'tis better to live on the hilltop and to listen to Beethoven in the womb (mother's or surrogate's), be bottle fed, go to private school, and have Mommy buy Daughter a training bra at five and a boob job at eighteen, and have Daddy treat Son to a hooker at twelve. Maybe. Sure, on the hilltop, you get glorious sunsets (not up for sunrises) and bracing air and you can see the church steeple. But in the valley you see the wonderful life in the crick (spelled creek by spoiled, rich city kids) and can see the roots of things. Those of us in the valley may see everything except the tops of the hills, those on the tops of the hills only see the tops of the hills unless they are looking down their noses – you can't see much looking down your nose. In those first eighteen years, I learned to keep my mouth shut even when I was right. I learned that I could never please those who mattered most to me. I learned that you could knock me down but not out. I learned that, when the dust settled, I was still standing there staring at the future. There's a downside and an upside to that kind of raisin'. Downside: I suffer fools silently but not patiently. Upside: from third grade on, I signed my own report card and no one noticed. There was never a parent-teacher meeting. I can take care of myself. And I can tell if you can or not. (I have never been caught in a forgery.)

I am not qualified to decide or to label "good" or "bad", "right" or "wrong", or "holy" or "evil". I never went to theological or divinity school. I am a Theo but I am not Divine. Now, I know what's "fair" and "unfair"; every third grader knows that; but every fifth grader should know – whether he does or not – that fair has nothing to do with life beyond the third grade. "Fair", after all is closely synonymous with "justice" and no less an expert than Clarence Darrow said, "Don't look for justice in court or out of court." Run from anyone who claims to be interested in "justice" or to be "tough on crime".

I am highly qualified to decide and to label what "works" or "doesn't work", "success" or "failure", "is it better" or "is it worse", or "does it operate better" or "does it operate worse". The trick is to carefully define the terms and to objectively and dispassionately observe, record, and compare the before and after conditions. (And that may just be what this book is all about.) Most people prefer the "good" and "bad" gambit and are distrustful of what "works".

I like the definition of "lie" (untruth) that I was taught in second or third grade: an intention to deceive. That is the definition that I will use. I know that it cannot be the legal definition because one can not determine the perpetrator's intention. However, the definition is still serviceable because one can usually sagely gage the perpetrator's intention.

Chapter Two

In Praise of Professional Liars

God, I'd like to lie like a Pro,
Then my money tree sure would grow.
But my mother was very bad;
She spank'd me when I was a lad
When I stretched things a tiny tad.
Lying then was a minor fad;
Now, like the Missouri flood flow,
Pro lying is a mighty show.

Some years ago Jack Parr was interviewing George Burns and Jack asked George if he had ever considered divorcing Gracie (Allen). George said, no, no the subject never came up in all their years of marriage. They never considered divorce. Then after a comedic pause he said, "Murder, Yes! ... Divorce, No."

At least I am not alone as a husband who has considered, at one time or another, murder as a reasonable alternative to the status low. The body; getting rid of the body was always a major difficulty; cutting it up would be easy; but a thigh it still a thigh. "You must remember this, A kiss is still a kiss, A thigh is just a thigh". People tell me that roast thigh sandwiches are good (maybe you could make a ham out of it) but I was always afraid of the elevated cholesterol levels. So if we, one of us, decided to take the O.J. path (I am not for one minute, not for a second, suggesting that he did it, although, as Chris Rock said, if he did do it, you could sort of understand why) but if we decided to play Richard III off the stage, we would want a good lawyer.

Does a good lawyer have to believe that we are innocent to defend us? Hell no! He has to be a good Professional Liar. Lawyers are taught to argue either side of any question – a valuable skill. They, in fact, get so good at it that they can no longer tell which is the "right" side in the sense of some abstract, obtuse, silly notion of "right or wrong". They learn the ultimate truth; "the right side is the fee side"! The trial is not over until Mr. Greenback has testified. "Justice" is to have your fee paid. It is the province of other professions to ponder the impossible imponderable of "Justice"; theology students are no closer today than three-million years ago; no two can agree. The better Professional Liar a lawyer is; the better he will be paid. Now, if you are innocent and he gets you off; that is a noble profession and well paid. If, on the other foot, you are guilty and he gets you off; that is a nobler profession and much weller paid.

One of the main jobs of the jury at trial is to appraise the lawyers and their performance and decide which one is the bigger liar and judge the accused accordingly (the bigger liar wins).

A trial judge on the other cheek enters the courtroom (usually) with his mind already made up and is just looking for the most acceptable sounding excuse to pronounce his judgment as law (particularly the Supreme Court 'Justices' ['Justice' has as much to do with those Justices as 'Reverend' has to do with Reverence or 'Honor' has to do with Honorable]). The judge, in fact, wouldn't be judge if he hadn't already proven that he was, indubitably, one of the finest Professional Liars. He wouldn't be the highest paid Professional Liar if he was not the very best Professional Liar. We live, after all, in a meritocracy I am told.

Our system of laws, saints preserve us, has made tremendous progress since this description of the law of three-hundred years ago by Mr. Jonathan Swift.

[Gulliver is attempting to explain to the Chief Houyhnhnm (his honour) the "rule of law" of which the Houyhnhnms have neither institution nor concept.]

> *"There was another point, which a little perplexed him at present. I had informed*

him, that some of our crew left their country on account of being ruined by law; that I had already explained the meaning of the word; but he was at a loss how it should come to pass, that the law, which was intended for every man's preservation, should be any man's ruin. Therefore he desired to be further satisfied what I meant by law, and the dispensers thereof, according to the present practice in my own country; because he thought nature and reason were sufficient guides for a reasonable animal, as we pretended to be, in showing us what he ought to do, and what to avoid.

"I assured his honour, 'that the law was a science in which I had not much conversed, further than by employing advocates, in vain, upon some injustices that had been done me: however, I would give him all the satisfaction I was able.'

"I said, 'there was a society of men among us, bred up from their youth in the art of proving, by words multiplied for the purpose, that white is black, and black is white, according as they are paid. To this society all the rest of the people are slaves. For example, if my neighbour has a mind to my cow, he has a lawyer to prove that he ought to have my cow from me. I must then hire another to defend my right, it being against all rules of law that any man should be allowed to speak for himself. Now, in this case, I, who am the right owner, lie under two great disadvantages: first my lawyer, being practiced almost from his cradle in defending falsehood, is quite out of his element when he would be an advocate for justice, which is an unnatural office he always attempts with great awkwardness, if not with ill-will. The second disadvantage is, that my lawyer must proceed with great caution, or else he will be reprimanded by the judges, and abhorred by his brethren, as

one that would lessen the practice of the law. And therefore, I have but two methods to preserve my cow. The first is, to gain over my adversary's lawyer with a double fee, who will then betray his client by insinuating that he hath justice on his side. The second way is for my lawyer to make my cause appear as unjust as he can, by allowing the cow to belong to my adversary: and this, if it be skillfully done, will certainly bespeak the favor of the bench. Now your honour is to know, that these judges are persons appointed to decide all controversies of property, as well as to the trial of criminals, and picked out from the most dexterous lawyers, who are grown old or lazy; and having been biased all their lives against truth and equity, lie under such a fatal necessity of favoring fraud, perjury, and oppression, that I have known some of them refuse a large bribe from the side where justice lay, rather than injure the faculty, by doing any thing unbecoming their nature or their office.

"It is a maxim among these lawyers that whatever has been done before, may legally be done again: and therefore they take special care to record all decisions formerly made against common justice, and the general reason of mankind. These, under the name of precedents, they produce as authorities to justify the most iniquitous opinions; and the judges never fail of directing accordingly.

"In pleading, they studiously avoid entering into the merits of the cause; but are loud, violent, and tedious, in dwelling upon all circumstances which are not to the purpose. For instance, in the case already mentioned; they never desire to know what claim or title my adversary has to my cow; but whether the said cow were red or black; her horns long or short; whether the field I graze her in be round or square; whether she was milked at home or

abroad; what diseases she is subject to, and the like; after which they consult precedents, adjourn the cause from time to time, and in ten, twenty, or thirty years, come to an issue.

"It is likewise to be observed, that this society has a peculiar cant and jargon of their own, that no other mortal can understand, and wherein all their laws are written, which they take special care to multiply; whereby they have wholly confounded the very essence of truth and falsehood, or right and wrong; so that it will take thirty years to decide, whether the field left me by me ancestors for six generations belongs to me, or to a stranger three hundred miles off."

The foregoing and other considerations may make it difficult to know just what is "that which is not" as the Houyhnhnms (who have no experience with speaking a not-real) are forced to call an untruth that we know as a lie. And, clearly, many people have different definitions of "lie". We better define our term before we get into a scuffle of misunderstanding.

I hate doing this but I better stop here and define terms. Boooring!

I am going to be speaking of the "Professional Liar" throughout this book. This is a highly technical term and has little or no relationship to the common street usage of "liar". The Professional Liar has been highly paid and highly respected throughout society ("society" is not to be confused with the "high society" of the debutant ball, the jet-setter, the well endowed ["well endowed" in this case is referring to the relatively large amount of wealth these persons have and not to the size of the ladies breasts or the gentlemen's penises], the country clubs, and the billionaire neighborhoods; in our sense "society" merely means modern homo sapiens) and throughout history ("throughout history" then we are referring to pre-modern homo sapiens). The image that the term "liar" may sketch in the mind might be of a seedy and untrustworthy person who looks dishonest (shifty eyes, conning ways, poor clothing, poor make-up, tobacco and/or alcohol breath, defensive, easily put-down, poor personal-hygiene, murders the Queen's English [like, "Ah ain't got to axe the ho"], etc.). The Common Liar makes things up on the run and often catches himself in his own web. When caught, he will often giggle and shift gears and plug the lie-hole with yet another, more unbelievable, lie.

The image of the "Professional Liar" is quite the opposite (steady, intimidating gaze; quick witted; sharp with the put-down; states data and assertions [true or false] with absolute authority, gravitas, and certainty; makes all observations perfectly fit preconceived assertions [made up as required]; exceedingly well dressed; shiny shoes; well coiffed; manicured nails, perfect make-up; minty, sen-sen breath; plays golf, maybe tennis, or hand-ball, sails; steady, well-paid employment that does not dirty one's hands [reporter, accountant, talk-show-host, foundation "scholar", or senator]; ample use of deodorants and cologne [not perfume], ups the Queen's English [like, "Ah have not acceded to make inquiries of the lady"], etc.). In short, "Professional Liar" does not construe anything negative and is, therefore, not libelous or slanderous. When the Professional Liar is caught in a lie, he will get ten other Professional Liars (from The Heritage Foundation or other ample supply) to swear to the factuality of his ass-sertion. He will never giggle when "caught"; he will ass-sert that there is no web and will declare that the web is actually the spinner.

Liar Type One: (what I was taught in grade-school Catholic catechism class) One who states (or writes) (deceptively) something that s/he believes to be false regardless of what you know or believe and regardless whether or not her/his belief is correct. (The Catholic Church, I understand, has since changed their collective mind about this. It is now acceptable – deletes the sin – if you do the equivalent of crossing your fingers [legs will do, mental reservation will do {say to thyself, "just kidding"}.] The Catholic Church changed its collective mind because it would be unsettling to think of all those Bishops and Popes stuck in hell. And, since the members of the Catholic Clergy are God's representatives on earth, what they say goes. Their law is God's law. That is why, to those of us outside the Church, there seems to have been changes inside the Church but to those inside the Church there has, in fact, been no change. It is much like a passenger inside a train [or plane {any moving vehicle |or object|}]. A passenger seated in a train chair experiences no relative motion between himself and the chair, whereas a dumb cow in a pasture beside the track sees, or thinks she sees, a great deal of motion [change] between herself and the seat inside the train. So, those of us outside the Church are like the dumb cow in the pasture along side the Church track, we think that we sense change inside the church (we may think that we sense the whole Church moving) but, in fact, there is no change or movement (when I was young it was perfectly O.K. to eat meat on Friday; it was only my active imagination that causes me to remember priests saying that it was a mortal sin – there has been no change, it is only my imagination) ("St." Christopher was NOT a revered saint when I was young – there has been no change, it is only my imagination as a dumb cow standing by the train tracks) (The earth does NOT revolve about the sun – there has been no change, it is only my brain addled from breathing too much train exhaust). It is neither a delusion on our part nor on the part of Faithful Catholics [those inside the moving Catholic Train] it is simply a matter of relative perspective.) Example (of Liar Type One) "You can't get to heaven if you are a member of their church!" Wait a minute! Sorry! Not a good choice. Try this: "I earn (am worth) $250.00 per hour (or more)!" (If you are being paid $250 or more this, of course, does not apply to you. You're welcome.)

Liar Two: One who attempts to convince you of something that you and he, openly, know to be false. e.g. "Jonah was swallowed by a whale!" No, no, sorry, not a good example; let's see. "Jonah swallowed a whale whole!" (That's not in the Bible, is it? [If it were in the Bible, it would be true, of course.])

Liar Three: One who attempts to convince you of a falsehood which he believes to be true (he is self deceived) regardless of what you know or believe. E.g. "Jonah was swallowed by a whale!" Um, maybe not a good universal example. Let's see, how about, "Global warming is true!" or "Global warming is not true!" Take your pick; one or both or neither of those statements may be true. The problem (the trick) with Liar Three is that most statements are not known with absolute certainty to be true or false. If you are a religious fanatic, of course, whatever your religion says is true, is true absolutely. And I do not doubt that whatever you say is correct and I am terribly sorry if I offended you.

Liar Four: One who attempts to convince you of reality which he believes to be a falsehood (he is again deceived) regardless of what you know or believe. E. g. "Hire me. I am one of the top brick-layers in America!" or "Hire me. I am paid $250 per hour (or more)!"

Liar Five: One who attempts to convince you of a falsehood which he believes to be a falsehood regardless of what you know or believe. E. g. "Hire me. I am the top brick-layer in America!" or "Hire me. I am worth $250 per hour (or more)!"

That may cover the field. I am not certain. Any rate, it is a pretty empty exercise because most of the time we cannot guess the speaker's intention or beliefs and often we do not know whether the material is true or false. But the more interesting and usual status is when we know or are pretty sure that the material is false but we do not know if the sender knows it is false (is he 'Puttin' us on?', 'Sportin' us?', 'Pullin' our leg?' or does he really believe that shit?)

Liar Two proves my point that there is nothing derogatory about my saying that someone is a Professional Liar. All fiction writers, actors, poets, dramatists, playwrights, screenwriters, journalists, editorialists, fantasy writers, sermon writers, and myself fall into this category. Did I say "novelists"? And none of these, other than myself, is considered a pariah out of society.

Let us look at an example of Liar Four or of Liar Five:

So there's this girl being raped on Pennsylvania

Avenue by a man (I know that "by a man" is redundant but I didn't want you to think that this was some sort of analog, allegory, or anti-homo harangue) and the pair on the ground ("in the street" more exactly) is surrounded by a mixed crowd. The scene is truly alarming (to me) and confusing (to me). Some people are cheering the man. Some women are screaming and trying to aid the woman (goddamn fem-Nazis). A bunch of guys are trying to get at the scene and pull the rapist off (god damn liberals). As we get closer we see that a ring of Military Officers has surrounded the pair on the ground and are preventing anyone from getting at the pair. The Military Officers are saying, "No, no! Let him finish what he started!" And, "The surge is working!" "Let's not cut and run!" "We cannot quit until we achieve victory!" "The consequences of not finishing the job are too horrible to contemplate!" "Quitting now is the same as surrendering!" "Only cowards quit under pressure!" So the man, possibly because of all the attention, can't seem to come (ejaculate for you purists). So the rape goes on. And on. Into the night and into the dawn, until noon the next day. The cops come (not ejaculate) but, seeing all the Military Officers who outrank them, the cops go (not pee). The crowd, too, has dissipated. Even something as horrible as rape cannot keep people from their daily appointed rounds anymore than can sleet or snow. We, ourselves, also exited the scene while the Military Officers still uphold that "we must maintain our course to victory!"

O.K., you know that I am the liar here because, of course, Military Officers would never egg-on a rapist. So, this is an example of Liar Two except that I am not trying to convince you of anything.

Now, of course, Military Officers do do that as regards to war (do say things like, "let's get started because you can't begin until you start" and, once started they say, "Let's not stop because that would be like quitting" ("Oops" is not in the military vocabulary). But, we know, of course, that rape is a far greater crime than war so Military Officers would never encourage a rapist. War is far, far less personal than rape. It is true that war, e.g. the Iraq war, may cause thousands of rapes, but it is not personal. It is the "fog of war". There can be, and indeed often are, (usually are, inevitably are, in fact) thousands of rapes (often, it is a weapon of war). But they (those rapes) are very, completely, absolutely excusable because they are not personal. I mean, they may be personal to the people involved, but to us they are not personal. So it is the Military Officers' duty to minimize the public knowledge of war-related-interpersonal-non-consensual-contact-with-physical-frictional-organ-peacemaking-interaction hereinafter to be known as WRINCCWPFOPI (jargon pronounced "rinkle cee clockwise pee foopee ee") or the like. (I remember riding in an Army Jeep and noting a posted sign something like, "This personnel vehicle will not be placed in motion until all personnel-vehicle body restraints have been placed in operation"; that's the short way of saying, "Fasten seat belts or no go".) No embedded buddy ("journalist") is likely to file a story about WRINCCWPFOPI. In fact, embedded buddies file the stories as written by the Military Officers.

Conclude: Military Officers do not encourage rape, nor, I might add, do the Military Officers applaud death. Death is merely a sidereal-like sideshow of war. It, death, is entirely excusable, indeed expected, though it is, in fact, not the purpose of war. The purpose of war, as we all know, is to achieve our national interests by means other than diplomacy. Another word for diplomacy is "talking" or "negotiation"; some people say "persuasion". But "persuasion" is not the way of Military Officers or of the U.S. State Department, of course. They, the M O's and the Staties, say that you must "negotiate" from a position of power or strength. You must be in a position (and the other guy must know it) to kick the shit out of the other guy (or, in the words of Bush I, to "kick some ass" [maybe he said "butt" – it's not important] – something that he never did in real life; he had his hired hands to do it). Then "diplomacy" is telling the other guy what he is going to do and he better like it and he god damned well better do it with a smile to show that he appreciates our "values". If someone doesn't share our "values", it is, obviously, silly to talk to them. What, I ask (rhetorically), is the sense of requesting someone to give us their oil (for example only), their land (for discussion purposes only), or for them to have a Regime change (in other words, asking the person to whom you are speaking to, basically, kill themselves) (suggested as a talking topic only)? Clearly, "talking" (or "diplomacy") is stupid. The ONLY solution is to go to war. And, naturally, a side effect of war is death. It is entirely excusable because it is unavoidable although not intended. And, if intended, not desired. And, if desired, not loved. And, if loved, not avoidable.

Conclude: Military Officers do not love death, nor, we might continue, do Military Officers applaud displacement and refugees. Refugees (millions of refugees in the case of Iraq) are merely an unintended, though not surprising, consequence of war. Military Officers do not deliberately go about creating refugees. They merely unintentionally create the conditions which make refugees unavoidable. In fact, given the opportunity, the Military Officers would encourage the refugees not to flee. They, the indigenous population, should remain in the line of fire and take the chance of being killed like brave men, women, and children instead of running like craven cowards. Eventually the shooting will stop, eventually there will be food, eventually there will be water, and eventually there will be peace. Not everywhere, of course, but once the buildings are destroyed, the infrastructure eliminated, the food gone, the water gone, and the population killed, there is little or no reason for the Military Officers to remain. They will move on to areas where there are other, more serviceable targets, other things to destroy, other people to be killed. These locations, known as a "target rich areas" are highly desirable as target areas because weapon efficiency is maximized. That is, more valuables can be reduced to rubble and more "enemy operatives" (sometimes known as "bystanders") can be reduced to body-count with the fewest stray destructive devices. "More bang for the buck" is the preferred expression among "Conservatives". Efficiently destroying active, usable infrastructure is more desirable than "making the rubble bounce".

> *"[A]nother part of military duty: our troops entering the enemy's territory, and putting all around them to fire and sword; burning farm, wasted fields, shrieking women, slaughtered sons and fathers, and drunken soldiery, cursing and carousing in the midst of tears, terror, and murder. Why does the stately Muse of History, that delights in describing the valor of heroes and the grandeur of conquest, leave out these scenes, so brutal, mean, and degrading, that yet form by far the greater part of the drama of war? You, gentlemen..., who live at home at ease, and compliment ourselves in the songs of triumph with which our chieftains are praised – you, pretty maidens, that come tumbling down the stairs when the fife and drum call you, and huzza for the* [soldiers] *– do you take account that these items go to make up the amount of the triumph you admire, and form part of the duties of the heroes you fondle?"* The History of Henry Esmond, William Makepeace Thackeray, set 1700, pub. 1852.

We know that for us to be safe we need military bases in 600 or 700 countries everywhere in the world. We are effectively told so by the Military Officers. No one says otherwise. Professional Liars are to be believed.

There is no one more patriotic than Military Officers. You can tell that they are patriotic because there are more flags per person in the military than in any other organization (except maybe congress if you count the lapel pins); their dress uniforms are always crisp and snappy; they can stand stiffly; they salute each other sharply; they work very hard to have the correct materiel and personnel to kill the maximum number of people with the least effort; they scrupulously avoid being distracted by any productive work; and they hold the people who are doing productive work (and supporting the Military Officers) in the highest contempt.

I must confess that I am apparently unpatriotic (just as, apparently, bees can't fly). We do have a couple or more flags in our possession but I don't fly them because I would be compelled (internally, from childhood respect) to take them down at sunset and put them back up at sunrise and take them down in the rain; and I am working so damn much (supporting the Military Officers) I just would not have the time to observe proper flag etiquette. My clothes are often un-pressed and often stained from cooking, baking, or cleaning the johns (for forty years I had to wear a god damned coat and tie but I sure as fuck don't have to anymore, free at last, free at last, thank god almighty I am free at last); I may stand a little stooped from so many years of labor; I don't salute any motherfucker, I seldom even high-five (when I do, I sometimes miss on purpose and half-fall-down [I don't mind playing the fool if it makes someone smile – another sign of unpatriotism]); killing is not uppermost in my mind (even when I think of congress); I have been distracted by productive labor all my life; and I do not hold laborers in contempt.

But my un-patriotism, I fear, runs even deeper. I (heaven's forbid) don't believe that we (the United States of America) need to be (almost) always in a state of war (declared, permitted, or otherwise just fooling around) nor that we absolutely must have a standing army when at peace (should peace happen to infect us by some weird unintended contamination). But here's what I find so frightening that it shakes me to my pith. The Founders, if you read about their deliberations at the Constitutional Convention or their attempt to sell the Constitution in the Federalist Papers, believed as I do. Damned unpatriotic Muthahs (in the case of Abigail) or Fathahs (in the case of Sam). The Founders feared the Military-Industrial-Complex more than Ike feared the Military-Industrial-Complex. But now we know that we don't have to fear it: Listen to the Military Officers (the Professional Liars [again, I repeat; no disrespect is intended by that Honorable Title {Professional Liar} nor should any offense be taken]):

What do we know for sure?:

This we know for sure: When George W. Bush (Bush II) came into office, the Military-Industrial-Complex was costing us about one-Billion-dollars-per-day! When George W. Bush leaves office (today is 7-22-08) the Military-Industrial-Complex will be costing us two-or-two-and-a-half-Billion-dollars-per-day. (And Bush and the other War Lords will be calling those god damn Liberals "Tax and Spenders") Those figures are necessarily approximate because the Professional Liars of the Military Officers hide as much of the cost as possible; large portions of the other budgets such as the Energy Department and NASA are actually Military Expenditures. This money is all borrowed. Most is borrowed from countries with horrible civil rights governments; from countries who are worse than Iraq was under Saddam Hussein.

From the root and bole of the previous paragraph, this Lying Tree grows so many branches in so many directions so fast that it is difficult to know which fantasies to follow in which order. This tree is more bountiful than the cigarette trees in the Big Rock Candy Mountains. It is crookeder than Harry Lauder's Walking Stick. It may be located in Camelot. Here are some of the Professional Lies:

A. A large Military-Industrial-Complex keeps us safe.
B. A large Military-Industrial-Complex makes us strong.
C. A large Military-Industrial-Complex keeps our economy rolling.
D. We get "more bang for the buck" from military expenditures than from other governmental expenditures.
E. We are fighting (or "we fought") for our freedom in Iraq.
F. We are fighting (or "fought") for Iraq's freedom in Iraq.
G. We are fighting to stabilize the Middle East by fighting in Iraq.
H. We are fighting the Global War on Terror by attacking Iraq.
I. We are (or were) fighting Terrorism in Iraq.
J. We attacked Afghanistan to kill Osama bin Laden.
K. Osama bin Laden was instrumental in the planning and execution of the attack known as 9-11.
L. We are fighting in Afghanistan for some logical, noble, sensible, or honorable reason or cause.
M. Victory in Iraq is defined as (to complete this sentence I went to the Internet and typed in "victory in iraq" and hit Google. Up came the White

House blogeria "Strategy for Victory in Iraq". A sub-title bullet was "Victory in Iraq Defined" Aha! I thought; the Mother Lode at long last. Going there [to that definition] I found Short, Medium and **"Longer term [notice, I am quoting]**, Iraq is peaceful, united, stable, and secure, well integrated into the international community, and a full partner in the global war on terrorism." Longer term is our interest and Short and Medium are only subs of the "Longer term" so I include only "Longer term" here. This reminds me of the hoary story of the missionary who reproaches the Native American for spending all of his time hunting and fishing and not being productive (to the Missionary's way of thinking). Missionary to Native American: "You should get a job!" Native American: "Why?" Missionary: "So you can earn money!" Native American: "Why?" Missionary: "So you can retire after working for forty years!" Native American: "Why?" Missionary: "So you can spend time hunting and fishing!" Hmmm! So after six or a thousand years (depending upon who gets elected), murdering a few hundred-thousand people, displacing a few-million people, destroying a country, creating nations of fanatics who hate America, and spending a few-trillion-dollars we are back to square one. Need I remind you that the very best that we can expect in Iraq "Longer term" if and when we pull our pecker out is an utterly intolerant theocracy [it is already in their Constitution] which is a sworn enemy of Israel [in their Constitution]? We can hope for anything we want; but that [a rigid, absolutely intolerant theocracy hating a neighboring theocracy] is the best that we can expect). So "Victory" in Iraq is defined as "returning to pre-9-11 conditions with a different dictator (this time maybe 'faith based', that'll make Georgie happy)". Like it or not, if you are not fully baptized as a Professional Liar you must admit that Pre-9-11 Iraq was "united, stable, and secure, well integrated into the international community, and a full partner in the global war on terrorism (which, 'the global war on terrorism' we admittedly hadn't started yet)." Saddam did not get-along-well with, he did not tolerate, and he did not like extremists or terrorists; for many years he was our ally, our client, and our supporter. I personally would not have liked him but Reagan and Bush I certainly did.

N. Iraq (Saddam Hussein) had something to do with the attack known as 9-11.

O. Osama bin Laden had something to do with the attack known as 9-11 (Yes, he probably was very happy with the success of the attack, but that is far different than "having something to do with it". I was happy with our victory over Germany [and the axis] in the second-world-war but few people have blamed me for it and no one tried to kill me for my unallayed joy.)

P. We didn't know that the attack known as 9-11 was coming.

Q. Saddam Hussein killed his own people (implying that he was not our friend and ally at the time and that we did not aid and abet him in the killings). (Bush II has signed off on 155 state killings in the United States and certainly killed more Iraqis than did Saddam Hussein.)

R. We must have victory in Afghanistan. I went on the internet and Googled "victory afghanistan" 7-30-'08. I received 12,800,000 site-hits in 0.31 seconds. You can look at them all; I am not including all of them here. I looked at the first 30. I found that John McCain has a "COMPREHENSIVE STRATEGY FOR VICTORY IN AFGHANISTAN" (bountiful, bigger, better, beautiful, bellicose belligerency – that is the one thing in which he has been consistent; he loves war). Then I was shocked to see how far behind the times I really was: "Coalition forces, including many brave Afghans, have brought America, Afghanistan and the world its first victory in the war on terror," President George W. Bush Tuesday, June 15, 2004. What a fool I am; I was searching for definition of "Victory in Afghanistan" when "it" already happened more than four years ago. Scary! Then here's another victory; "Apparent Karzai Victory in Afghanistan a Big Win for Democracy" - American Forces Press Service WASHINGTON, Oct. 28, 2004 (we are piling up victories, this one just four months after President Bush's big victory as reported by our own propaganda service which I pay for). Here's another Victory in Afghanistan from The Heritage Foundation; it's an even earlier Victory (fourteen years earlier, my goodness, Toto), (Didn't Yogi say, "It's amazing what you can see if you just look") "February 20, 1990; [please notice that I am quoting] Consolidating Victory in Afghanistan; by Phillips, James A. [Heritage Foundation Professional Liar]; The Afghan Mujahideen freedom fighters scored a great victory when their fierce resistance forced the Soviet Union to end its ten-year occupation of Afghanistan on February 15 last year (1989)... at the cost of 1,200,000 Afghan lives...the [Moscow puppet] regime survives largely because of the $250-million to $300-million... every month from Moscow." While we are here, keep this in mind: we (you and I, the American taxpayers) are sending billions of dollars (probably more than $10-billions; the amount is classified – our employees think that we are too stupid and unpatriotic to know how much money we spend) we are (were from '79 to '89) sending $-billions to the Mujahideen (holy warriors) freedom fighters who are identical to the al Qaeda and the Taliban; remember this now because it can get confusing. And please remember that this Patriotic man from Heritage said "The Afghan Mujahideen freedom fighters". While, at this time, the Saudi national, Osama bin Laden, was not openly our ally although he too was supporting the Taliban "Freedom Fighters" that we (the U.S.A.) were supporting. We were absolutely, certainly backing and giving material support to Osama bin Laden. So we are or were on the same side as Osama bin Laden. (Osama bin Laden is a billionaire Saudi Arab who wants foreigners out of Arabia; all foreigners whether U.S.A. or U.S.S.R. I agree with him on this so perhaps I am a terrorist too!). I want to give you a short time-line of Afghanistan but I don't want to go back too far because it can get very wacky, confusing, and ridiculous. If you want to read "Kim" by Rudyard Kipling you can see that the "Great Game" has been going on for hundreds of years; we, the United States of America are goddamn amateurs. Goddamn fucking amateurs, amateurs, amateurs. We are fucking goddamn idiots to be over there getting chewed up and pissing away my money just to make our War Lords happy. The Middle East borders have not been stable since biblical times. The Middle East is the land of the Old Testament with its constant wars. This is the Persia, the Bagdad, of the king who has a new wife every night and executes her in the morning (or else she might be unfaithful) until Sheherazade of The Thousand and One Nights or The Arabian Nights (Aladdin's Lamp, Sindbad the Sailor, and Ali Baba and the Forty Thieves). Now we are waving our pecker around there too in a pissing contest. We are bound to be pissed on, watch and see; here we go over the river and through the wood to Grandmother's house with Little Red Riding Hood. Bear with me; the first few entries don't seem on-message but think about it for a moment.

Time Line For U.S. Involvement in Iraq and Afghanistan:

1950s two planes hijacked from Cuba to America. An article on the internet suggests that these were inspired or arranged by the C.I.A. to destabilize the Castro Regime.

1960s Fifty planes (attempted, most successful; only a few deaths, a few planes lost at sea) hijacked to Cuba (almost all from the U.S.)(Average of five per year). One from Cuba to U.S. (Cuba seems to be a more popular destination than the U.S.) No one (not the airlines, not the F.B.I., not F.A.A.) does anything to prevent hijackings (not even hardening the cockpit door). (Oops, I'm sorry, they did too do something, they talked, officials talked, Military Officers talked, Diplomats talked, Politicians talked, Media talked, Editorialists talked.) (And talked, no one hardened the Cockpit door! No one hardened the cockpit door! Dah!)

4-27-'78 Military coup installs "Democratic" (communist?) government in Afghanistan.

12-7-'79 Soviet Union (Russia); invited in by the "Democratic" government; attacks Afghanistan with whom they share a 3,366 mile border (one-and-two-thirds times longer than our border with Mexico). We (the U.S.A.) begin supplying the "Freedom Fighters" (the Mujahideen aka al Qaeda aka Taliban) with $-Billions of equipment, training, and support. Russia gets their ass kicked.

9-22-'80 Iraq invades Iran. The United States supplies arms to the Iraqis. Kuwait, too, supports Iraq.

6-'82 President Reagan stated that the United States "could not afford to allow Iraq to lose the war to Iran".

'85 U.S. sells weapons to Iran. (Yes, we are arming both sides!)

'85 – '86 Iraq and Iran exchange some 700 missiles directed at civilian targets. (Most likely, all supplied by the United States of America.)

4-'85 to 1-'87 Soviets devise exit strategy from Afghanistan. (Yeah, took two years.)

'86 Afghan constitution installed the Republic of Afghanistan (ROA).

'87 – '88 U. S. attacks Iranian oil platforms. Destroying about a half dozen platforms and sinking about the same number of Iranian ships. (Another undeclared war instigated by the United States of America.)

7-3-'88 USS Vincennes, laying mines in Iranian territorial waters, shoots down civilian Iran Air

Flight 655 killing all 290 passengers and crew. (Our Professional Liars [the Corporate Media] lie about it until the next news-cycle buries it.)

1-'87 to 2-'89 Soviets (declare victory) withdraw from Afghanistan. (Yeah, took two years.)

7-25-'90 The U.S. Ambassador to Iraq, April Glaspie, told Iraq that Washington, "inspired by the friendship and not by confrontation, does not have an opinion" on the Iraq-Kuwait argument "we have no opinion on the Arab-Arab conflicts, like your border disagreement with Kuwait". Naturally, Saddam Hussein took this as a go-ahead. (Remember, we did not object when Iraq invaded Iran just ten years ago, we helped!) Sounds, to me, like a promise of non-intervention on our part. Yet another un-kept promise.

8-2-'90 Iraq attacks Kuwait.

1-16-'91 U.S. Attacks Iraq. 4-1/2 months later.

'92 – '96 Afghan Civil War.

9-9-'01 the Mujahideen aka al Qaeda aka Taliban (our clients) gain upper-hand in Afghanistan. (Good, we kicked out the legitimate government.)

1999 – 2000 Flight trainers (in the United States) notify the F.B.I. that Saudi Citizens are learning to steer commercial jetliners but have no interest in learning to take-off or land. The F.B.I. does nothing; it does not notify the airlines, it does not notify the pilots, it does not notify the flight attendants, it does not notify airport security, it does not notify airport management, it does not notify local police, it does not put agents on planes, it does not harden cockpit doors, the F.B.I. does nothing.

6-15-'01 U.S. War Lords insulate themselves from effects of war by eliminating the draft (previously) and giving themselves a tax break.

9-11-'01 we are attacked by Saudi Arabian nationals; by 19 men commandeering four commercial planes and flying them into the Twin Towers in New York and other targets (15 of the men were from Saudi Arabia, two from the United Arab Emirates, one from Egypt and one from Lebanon, none are from Afghanistan, none are from Iraq). Surviving members of the group which planned the attack say that their group within the U.S.A. did all of the planning with no help, communication, or direction from anywhere else. (Including not from Osama bin Laden.)

9-11-'01 onward. Having done nothing sensible thus far about air (port; plane) security we do not wish to break our ninny streak. We seemingly everywhere put in charge nothing but brown noses ("great job Brownie" - Bush to Brownie about New Orleans/Katrina/Bush disaster). We install an inspections system that has failed every time that it has been tested. I am quite sure that I could bring a bomb on any plane that I choose to. The sole purpose of the inspection system appears to be to demonstrate to the American Public that the Government has the right to invade your most personal business, person, property, communications, and thoughts anytime and anyplace that it decides to. And it certainly does. If the government decides to play with your balls or your wife's tits, you better spread your legs and loosen your wife's bra and smile. We have installed an inspection system which has, and continues to, cost billions-of-dollars and causes hours of delay for each person on each flight and serves no purpose except to intimidate the Americanus Publicus Boobus. (When my wife and I flew to Florida, they [the "inspectors"] confiscated her half empty six ounce bottle of Oil of Olay. I was wearing a medical prescription catheter and a urine sac attached to the inside of my thigh which was completely undetected. As it happens, urine contains all of the elements and many of the compounds found in most explosives; including percussion detonated explosives. I had one sac of urine attached to one thigh; I could have had two large sacs of explosives [easily twenty pounds] attached one to each thigh and gone completely undetected.)

10-7-'01 (less than one month after 9-11) the United States attacks Afghanistan. It is almost certain that this attack was planned well before 9-11-'01. We are told that the purpose of the invasion is to capture Osama bin Laden, destroy al-Qaeda, and remove the Taliban – you remember the "Freedom Fighters" who we were supplying with missiles and other weapons and who we were training how to fight and how to kill?

10-11-'02. Senate votes 77-23 to authorize President Bush to attack Iraq if Saddam Hussein refuses to give up Weapons of Mass Destruction as required by U.N. resolutions. (There were no Weapons of Mass Destruction.)

3-20-'03 with our flawless logic, our wry sense of humor, our love of irony, our passionate adoration of massive deficits, and our worship of war; we attack Iraq. Afghanistan and Iraq had no more to do with the 9-11 attacks than Canada or Mexico (or hundreds of other countries.) no Military-Officers resign in protest or in disgust; they all love their pensions more than the Constitution. Here's the last word on the meaning of "Victory" in Afghanistan:

07-16-2008 "Wednesday morning, Mujahideen of Islamic Emirate Afghanistan, shot down an American invaders helicopter with anti-aircraft rocket ... in which all the American terrorists onboard were killed" Reported by Zabihuallah Mujahid on the internet. I'll bet dollars to elf shit that that was an anti-aircraft rocket that we supplied to the Freedom Fighters; remember them – the Mujahideen Freedom Fighters that we trained and supplied. This is not the Twilight Zone it only seems that way.

09-12-2008 I am revisiting this time line because there has been another horrible outrage. Apparently we (you and I as citizens of the United States of America) have been lobbing missiles into yet another country, Pakistan, since at least January of this year! Have we been killing Taliban?

Who knows? Who cares? That is not the issue! For certain we have been killing innocent women and children. Now finally on September 3rd we have invaded Pakistan; "boots on the ground" as the idiots who are doing and reporting this like to say. The American War Lords who own the U.S.A. Corporate Media have avoided reporting these outrages as much as possible. This Act of War has barely been mentioned at all. Act of War? I would say so. Suppose Russia (for example) lobbed a few missiles into New York (or Canada lobbed one or two into Minnesota); wouldn't we be a bit upset? Yes military invasion, murdering civilian citizens of a foreign nation is an Act of War. We have gone to war yet again without Congress Declaring War. Some of you may remember when we used to be a Constitutional Republic. The bad old days apparently. We no longer even bother with formalities. I have not heard of anyone who has raised any objection. "When the President does it, it's not a crime." As an engineer, I can only think of three possibilities: 1. I am insane. 2. Everyone else is brain-dead. 3. We have been inured against outrage by outrage (we expect outrage and, therefore, outrage is no longer outrage). Then: people died to save and support the Constitution; now: people die to salve and abort the Constitution. One great wonder has emerged from this latest outrage: All honorable military officers have resigned in protest.

10-26-2008 Who could ever have thought that I would have to come back here? What could top invading yet another country, invading Pakistan? What? What? What? Today we have invaded Syria! Lord! I'm not even outraged this time; the World Series is on; who gives a shit if we are going to war again. I'm drained. This is like Pearl Harbor and no one is paying any attention (remember the one-word four-inch headline punctuated with an exclamation-point: WAR!). This is our day of infamy. Another one. Yet, another one. We have no news media. We have no congress. We have no Supreme Court. We have no constitution. Do I love my country? Where is it? We have a criminal government. If the government does it, it is not a crime. Therefore, it is not a crime and we do not have a criminal government. Presto! Change the definition, change the meaning, change the structure: change the act. We are down the rabbit hole. We kidnap. We torture. We murder. We invade. The Goths had a reason. The Mongols had a reason. The Romans had a reason. The French had a reason. The Russians had a reason. The Germans had a reason. The Japanese had a reason. We don't have a reason. We have no reason. We have no rationale. We have no plan. We have no justification. We make no sense. We are nonsense. We are horror. We are Godzilla; only ugly. Do I love America? Do you love Godzilla?

10-27-2008 The Saint Louis Post-Dispatch put the article about the attack by the United States of America against Syria on page A-11. During this sneak attack, we murdered Syrian citizens some or all of whom were innocent of any crime, aggression, or antagonism against the United States of America. Imagine opening the paper on December 8, 1941 and finding the strike on Pearl Harbor on page 11. Yessss, I know that there are differences; but the essence – an attack by one sovereign nation on another sovereign nation's citizens and property in the second sovereign nation's territory – the essence is the same. It is an act of war. It is a sneak-attack! An act of war carried on page A-11. Not called a "sneak attack". Syrian spokesperson said that the raid was an act of terrorism. And "said the raid on the town of Abu Kamal had killed a father and his three children, a farm guard and his wife, and a fisherman." Here are the articles that the Post-Dispatch thought were more important than Our Pearl Harbor: "Nixon Pulling Away From Hulshof"; "No Bootheel Footholds"; "Point Man for A-B is Brewer of Consensus"; "Prescribing HIV Drugs Sooner is Better, New Study Suggests"; "$878 Bill? Unlimited Long Distance Has its Limits"; "Former Landfill Replanted With Native Seedlings"; "Halloween Party Fits Kids' Needs – Without Sweets"; "Off-duty Officer Kills Carjacking Suspect"; "Law & Order"; "Drinking Fountain Gives a Good Drenching"; "MSD and U. City Will Face off Tonight Over Flooding From Ike"; "Candidates are Focusing on Battleground States"; "Underclass Grows in Japan"; and "Global Financial Crisis Spreads to Kuwait". Then came: "U.S. Launches Attack in Syria" – two columns nine-inches long for our Pearl Harbor. On page A-11.

10-30-2008 The Post-Dispatch runs an editorial on the bottom of the Editorial-page. **"On to Damascus"** "[We R]eserve the right to pursue terrorists [we were not 'pursuing' terrorists] across borders; with or without the permission of the country where they are hiding [no one was hiding]. This is the new reality that terrorists have forced upon the world. [There is no evidence that there were terrorists. No one 'forced' anyone to do anything. The 'world' didn't attack another country, we, the United States of America, did.] Countries such as Syria and Pakistan will have to get used to the idea. [They don't have to and they won't, you fucking idiot. If you, because you are bigger than me, came into my house and raped my wife, robbed me, and killed my son, I would have to 'get used to the idea'? I don't think that I would.] So will the people of the United States." Do we? Do we? Do we? Is that what we have come to? Get used to being an insufferable bully? Get used to being deranged? We might as well get used to living in a Depression then too. Or have we? We might have to get used to having a dictator then too. Or have we already? Have no military officers objected? Have none resigned? Have none committed hari-kari like honorable men? Do military officers have no knowledge of the Constitution? Are military officers so drilled in obedience that they have no conscience? No free will? No sense? No sense of decency? No decency? What do they teach in the military academies? Is there no class? No class in the Constitution? No Constitution? We know of the persistent scandals at each and all of the military academies. What is to be expected of young, impressionable men looking for a free lunch and getting it? The fear of having to struggle; of having to yearn, of having to work, of having to earn must be overwhelming when you are expecting and are getting a free lunch. No wonder there is a climate of religious bullying and intimidation. All student admissions at the Military Academies are based on politics. All of them! Political corruption. Politicians, lobbyists, and military officers choose based upon political considerations. When no one is admitted on merit, there is no merit. When everyone is admitted on corruption; everyone is corrupt. Education at military academies is free. No one pays for education at military academies. No wonder McCain knows nothing about economics. No wonder he wants to 'strengthen' the military. It's free. No one pays. Are the military academies broken beyond repair? Is this all a big joke like a Marx Brothers movie? Will the last reel be played? Please? Do I have to beg?

1-14-09. Dick Cheney admits to being complicit in the torture of fellow humans. He claims that he is proud of torturing fellow humans. He, likely, does not think that the people that he caused to be tortured were human; not like him. He may be correct. He may not be human.

I was weaned on the Second World War so that is the basis of my thinking. (I really was weaned earlier; I did not continuously suckle until I was ten, and I did not begin again until I was twenty.) Yes, there were moral dilemmas concerning the Second World War; and, yes, there was propaganda and, yes, there were lies.

But, at the time, I remember no one questioning the internment of Japanese U.S. citizens; no one objected to the firebombing of Dresden; no one second-guessed dropping the atom bomb (twice) (Tojo still didn't want Japan to surrender); no one was appalled when Paton said something like, "we grease the treads of our tanks with the guts of our enemy" (if, in fact, he did say it). We wanted as many Krauts and Japs killed as possible and if they suffered as they died, good; well deserved and good riddance. We sat hypnotized by the little Cyclops green eye on our radio during the Battle of the Bulge (fucking static). We thought that we were closing in on the Bastards in Berlin, and now the sons-of-bitches were murdering us; maybe we could lose yet! No hyperbole; this was life or death. Kill the no good sons-of-bitches, kill their wives, kill their children, kill their cows, kill their dogs, destroy their cities, destroy their farms; kill, kill, kill the dirty, filthy sons-of-bitches. "Loose lips sink ships", we believed it entirely. Don't talk about what you do on your job; the enemy may be listening. When we heard that milkweed seed pods were needed for Mae-Wests (no relation) we took gunny sacks up and down the railroad tracks and gathered hundreds of pounds by ourselves. (I mention elsewhere that my brother Al was shot down over the Pacific and only three survived from the bomber crew and were picked by a seaplane. This war was personal.) When lard (bacon drippings) was needed for ammunition we went without butter and lard. I still have half filled books of dime savings bonds that I bought to fight the war. Our lives depended upon it.

But since then, since then, my god, since then what has happened? These fucking half-assed wars that are fought on lies to satisfy vested interests to enrich the rich and to provide pleasure to the President are disgusting political posturing to enrich the few at the expense of the many and no one gives a shit if a bunch of people are killed? Make the War Lords happy. I feel sorry for the soldiers. Korea was still fought by draftees (my brother Leo was on his way there when the god damned papers were signed ending that war); but since then it has been the Roman Legions who are/were so poor that they had to trade murder for bread to fight the Gauls or the Picts or to suffer the ignominy of petty ghetto life or the equivalent.

Wars will defeat the mightiest nation. Wars will defeat the mightiest nation. No one can be victorious in war. I think someone said that you can no more win a war than you can win a hurricane. (There were three boxers in my family. Dave and Leo fought in the Fox River Valley High School Catholic Conference in the '40's [often fighting each other because both of their opponents didn't show, forfeited – always a draw {both meanings}] [fortunately, Dave knocked a nun down a stairwell and I didn't have to go to St. John's Catholic High School in Little Chute {I hit my nun when I was in third grade ||she hit me first; what was I to do?|| – I was always a bit ahead of Dave. This had two results: First, I sure as hell never hit another nun; I never wanted to get in that much trouble again. Second, the nuns must not have known that I would never hit another nun; they certainly were all very nice to me after that.} and I fought in the Golden Gloves and varsity at the University of Wisconsin. Leo had 47 ring-fights and a great win-loss record [But didn't make varsity at the U.W.]. Dave actually turned pro. I, at 135#, sparred hundreds of hours with Dave, at 220#. I had only a few fights and not a great win-loss record [50%, one knockout, I was never knocked down in the ring]. Dave and Leo were fighting high-school kids; a high-school conference; I fought just below the pro level; a university conference during college-boxing's "last hurrah". One time someone came up to my brother Leo in Whitey's Bar in Little Chute and said, "I hear that you've been bragging that you can kick the shit out of anyone in the Fox River Valley!" Leo said, "That was probably my brother Dave but it doesn't make any difference because I can kick the shit out of him. You wanna try me?" I only had one street fight after grade school [I was jumped by strangers who regretted it]. Dave had a lot of street [bar] fights. He 'won' them all. He was buried with a bite scar on his chest and a glass ball in his eye socket and a scar under his eyebrow that I gave him. You can't win a fight. Dale Carnegie said you can't win an argument

(I was in a store today and 'How to Win Friends and Influence People' is still in print after 70 years. I must have read it 60 years ago). You certainly can't win a war. Who won; the Hatfields or the McCoys? Did Aaron Burr win? Hamilton? Who won; the Capulets or the Montagues? Or, more to the present, who won in Afghanistan; Russia or the Mujahideen 'Freedom Fighters'? Who wins death and destruction? The North, you say, 'won' the Civil War. The South surrendered and the Union was preserved. There was jubilation that the war was over. Did Grant and Lincoln have a great celebration or were they profoundly sad? How many rotting bodies of young men make you happy? How much gangrene is a joy? How much starvation is a blessing? Yeah, I'm terribly, terribly naïve! And the American War Lords [and Professional Liars] who bring you death and destruction on a silver platter are intelligent and sophisticated.) War is a destructive force. I feel like such an idiot saying that; it is so damned obvious. But not many believe it. It's like saying, "Poking your eyes out does not help you to see better." And then having some neo-con person look at you as though were some sort of idiotic traitor. "What do you mean, you fucking Liberal asshole, 'poking your eyes out doesn't help you to see better'; are you fucking nuts. May God forgive you! I certainly won't! I mean that's just how I feel! And, and I say, we can fight and win two wars simultaneously. Let's get started. And, and I say, you shut your fucking mouth, you traitor. You God Damn war protesters all hate America."

There are some odd coincidences in history that have no deep meaning but haunt me nevertheless. When I was very young, very, very young, our George the First was bleeding the invading G.B. (U.K.)s' George the Third with the war of a thousand small cuts. Our George the First was leading the insurgent terrorists against the Hessians. You remember the Hessians, the People of Hesse, hired out by the German Nobility (the Lords) to the King of England. They were great fighters. They were paid in food. They were basically slaves. The English Lords paid the Hessians' Lords for the fighting Hessians' service. These were the guys that George the First (Washington to you) beat when he crossed the Delaware River and attacked them at Trenton on Christmas night. George the Third originally had about 18,000 Hessians shipped to "his" Colonies. Then George the Third had a surge and increased the Hessians to about 30,000. But George the First only had to hang in there and eventually even the Lords of England couldn't have someone do their fighting forever. It cost money. Eventually they had to back down. The rest is history. (Franklin ran into Gibbon at a cocktail party and suggested that he, Gibbon, write a sequel and call it "The Rise and Fall of the British Empire". Gibbon was not amused.) (Now, I fear, someone might do well to write, "The Rise and Fall of the American Empire!")

And how much difference did it (our Revolutionary War) make? ("History does not disclose its alternatives.") Are Canada and Australia less free than we? They didn't fight a Revolutionary War! Do they have better or worse governments? Don't get me wrong; I am glad our George the First, and we, won and England had to lose. War will destroy the mightiest nation. The Lords of England had already fattened themselves mightily on the slavery of others. Whereas Hitler killed 6-Million people, the Lords of Great Britain killed 6-Million Indians at a crack and then went back and did it again. And, the Lords of Great Britain killed a million Irish and never wept a tear. That was after they had starved and impoverished their own countrymen. The Lords of Great Britain make Saddam Hussein look a sweet Kindergartener.

Now our George the Third (He's Bush the Second; but he's our Third George President; George the Third) has attacked the terrorist insurgents in another country. We don't know the outcome but it is likely that it won't make much difference. Except for all manner of tremendous losses all 'round.

Now I have worked my way around to our George the Third; perhaps the greatest Professional Liar in history. The fact that all of the Moneyed Religions classify George the Third (Bush the Second) as perhaps one of the greatest Professional Liars both tends to prove my classification and to explain why they supported him in his campaign for election and in his efforts to bring about the End-Times.

I was raised Catholic and the Catholic Church and School that I attended did not preach a great deal about the end-times in the sense of eschatology. Yes, there was always the "final judgment" when we would rise perfected physically and spiritually. I have a business associate who studies the Bible and is guided by the Holy Ghost so he understands all this stuff. Now, you and I know that everyone has always believed that he lives in extraordinary times usually something like the End-Times. Thousands of times whole sects have gone to this or that hill to await the end, then – oops – had to come back to the flatlands with the rest of us.

Professional Liars will set you free
I know they've done a lot for me.
I'd be idle at seventy
Pickin' bucks from the money tree
But with all their help, luckily
I'll keep workin' till ninety-three
I will be productive and see
That they can live in luxury.

Chapter Three

Our Credit Card

Today is September 19, 2008. We have a 13-trillion-dollar economy. Our national debt is a little less than $10-trillion (your share is about $32,000). The debt was about $3.6-trillion when Bush took office. "Way to go Brownie!" If Bush had kept on the Clinton budget, the National Debt would be about $1-trillion – almost getting rid of the Reagan debt. In the past week the national debt has increased by about $200-billion (by the end of this week, it turns out, it will be increased by about $1-trillion; so Bush will have increased the National Debt by about 9-trillion [Bush multiplied the National Debt by almost 3-times; 10-times what it should have and could have been]). (We've been buying bankrupt corporations like they were ice cream cones.) (Well, we didn't actually get any ice cream cone.) We just give the money to the criminal class (aka Professional Liars) to do more of the same. (Not to be confused; the criminal class is different than organized crime. Twain, or someone, said that the only organized crime in the U.S. is Congress. But he didn't know how bad it could get; he didn't know about the Republican congresses of the past dozen years composed almost entirely of Professional Liars – Santorum, McCain, McConnell, Jefferson [Dem], Frisk, Young, Gramm, Army, Sununu, Hatch, Lugar, Kemp, Gingrich, Helms, Bond, Warner, Hagel, Graham, Lamar, Hastert, Lewis, DeLay, Sensenbrenner, – the puke inducers. Rot! Decay! Poison! Corruption! Theft! Take the money and run.) We will do more of the same. I'm not finished with this.

I mentioned earlier that a car driven by a dead man smashed my wife's car about five weeks ago (I haven't been feeling well; that's why I haven't written much between then and now – I might tell you about that later). The previous paragraph, this and the next few paragraphs will be tied together 'though they seem disparate now. Naturally we have been paying for car insurance for fifty years, maybe one previous claim; so "the" insurance company has made a bundle off of us. Since we were asleep in bed when the car hit my wife's car and her car, of course, was stationary; it definitely was not her fault. My wife's car was totaled; there was nothing right on it. In our restaurant when some one orders a meal, we deliver it as fast as we can as good as we can make it. What a great business it would be if we could just take orders, take the money and never deliver. :::That's the insurance business! Or deliver only part of what we promised. :::That's the insurance business! Owned and operated (and regulated) by Professional Liars. The insurance adjuster found a real cheap car down in central Indiana the same make and model as my wife's car. (Who knows what the condition was!) There was no car like that within a hundred miles of us. That was their settlement offer; an inaccessible car hundreds of miles away. Yes! You guessed it; insurance adjustors are Professional Liars. If every two or three days they screw someone out of a few thousand dollars, they earn their money. Why do they have to steal a few thousand dollars every few days? I think I read that Warren Buffett has slipped to the SECOND richest man in the world. NO! Say it's not so! So, of course they have to steal a few thousand from us to ship to Warren; maybe he'll send us a thank-you-note? Naturally, Warren didn't personally steal the money. No! He's an innocent "holder in due course". He's "The Oracle of Omaha". His hands are clean. He doesn't personally steal money directly. He is innocent. Just like Hitler didn't personally kill anyone. He is just as innocent. He was "The Oracle of Berchtesgaden". Oh! What Oracles they are! Oracles, Oracles; Oracles got balls. Their hands are clean!

The car that was driven by the dead man also caused damage to our house and sidewalk. My wife and I attempted to get some information – the name of the driver, the insurance company; anything. The two-inch article in the paper was taciturn. Nothing! No go. We tried formal and informal channels. No go. We concluded that the dead driver was an undercover police officer or a federal narc agent – another casualty in the war on drugs. So we will just have to pay to fix our property ourselves. (10-23-08; my wife finally got the name of the car owner; the "girl friend" of the dead man. She, my wife, also got the name of the insurance company and the policy number. The insurance company [surprise, surprise] says that the man was dead and, therefore, they are not paying. Gosh, am I surprised. Sell a product and not deliver; why didn't I think of that!) (3-30-9; "The City", St. Louis has now issued a warning to us that we have to fix the front wooden stairs and hand-rail and re-pour the concrete steps or we will be ticketed!)

Within the past few weeks we paid off the only credit card that we have. (I had used the card over the last couple of years "as a last resort" to finance the business. I know that using a credit card to finance the business is a dangerous, desperate, and stupid thing to do. It was also the only thing to do. But it worked.) We saved the business and paid off the card. We have also paid our trade debt down to "current". We still have a mortgage and a line-of-credit but we pay on time. My wife has always paid our household bills on time. So! We were surprised when three loan companies turned down our application to buy the new (used) car (even Anheuser Busch Employees' Credit Union where we do most of our banking turned us down) (The loan was at eight-percent when the bank was getting nearly free money from Treasury). Apparently we were hit by the credit melt-down. One positive result of the credit crash is that the ten calls per day (three at dinner time) offering us money have stopped.

We hired three guys named Ben, Hank, and Chris to watch our house when we were gone. Each to do his part and to take his turn. Water the plants; feed, water, and walk the dogs; feed the cat, etc.; you know, "oversight". What a surprise when we returned. It's a two story house. From the basement you could look straight up and see the sky in several places. The place was trashed. The dogs' ribs were showing. The house was full of dog shit. The cat was so hungry that it was actually catching mice; that's desperation. The plants were dead.

Does that describe a mess? We figured it would cost about ninety-thousand-dollars to repair the damage. So we figured the fair thing – since they had caused the damage, they were experienced – that they; Ben, Hank, and Chris; should repair the damage to the house. So we gave them each a raise and thirty-thousand-dollars to do with as they pleased – everyone knows that paying lots of money makes people honest and motivates them to work harder and smarter. We promised that we would not interfere with them whatever they did – They're experienced, honorable men.

Now some people might say, "Fire the sons-of-bitches; bring a lawsuit, put the bastards in jail". But that is un-American; that is not the American-Way!

O.K.! You're way ahead of me; you guessed it; it wasn't our house; it was the American Economy, Investment Banking, and the Stock Market. And Ben, Hank, and Chris are Benjamin Bernanke, Henry Paulson, and Christopher Cox. Certainly in normal times they would each receive an Oscar for greatest Professional Liar (if the Academe had not been remiss by missing this category). But these are End Times. Times that call fourth the greatest. No one can successfully compete with Bush, Cheney, and Rove!

As an engineer, I am personally against bringing back the Guillotine. Not that they and all their Republican buddies in the Big Bucks Bubble Bath don't deserve it; they certainly do. It just hasn't worked out well in the past (from an engineering standpoint. No, no; the Guillotine works fine and would do a fine job on Ben, Hank, and Chris; but, for the remainder of us, things can go terribly wrong like a Coen Bros. Movie – who wants, oops, damn, shit, oops, damn, shit!) – look at France's experience (or Russia's similar experience with poison and lead) (this is discussed more in the Life and Sex chapter). The F.B.I. is (finally) investigating; we can all rest in peace. I'll bet dollars against a witch's-wand that they find someone. Yes! One of the poor little sweaty fat guys (who you never heard of before who only stole a couple-hundred-thousand-dollars) manning a bottom oar in the triremes will be found with some food hidden under his bench. He'll be tried in a court of law; the corporate news people will be all over it like flies on a dead fish. The story line will be "we are getting all the bad guys who caused The Second Great Depression and the Death Dance of the Dollar and the Large Liquidity Leak, yes we are getting them all". The little sweaty fat guy will be severely sentenced (basically to time served in a Country Club) (which, after the story has run out of gas, will be overturned on appeal or pardoned by G. W. Bush just before midnight).

To satisfy the public's blood lust, there will be "Oversight"; there will be "Regulation"; there will be "Monitoring". The Democrats will demand it; the Republicans will accede (as long as the unions are punished); the corporate news will praise the "Solution"; Democrats, Republicans, Corporate News: three groups of Professional Liars. I have given two synonyms for "Oversight" but there is a third: "CORRUPTION"! Here is one example of the most recent: "**Rampant corruption at US agency responsible for collecting oil royalties**: By Kate Randall: 13 September 2008; ... employees at the US agency in charge of collecting royalties from energy companies have been involved for years in inappropriate and illegal behavior, including accepting gifts, handing out sweetheart deals and engaging in sex and illegal drug use with oil company employees." This case is a little unusual in that the Regulators were fucking the company that they were regulating; usually they are just fucking us. But, like the word "cleave", the word "fuck" in this case has two opposite definitions. When "fucking the company" they had the literal ecstasy of having their dick in the companies' employee's pussy; when "fucking us" they merely had the pleasure of having their hand in our wallet. EVERY regulatory agency ALWAYS goes this way!

(In L.A., I was on the Board of Directors [we were the 'oversight' & 'regulators'] of our Condo Association. We served gratis; we all knew that we were not paid when we "ran" for office. But at the suggestion of our hired "Manager" we began going out for an annual dinner [taking along our 'life partners'] with the Condo Association paying in secret. We went to a mighty fine restaurant and drank plenty of fine wines [I was on the wagon]. It was over-the-top-expensive. That's corruption! I went along without saying much. That, too, was corruption. EVERY regulatory oversight monitoring board degrades in the same way. There is always 'justification'! There is always corruption! [We had 'auditors' checking on us {another layer of 'regulators'} who checked our arithmetic but never bothered to check our management procedures {did we go out for three bids for gardening, maintenance, etc.?} this was no more 'oversight' than rubberneckers at a construction site {sight}].)

There is not an exception. Utilities. Mines. Food. Broadcasting. Government contracts. Meats. Drugs. Railroads. ALL Privatization Always. Music. Charities. Churches. Roadbuilding. The regulators and the regulated are always in a 69. The only time that they can breath is when their partner farts. Professional Liars are the norm.

Regulation does not work! Professional Liars do.

Then what the hell ya gonna do to prevent... Ah, um y'know. How can you stop... you know, ah, um, you know, c'mon, you know. What are you going to do to prevent – how shall we say? – excesses?

Couldn't say it, could ya! Men or women in designer suits don't do it, do they? Go ahead, say it! How ya gonna prevent gittin' fucked? How are we going to prevent crime? "Crime" is the word/concept/idea that tied your tongue.

I am so glad that you brought that up! I feel downright un-American when I bring it up. We don't jail people in designer suits unless they steal from the rich. What can we do about it?

How about decriminalizing non-criminal behavior like kids smoking pot or women prostituting themselves and criminalizing criminal behavior like felony stealing or mass-murder? That, strangely, is the opposite of our present order. No one went to jail for deliberately torturing to death a thousand people a day with cigarettes. (Oh! I forgot! Those weren't people; those were commoners!) No one went to jail for the horrors of Thalidomide. No one went to jail for the deaths and injuries of the Dalcon Shield. No one goes to jail for deaths of miners from easily preventable mine disasters. Here's one now: SL P-D 10-4-8; A6: "... [S]entenced ... to three years probation ... cost the company $20 million ... net worth of $80 million ... pay a $40,000 fine and do 40 hours of community service." Poor bastard will probably have to play golf with the judge too. Aw, he had to pay a fine of 2-tenths-of-one-percent of what he stole! He got a letter of praise from a catholic priest and many other village idiots. He wears a three-piece-suit. He's a "pillar of the community". How could you possibly put him in jail with someone who doesn't wear a three piece suit and stole only say $100? That would be insulting. That would be un-American; we just don't do that sort of thing!

Here it is Thursday, September 25, 2008, the President has spoken; the economy is going to hell in a luge he says, he wants $700-Billion given to Benjamin Bernanke, Henry Paulson, and Christopher Cox to do with as they please without any kind of "interference", with absolute immunity from any responsibility. These guys do believe in Free Enterprise after all ("Free Enterprise" is a synonym for "Communism" for the rich). Like the days of Lords of old England, for us not to bow and kneel in their presence is to be beheaded. They love Free Enterprise. If the Supreme Court can appoint Bush President, I guess Congress could easily make these guys Jupiter, Thor, and Jesus. I was mistakenly thinking that when you've fucked up everything that you have ever done in your life, that maybe, just maybe your ass should be fired. Instead we are to give them $700-billion. You want to know how many cups of coffee I have to sell to pay for that? A lot. But what the hell, if you have never had to do anything in your life, it's just – what? – It's just money, dollars, green backs, bucks, folding-paper, filthy lucre. It is not putting in plumbing. It is not building cabinets. It is not laying brick. It is not milking cows. It is not frying eggs. It is just paper. Fuck it, it's just paper. These guys are criminals. Put them in jail! Especially that Cox sucker; he has a long rap sheet; he's a lawyer; he's a Harvard M.B.A; he was in the Reagan administration (probably the Savings and Loan crimes that cost me [as a taxpayer] $124-billions directly plus other costs; Presidential Candidate

John McCain and Bush's brother Neil were two of the miscreants [without even a wrist slap]. Surprise? Hell no! Laws are passed to protect the rich not to hobble those thieves!) These guys; like Bush, Congress, and C.E.O.s; know nothing about economics. Theory, yes? Reality? Nothing! Nothing! Nothing! If you have not been forced to do something creative for money, you know nothing about economics. Drive a thousand nails because you must; learn. Paint one-hundred paintings because you must; learn. Pan a thousand loaves of bread because you must; learn. Weed fifty rows of beets because you must; learn. Review a case study because it is in the curriculum of a professor who has never done anything productive for money because he had to; waste your fucking time.

That's all that we have in all "high" places: theorists who have never done anything productive in their lives. The McCain Campaign says that we are a bunch of whiners who have a mental depression. He has never done anything productive in his entire life. He says the government can't do anything good and he has been in the government all his life. He is running against himself. He says that the base of the economy is very strong. I was with a friend the other day when this friend had his car repossessed. The guy who was doing it was an insulting asshole like Gramm/McCain. Compassion? None! Empathy? None. Understanding? None ! Like Bush. Like McCain. Like McCain's economic adviser Phillip Gramm. Gramm has brain clap: rotting and putrid drainage from the mouth.

Our police department (yes, here in St. Louis) has been a car theft ring along with the police towing company. It is unfair to call it "the police towing company". It is, rather, a Saint Louis towing company although privately owned (you remember that 'privatization' thing that is sure to solve all of our problems?) a towing company that had a special relationship with the police department; a towing company that the police used all the time. It, the Towing Company, would steal cars and then sell them (or 'loan' them indefinitely to 'special' people like the Police Chief's daughter). This went on for years; it is not clear now just how many years or how many cars (maybe there will be an 'investigation' [whoever brought it up will be destroyed]). The Police Chief was involved to some degree. He was given $700,000 and told to walk. The towing company allegedly stole $700,000. Over how long a period I do not know. The stories of people whose cars were stolen are extremely distressing. When a poor person is a victim of a theft of that magnitude it is a life altering and destroying event. No one would help them, the victims. Not the police. Not the mayor. Not the courts. Certainly no lawyer. The mayor was livid because he (the city) did not get his cut of the swag. I did not hear of him being upset because of the distress suffered by the victims. The victims had no clout. The mayor is from an old established family. There's a difference. There's a void. There's a chasm.

What do we know for sure?

Monitoring = Corruption.

Regulation = Corruption.

Oversight = Corruption.

Privatization = Corruption.

Alright then, Smart Ass, how do you prevent murder, stealing, and stupidity?

How do you prevent murder and stealing any other place or time?

With cops!

No! You don't prevent it. Well, maybe you can prevent some but most of the time you punish it after it happens (as a deterrent to like-minded pig's asses). And yes it takes cops and, if you want to call that "regulation", so be it. But, and the cops have to be policed also. Because if a business can save a million dollars by paying a cop a hundred-grand they sure as hell will do it. It is done all the time, it is de rigeur. No question and no doubt. So the cops have to be well paid and they have to be rotated so they don't get friendly with management. They must somehow be aligned with the public interest. They must not be allowed to spend time with the corruptors. They must work at arms-length. And the criminal acts by the rich, which are now quite legal, must be made criminal. It is not fair to have only poor kids who committed petty crimes in jail, while the major thieves spend the winter in Acapulco.

When I worked for DuPont in Circleville, Ohio, I ran the contractors for a couple of years. This was at a plant that had, at the time, I believe about 2000 employees so they had many acres under roof; a flat roof that was loaded with equipment, work-crews, and machinery; so we spent many $Thousands on roofing repair each year. When I first took the job, the roofing contractor foreman offered me a bribe which I turned down. A couple of days later the contractor owner came in and said he was embarrassed about how small the "consideration of appreciation" was and he could understand how I could be offended and turn it down. He made a more "appropriate" offer. I turned that down too. He made it clear that all of the previous engineers that he had "worked with" had taken the "offer". I turned him down and found a new roofing contractor. I informed my boss what had happened. My boss gave me one of the most ignorant lectures that I have ever heard; the implication seemed to be that I was pretty stupid not to make a buck when I had the chance and "no one would be hurt" (he must have been on the take). At an earlier time at that plant, when I didn't pad my expense account, another of my supervisors there was completely disgusted with me; I was spoiling the system "you need to learn to take care of yourself", he said. Bribery, kickbacks, and the like corruption are endemic. They are systemic. They are universal. Corporations understand "it" little (or maybe they do and that's the way that they want it). Corporations make almost no effort to prevent or stop "it" (Corruption, after all, is rampant at the top). I could tell dozens of stories where I personally know "it" was going on and dozens more of which I was told "it" was going on. Professional Liars rule the day. Honest guys rue the day. Corporations do not want someone around who is incorruptible. That is dangerous. What else might they do? Honesty cannot trump loyalty and self-interest. The corrupt live in that Shining City on the Hill. The resisters live in Mildew Valley.

Yesterday the President signed the $700-billion bail-out of the crooks, for the crooks, and by the crooks. The crooks who cooked the books about mortgages. Seven-hundred-billion-dollars.

With our time travel machine it is now November 13, 2008. Secretary Paulson has now pissed away about $350-billion of the $700-billion that we gave him; squandered it on the Troubled Asset Relief Program (TARP). The Troubled Asset Relief Program reminds me of the Holy Roman Catholic Church. 'The Holy Roman Catholic Church is not Holy, is not Roman, and is not Catholic'; the Troubled Asset Relief Program is not Assets; is not Relief; and is not a Program. Paulson has, he says, changed his mind about buying more Toxic Assets. If it were Dr. Frankenstein changing his, Paulson's, mind and replacing it with that of a higher primate, we might have some hope. If we replaced a Troubled, Toxic Asset such as his mind, one could be excused for rejoicing that Happy Days Are Here Again.

Paulson says that he will not apologize for changing his mind when conditions have changed. But, conditions have not changed except that he now has half the assets that he had when he began. But other conditions have not changed; he has made no progress; he has given $350-billion to thieves; the economy is still unzipping at the same rate (the zipper is slightly more open). The rich are richer; the poor are poorer (to Paulson that's progress). But Paulson has expressed a desire to throw the program into reverse; he intends, he says, to allow MORE credit card debt, MORE auto loan debt, and MORE student debt. Someone should whisper into his ear (after getting his attention with a 2X4) that it was TOO much debt to begin with that got us into this mess. He also intends to spend $250-billion ("to spend" is what a drunken sailor does when blinded by red lights reflecting off firm nipples) he, Paulson, is going to buy stock in troubled banks (with our money). Really. Honest. We, us taxpayers, will now own bankrupt banks. That's Republican progress. They would be outraged if someone suggested that we Nationalized the oil companies and made a few $Trillion; but they are all smiles when we

Nationalize failed banks so that they can take their money and run, leaving us with the shells. Now travel back to late September or early October 2008.

Our son, Paul, has a house on Bainbridge Island, west across Elliot Bay from Seattle; the Northwest corner of the country. Our son Kevin has several properties in Fort Lauderdale Florida; the Southeast corner of the country. All the properties of both sons are in financial trouble. Both sons attempted to talk to their banks. The banks won't and can't talk to them about the contracts because the banks sold the contracts.

What?

The banks sold the contracts.

What?

Yes, dammit, the banks sold the contracts.

Who were the contracts with?

Look, Stupid, the contracts weren't "with" anyone; they were just contracts.

You can do that?

Certainly! Suppose, for example, I knock on your door with my little push lawnmower and my little weed-wacker, and my little hand-shears and I tell you that I would like to contract with you to do your yard work next summer. You are very concerned because you have many tender trees and wonderful flower beds. I assure you that I will take special care. We sign a contract. It would take me more than day to service your lawn each week. I really wouldn't make much money. So I sell your contract to a guy who has a tractor pulling a five-foot-wide mower who can cut your grass in fifteen-minutes and will make a very good per-hour-rate so he is willing to pay me a premium. HE sells the contract to Somber Corporation down in the Cayman Islands who have some Indian Indians service the contract. You have to pay. Maybe some Jamaicans will cut your grass. Everybody is happy.

I sure as fuck am not happy! How is his great big tractor going to avoid my trees and protect my flower beds?

I'm happy. I made a bundle in twenty minutes without doing any work. Fuck you! The guy I sold the contract to is happy; he's gonna make a bundle. Fuck you.

I'm not happy. I'm not going to pay you rascals! Swindlers!

Your credit will be destroyed. You will lose in court. (Judges belong to the same country-clubs as bankers and lawyers. They are not in your corner and don't give a shit about you. They consider you just another god damn trouble-maker like the 9-11 terrorists.) Your paycheck will be garnisheed. A lien will be placed on your house. We will do everything that we can to destroy you! Fuck you. We have more money than you. We have better lawyers than you. Our lawyers know that justice is winning the case and getting their fees paid. I play golf with the judge; we both belong to the same country-club. You on the other hand, have a nice flower bed. Ha! Fuck you, you little prick!

That seems dirty but the law is the law!

"Speculation is a round game; the players see little or nothing of their cards at first starting; gains may be great – and so may losses. The run of luck went against Mr. Nickleby. A mania prevailed, a bubble burst, four stockbrokers took villa residences at Florence, four hundred nobodies were ruined, and among them Mr. Nickleby.

"'The very house I live in,' sighed the poor gentleman, 'may be taken from me to-morrow. Not an article of my old furniture, but will be sold to strangers!'

"The last reflection hurt him so much that he took at once to his bed; apparently resolved to keep that, at all events.

"'Cheer up sir!' said the apothecary.

"'You mustn't let yourself be cast down, sir,' said the nurse.

"'Such things happen every day,' remarked the lawyer.

"'And it is very sinful to rebel against them,' whispered the clergyman.

"'And what no man with a family ought to do,' added the neighbours.

"Mr. Nickleby shook his head, and motioning them all out of the room, embraced his wife and children, and having pressed them by turns to his languidly beating heart, sunk exhausted on his pillow. They were concerned to find that his reason went astray after this; for he babbled, for a long time, about the generosity and goodness of his brother and the merry old times when they were at school together. This fit of wandering past, he solemnly commended them to One who never deserted the widow or her fatherless children, and, smiling gently on them, turned upon his face, and observed that he thought he could fall asleep."

---Nicholas Nickleby, Charles Dickens---Published as a serial from 1838 to 1839---

But if they sell, or rather sold, the contracts then why are the banks in financial trouble?

Well, when the contracts were sold, the value went up. Then someone bundled a bunch of these contracts and called them by one or another of a dozen different names like "mortgage based (or backed) securities"; "collateralized debt obligations"; "pass-through mortgage-backed securities"; "pooled investments"; etc. These mortgages were shuffled like cards; they were cut and dealt like cards over and over into different "hands" and each "hand" was called a different name and each hand was sold for more money and then reshuffled and resold for yet more money and finally your bank bought a bunch of "securities" which were based on the bad mortgages he had sold. They weren't worth the paper that they were printed on (as Yogi said about verbal contracts) but their price had multiplied by thousands.

Some dealers became worried about the lack of value. Someone else saw a buck to be made, so they guaranteed the value of the worthless 'structured securities'. Yup! They 'insured' the securities so that the holders couldn't lose. But they couldn't "insure" them because that was against the law so they waved a wand and called the "insurance" policies "swaps". Sort of like Genesis; it is what you call it. A laughing hyena is a laughing hyena. Take the "insurance" policy, pour holy-water over it and say, "I baptized thee Swaps; thou art forbidden to be an "Insurance" policy." Maybe they used Latin? So for every dollar of (doubtful) mortgage, about a hundred-thousand dollars of derivative securities was created. Why should your bank care if the mortgage was sound, it had already made money selling the mortgage; why should anyone care if the derivative securities were any good; everyone was making $M/Billions. Keep dealing!

This wasn't the mutha of all Ponzi Schemes; this was the GOD of all Ponzi Schemes. This was the big bang of bucks. A Billion sheets of paper worth $0.001 were each turned into $50,000 each. God, himself, could not have done better. Bankers can create. Bankers can create (the appearance of) wealth.

Eventually, naturally the house of cards had to fall. (See the Chapter "The Life And Sex Island".) Now, 10-29-'08, I'm back, we have come to believe that these crooks were even more creative. It now appears that they took a sheet of plain 20-weight white paper and printed on it that "this is an investment grade certificate of value worth many $K-bucks" and on the back printed in 5-point font "this security entails significant risk" and sold them to investors as investment grade securities (for your retirement fund) and that the crooks got a 30% to 60% commission for the theft. What a country! I just love free enterprise! Isn't this just the greatest country! I just hate these god damn socialists who are always bitching about the Capitalist System. Let's Privatize Social Security and put all your retirement money into these "Certificates" with "Significant Risk" you'll make a killing; we will 'save' Social Security. (Come to think of it; I haven't heard anyone say that, Lately.)

Now my employees in the government are going to take my money and buy these nearly worthless contracts from the bankers and dealers who hold them now (toxic assets). The crooks are off the hooks. Not one had the limited decency to jump out of a 40-story window.

Will this help my sons with the properties that they "own"?

You mean, "Will the $700-billion bail out help your sons?"

Yeah; that's a lot of money! Will it help my sons?

Nope! Not a whit! It won't help your sons or anyone else who has a troubled mortgage (Paulson is paying $Billions of our money for shit! How can that help anyone but the thieves? Where was Paulson when Jesse James wanted to get 'off the hook'?) It won't help anyone who gets mildew on his wash. It will help a few who live high on the hill. It'll help some of the thieves. Remember,

America is the land of the thieves, by the thieves, and for the thieves.

Well, it will jump-start the economy; won't it? And that will help us all!?!?

No. Nope! It is estimated that the amount stolen is about $62-trillion. That's trillion dollars. That seems very high but it could be, might be, far worse; nobody knows. (Now, 10-29-'08, that $62-trillion figure has been repeated many times so that it now appears that the theft did actually get to that Bubba The Hut size.) $700-billion is only about one-hundredth enough. That's like trying to pay a mechanic seven-dollars for a $620.00 engine repair for your car. It ain't agonna go. We need a hundred times more; we ain't got it!

Wait a minute! Wasn't $13-trillion about our whole GDP for an entire year? The money stolen is four-and-three-quarters times everything that we produce for a whole year?

Yup! Yup! Yup! Setting aside the fact that the $13-trillion is not production; more than half is "service". These are no minnows we're trying to fry. It's more like a 620-pound shark shank you're tryin' to put in the frying pan sized for a seven-pounder flounder; tryin' to put it in all at once. It's not going to fry. The people who committed this giant fraud weren't pikers. They were massive thieves.

But that's $700-Billion being dumped into the economy! It has just got to help or we are all shitted!

Look; calm down! This is a difficult thing to think about. Like some rehabilitation, it requires a twelve-step program to think about it. Let me walk you through it: Step 1; sit down. Step 2; relax. Step 3; examine your navel. Step 4; reflect that the cause of the First and Second Great Depression was the fantastic, mean, cruel, deliberate, horrible, unnecessary, inequality of wealth. The rich have too much wealth (see chapter "The Life and Sex Island"), the poor and middle-class have too little to sustain life. Like now! Step 5; consider that the lower classes have to borrow to live. Step 6; remember that the debt of the lower classes becomes unmanageable (they cannot pay). Step 7; observe the rich turn the screws to torture the lower classes. Step 8; watch with horror the lower classes escape (change names, drink, do drugs, sell drugs, beat their spouses, torture their children, commit suicide, throw themselves on the open-fire of religion, 'declare' bankruptcy, work four jobs, steal, move leaving no forwarding address, etc.). Step 9; notice the rich demand that the law punish the lower classes. Step 10; see the politicians say 'ohmygod, we might not get reelected, we maybe should do something, but I don't know what-the-fuck'. Step 11; gawk while the politicians give $700-billion to rich thieves, dah. Step 12; be delighted to see that then things really go to hell (there's a fire in grill, throw gasoline on it!).

But some experts are saying that "lack of faith in the banks" is the root cause of the financial freeze.

That's like saying that vomiting is the root cause of drunkenness.

Maybe so, but other experts are saying that the "bad" mortgages are the root cause of the financial meltdown.

Experts? We've had "Experts" (also known as Professional Liars) running our economy and look what happened. To say that "bad", naughty mortgages caused the Second Great Depression is like saying; let's see; what? Remember I told you about the speeding car driven by a dead man, shot in the head, crashed into the car behind my wife's car, then that second car smashed into my wife's car, then my wife's car smashed into the car in front of her throwing her car into the middle of the road, then, finally, the speeding car driven by the dead man hit my wife's car; all in an instant. Well, to say that the naughty mortgages caused the Second Great Depression is like saying that my wife's car caused that crash. The massive inequality in our economy is a speeding car driven by a man shot in the head; it is going to crash into something. If the speeding car driven by a dead man hits a tree, the "Experts" would say that the tree caused the crash. If it hits a house, the "Experts" would say that the house caused the crash.

C'mon, the freeze had some causal effect!

What is it? Freeze or Meltdown; make up your

mind. What is it? Cause or Effect? "Did you ever have to finally decide? Say yes to one and let the other one ride."

I don't know! You hear all kinds of terms: hump, slow-down, hic-up, recession, market-correction, bear-market, financial-crises, or bank-crisis but a dead mouse by any other name would smell as sweet.

Nobody wants to say it: Depression, Depression, Depression, The Second Great Depression. To say that the root cause of the "financial meltdown" is the "bad" sub-prime mortgages is like saying the empty bottle is the cause of drunkenness. Drinking causes the empty bottle; drinking causes drunkenness. Mal-distribution of earnings/wealth; the middle-class having sub-subsistence wages caused the First Great Depression; causes "bad" mortgages; causes "financial meltdown"; and causes the Second Great Depression. Dumping $700-billion at the top is like curing the drunk by giving him another drink. It's like giving the bartender another case of booze to give to the drunk. In a Three-Stooges Movie this would all be very funny but the acting would be better and, about the time it became tiring, you could walk out and get a breath of fresh air. Pretty soon we'll be screaming at the projectionist to cut the god-damn film this isn't funny anymore.

We're screwed. You're sayin', we're screwed.

Yeah, we're screwed but look on the bright side.

(Laughter.)

No really! Until we have a severe Depression, we are just heading toward a Depression.

Oh! Wow, that's really consoling. Gosh, you're really cheering me up! Buckle-up, a Depression is coming; smash, oh! Good! It's here!

That didn't come out right. We have been going down hill since the last major Depression. We have been heading for a depression for fifty years. But the Class Warriors, Aristocrat Class Terrorists owned the Congress, owned the Corporate Media, owned the Guppies (Professional Liars) in the Think Tanks, owned the Goodie Foundations, owned the President, the Moneyed-Religions-Businesses, and owned the Supreme Court. They were all very happy with the massive unfair inequality. The public was distracted with-and-by Sports, Frivolous Moneyed Religion Nut-cakes, Tits and Ass, Fear Factor Wars on This and Wars on That (the Republicans have been winning on wars of one kind or another for more than fifty years; it works and works and works; and Americanus Publicus Ignoramus never seems to catch on; meanwhile, the only war worth noting has been the War On The Middleclass [the Middleclass lost]). The Class Warriors, Aristocrat Class Terrorists were in complete charge of everything. They made certain that the guns of the law were pointed at the poor and middle-class; and the Judge Seats were stacked with Midgidiots. They made certain that the poor and middle-class were sinking in a financial morass. There was no chance that the downward dash could be stopped. If we have another Real Depression (which, for several months, I have been saying was coming while Paulson was saying, "the worst is over") there is a slight chance that things may change.

That's why both presidential candidates are running on change?

Yes, they both have a slogan along those lines; something like, "change you can trust", and "change you can rely on"; something like that.

But McCain is the incumbent party; he's a part of it! Why is he not running on his record? Why is he running away from his record?

Well; it's the worst record in the history of the United States; maybe in the history of the World. He's hoping that the American People are too stupid to notice that he's running against himself. And about half the people ARE too stupid to notice. They must like being pissed on (trickle-down) or they are too stupid (or too distracted or too lied to) to notice. And McCain is an utterly guileless liar; it just comes naturally to him.

He says that he would put America first.

I think that that is correct. Whereas George Bush says, "Fuck you America". McCain puts America first and says, "America, fuck you."

That's putting it pretty strong. There were other important issues; like abortion. That minister someplace asked, "When does life begin?" McCain said, "At conception". Obama said something like, "The answer to that is above my pay grade"; which sounds pretty stupid.

I break in here at a later time: 11-5-2008, the day after Obama has been elected.

My wife and I can both speak with insight about the issue of ABORTION.

I'll let my wife go first:

She can remember huddling with her two sisters on a couch while her father beat and beat and beat her mother over and over and over. This was a scene to happen at any moment; to jump out at you like Freddie Kruger or Jaws. A childhood giggle could be shattered like a pane of glass by an unexpected rock – the drunken father.

Later she would 'find out' or 'come to realize' that those two other children were her cousins and the 'father' was her blood uncle and her 'mother' was her aunt (-in-law). Those three little girls wandered the city completely unsupervised. Yes, my wife has never seen nor known her biological father. Her mother did not want her, my wife, at that time. I have never called my wife, no matter how angry I was, "bastard". That would have hurt too much. She is a bastard. Today, it seems, about half the kids being born are bastards; but back then "bastard" was an extreme derogatory term and situation. Calling someone a bastard was solid grounds for a slander suit.

Later, my wife's mother was married and my wife was adopted (with a payment of $5,000 from the biological father [about $72,000 today]). My wife was very fortunate that her step-father was a great guy. Life was better but she was still and always the "other". My wife was, obviously, the eldest of her (half) siblings by several years.

My turn: Some of this, I apologize; will repeat some things mentioned elsewhere.

I am the youngest of my living siblings. I had one younger brother who was still-born. (How much has the world missed him? Not at all! He might have been... god knows what. But he wasn't. He died. He was never a child. He wasn't forgotten, he is and was unknown. The

The same as an aborted blastula. Say any idiotic thing that you want; it is not a child.)

Twelve or thirteen of us grew to first-communion age; ten of us to voting age. I apologize that I don't know the complete family history. A lot happened before I was born; and I was born a non-person in the depths of the First Great Depression. My parents had been trying to kill each other for at least twenty years before I was born. My oldest brother, Al (twenty years older than I), onetime described to me how the Old Man had gotten the scar on his nose. Al as a teenager had a broken arm which was bound with a metal splint. There was a stand-off between him and the Old Man. The Old Man thought he might be safe because Al was incapacitated with a broken arm. The Old Man took a chance and started to beat Mother. Al hit him a couple times. Ergo, presto, the gaping nose wound from the metal splint.

So, if Al, at that time, was thirteen or fourteen, there must have been at least three or four, maybe five of us born after that yet. So, despite the outrageous enmity that was evident, there was still a lot of fucking going on in that house. My memory is of a relationship that could not go lower but did. The atmosphere was as I have heard the front-line of a battle described. Long periods of idle tension broken by surprise violence, blood, body blows, beatings, and broken bones. Then the slicked down parade into church on Sunday. My parents, in my opinion, were peasants in the worst meaning of that appellation. The Old Man had the lowest of the mill-jobs. He often drank his paycheck and come home penniless. I remember once my Mother called a cab and went to the bar where the Old Man had cashed his check (how did she know which one?). She came home with the check. (I once began to read Angela's Ashes but it was all just too, too familiar. I could not go on!)

My parents followed all of the trappings of the Holy Roman Catholic Church and only those tenets which were convenient. Anything requiring moral effort was unknown. When I was a pre-schooler and was home alone, there was a man I knew as Nicky who would visit our house, coming across our back acres from the railroad track.

I would be given a treat and told that I did not see anything and given some long task in the garden or barn and Nicky would disappear into the house with my Mother. One time, walking with some second grade friends near St. Mary's School which we attended; we almost bumped into a drunk who was with a painted lady; he was so attuned to her that he did not see me. I must have grown pale but I kept 'my cool' and did not let my friends know that that was my Old Man. My Mother was always smugly proud when she knew that "her boys" were fucking some of the local girls. I was not one of her boys. From third-grade on, I signed my own report card and no one ever questioned me about it. I think that I should be proud that I was a good forger. I had malnutrition anemia. As a child, I wandered the country-side completely unsupervised. Shoes and shirt came off first day of vacation and not on again until first day of school (except for Sunday church).

I never, ever got approval from either parent or any of my siblings for anything. Lots of disapproval, Yes! I think that I accomplished a lot in life. When I graduated from high school, no one showed up. When I boxed varsity at university, no one came. When I graduated from Engineering School (U.W. Madison, January 1960) I didn't even do the cap-and-gown bit. No one mentioned it to me; no one, except my in-laws, congratulated me. One time when I complained to my father-in-law about not making a mark in life, he said, "You raised four kids!". Implying that I (we) had done a pretty good job of it. And, one time – I have to make a correction – about three years ago, I was visited by my last living (of course, he's living how else could he have visited – I don't believe in ghosts) sibling, Jim, and he said after seeing our restaurant, "I'm really impressed by what you guys have done here." He let me buy him dinner.

Being unwanted affected my wife and me in opposite ways. She's the eldest; I'm the youngest. She's the boss; I'm submissive. To a point. (My wife would not agree with those last three sentences). You cannot hurt me in body or soul and I know it; lots of people have tried and failed (Failed finally to defeat me. Hurt me? Yes.

Made me give up? No!) I have, unfortunetely, insulated myself from hurt. I keep my mouth shut. I don't speak my mind until I have had a long time to think about it and make sure that I am right and cannot be challenged in the matter in hand. Sometimes, I bring up a 'question' that my adversary thought had been 'put to bed' the day (or more) before and s/he is pissed-off. There are also lines over which I cannot be pushed. This, regrettably, gives the impression that I am slow and will not stand up for myself and then an adversary finds that I am immovable to his surprise and dismay. Still, people are fond of and admire me when they don't have to compete with me.

If you are born and raised in a snugly atomic family (not "atomic family", you idiot; "nuclear family"), perhaps you cannot understand what abortion is all about. Perhaps, then you should recuse yourself from the discussion. You just may be ignorant. How can you know? You almost must be ignorant of the subject matter. (If you were born and raised rich, perhaps you should not pretend to know poverty either. I, in return, will not pretend to know what it is like to be raised rich.) I will, in turn, recuse myself if you are talking about a warm, furry family.

So, what if I had been aborted or been delivered still-born? What if? What if?

(I remember reading a Science Fiction story about someone who had invented a time machine and guided "big game" hunters back in time to kill dinosaurs. The guide was always careful to pick the exact instant when the dinosaurs would be killed by lightning or such because they knew not what might happen if they changed the past. Would changing the past, change the present or future? Coming back from the hunt they found that Obama had not been elected; Bush had staged a coup and was 'serving' a third term. The guide examined his shoe and found that he had stepped on a tiny little yellow butterfly. The future had been changed. [O.K. It wasn't about Obama and Bush. I made that part up, now calm down, for Christ sake!])

So, if I had been aborted, the world would be

changed in unknown ways. Would I care? I certainly would not! Would god care? Get real! Would my wife care? She might be married to the man of her dreams! I can tell you it is no fun to be an unwanted child; it is life stunting; it is a night of nightmares; a life of never a peaceful dream. When my parents died at different times, in different cities, their property and valuables were divided up; there was nothing for Teddy. Being an unwanted child does not miraculously end at eighteen months or eighteen years. Being unwanted has no end. Unlike the Sword of Damocles; it hangs by a horse-hair over you always.

If you have not walked there; you know it not. So, if you are not or were not an unwanted child, shut up about abortion. You are an ignoramus on the subject and it is none of your business (unless you are pregnant and it is your abortion that is under consideration. In which case, it is none of my business). Just shut your mouth, you stupid asshole. It is none of your business. It is the business of the hapless girl, lady, or woman who is pregnant. She can get advice from whomever she pleases but she should not be coerced or shamed into doing anything other than what SHE decides. She should not bring an unwanted child into this coarse, unforgiving, un-understanding world.

If you want to stop abortions, make sure that we have lots of real education about sex and birth-control. Got that! Limit yourself to making sure that boys, men, gentlemen, girls, women, and ladies know what they are about when their dick gets hard and their pussy gets tumulose pink and wet. And the pecker will absolutely, simply die if it doesn't get cuddled in that nice warm, moist cunt. And that vagina will spin into oblivion if it is not resuscitated by the stroking of that manly tool.

One abortion eliminates one unwanted child, one compromised ego, one victimized youth, one beaten lad or lass, one lost soul, one incomplete adult, one no-self-confidence-human, one struggling bugger, one sliced human, perhaps one frustrated, manic, cruel, victimized, frantic, confused, troubled, wanting, bewildered half-person; one burdened mother, one incomplete lady, one resentful woman, one harried father, one troubled father, one rueful man; perhaps a ruined, forced, resentful marriage.

An abortion is usually a blessing. A million abortions eliminates three million unfortunate, partial, troubled humans; and three million troubled relationships. An earth populated by unwanted children is not a happy earth to contemplate; an earth of crime, distress, and trouble. Not a month goes by without a story of some child(ren) being tortured; often to death; most such stories are hidden. (I have heard of dozens that never made it to page three or further obscurity.) Do not bring nor let others bring into the world unwanted child(ren). Eliminate abortions by eliminating unwanted pregnancies. Eliminate unwanted pregnancies by eliminating conceptions. Fucking causes conceptions. The only way to eliminate fucking is to eliminate animals. Say your matins for birth control.

Since this is called a free country (particularly by men who do not wish it so) I must confess that there are quasi-homo sapiens with debauched craniums who hold an opinion opposite to that which I have just expressed. And as Patrick Henry might have said, I will fight to the death for their right to hold any dissolute opinion that they wish. However holding an incorrect opinion and screaming the same along with foul obscenities at young girls engaged in lawful activity are two contrary situations. Though both the holding and the screaming in that situation clearly reflect sourly upon one's parents and upbringing, as well as indicating a depreciated intelligence, they are rarely arrived at without the erroneous reading and interpretation of one revered, claimed holy book or another. As we all know, every ludicrous opinion and teaching since the dawn of language has been documented and sworn to by such revered claimed holy books. There is, in fact few if any outlandishly stupid claims which cannot be proven by such books. Since asses will continue braying, such contrary and erroneous opinions will continue to be sprayed over the land. The Catholic Church in particular can be forgiven for extolling the breeding and production of compromised children as this gives them ample material for their rump affairs.

The Catholic Church must bear responsibility for the near destruction of the earth because they have been actively supporting and demanding the election of duplicitous, compromising Republicans including George W. Bush. They have done this linked arm in arm with such Professional Liars and Aristocratic Class Warrior Terrorists as The Wall Street Journal and Forbes Magazine. It is not just the Catholic Church; it is nearly the whole of the Religious Industry which has fought for the destruction of the earth. I bow to Religion as it is a richer and more adroit business even than the Insurance Business. The Insurance Business sells a product which it has no intention of delivering. The Religion Business sells Fear-Relief; Fear which it creates from the depths of beast side of man. The Religion Business creates the Fear and then promises to maintain that Fear with the distant and non-achievable Fear-Relief that they promise will never come. The only Fear-Relief is Death. And they charge for that. It is a great business and I am green with envy. I wish that, in our restaurant, we could create a maddening desire for our food and then we could go around among our customers and collect money by promising that their hunger would continue and, therefore, they should continue to give us money.

I was imperfectly happy to pay for the Religion Industry as long as they didn't try to destroy me. But now that they have attacked me personally I chafe at having to pay them while they abuse me. I concede that the Religion Industry has the 'right' to say whatever they wish about any subject. And, since they have the 'right', I believe that it follows that, if they so believe, they also have the 'duty' to say whatever they desire. However, when they say that to which I object, I then object to having to pay them to say it.

How do I have to pay them? The City must obtain funds to operate. I am forced to pay (what the City considers) my share. But, since the Religion Industry is excused from paying their share, I must make up the difference. My share is, therefore, increased to make up for the Religion Industry's shortfall. This, I believe, abuses me. And, were the Religion Industry fallen on hard times, I might relent and pay their share. But, in fact, the Religion Business is a highly profitable business and it is eminently able to pay its share. Why are they excused from paying? Likewise, the Federal Government requires funds to maintain and increase operations – to wage war, to reward thieves, to pay miscreants, etc. I must pay to provide funds for my employees to do what they do even though they do the opposite of what I would have them do. Again, the Religious Industry is excused from paying what is their share (when they, in fact, approve and urge the insane acts of the Federal Government) and I must make up the difference. This is clearly taxation without representation. I find it repugnant that I must pay for activities which are not sanctioned by my Government and which, therefore, I can have no influence upon such activities, and thus it seems radically unfair that I must support these activities of the Religion Business. The Religion Industry should, I firmly believe, lose their exemption from paying taxes when they engage in political and social activities which go against my fundamental rights and my core beliefs.

That minister someplace asked, "When does life begin?" McCain said, "At conception". Obama said something like, "The answer to that is above my pay grade"; which sounds pretty stupid.

Yes, it is very stupid; both answers are very stupid; ignorance at its most shallow (or deepest, if you prefer). But somehow, difficult though it seems, the question (made-up by a Professional Liar) is more ignorant than the answers. Life began 3- or 4-billion years ago. Since then, it has been a continuum (although it may have begun again and again spontaneously just as flight and sight have evolved several times each). I did not create life when I fucked my wife. That would put me in a class with several gods around the world. As my wife will be happy to tell you, I am definitely not a god.

But when the sperm combines with the egg, isn't a new life created?

Don't be silly. The sperm and the egg are both alive and each contains a half compliment of DNA. Although the egg is more equal than the sperm since it also contains the mitochondria which are also essential to human life and only come from the mother as the sperm has no room for such nonsense.

"Nonsense!"???

Well, not nonsense. But the sperm is stripped down because it has a lot of work to do. It has to go searching for the female. That's one hell of a lot of work. That's why I've been married for over half a century; I never had time to go looking for another female.

But some females must have come to you.

Yeah; but I didn't have time for that.

There's more to it than you're telling.

Maybe.

But a lot of people talk about life beginning some time at or after conception. Are they all Professional Liars?

No, but they are not correct either. Even if a majority believes something, it is not necessarily correct. Might does not make right.

Minorities are less often correct.

Maybe. Maybe not. But, for me, an engineer, facts rule. Reality trumps superstition.

That the egg combined with the sperm is a complete cell is not "superstition".

True, after conception the egg combined with the sperm does make a cell with a complete complement of DNA. But every cell in the body (except red blood cells and maybe a few others) is, likewise a similar cell in that it contains a full complement of DNA. I said that I had recently been to the doctor; well I had a urinary track infection. Every time I peed, I peed away, I don't know, hundreds maybe thousands of white blood cells; each with a full complement of DNA. Was I murdering hundreds or thousands of babies? Every time I spit, I spit many cells with complete bunch of DNA, I spit potential babies. Am I a mass murderer? When I shower I schluff off "many" complete cells; just as complete as a fertilized egg. Every one capable of being a complete human being under the proper circumstances. Am I a mass murderer?

You can't put a damn skin cell in a uterus; a womb, and make a damn Jesus Christ baby!

That's a claim, not a fact. I don't think that it has ever been tried. It is very easy to get pregnant; it is difficult to avoid pregnancy. If you took the DNA from a skin cell and replaced the DNA in a fertilized egg with it and put it in a human uterus, you probably would have a baby. I think that we are off on a non-productive tangent anyway. Remember, the real fanatics think that birth control and even masturbating is the same crime as abortion.

That's not so!

It is. I have been thoroughly lectured on the subject more than once. They don't talk about it much but if they succeed with outlawing abortion, they will go to the next level until they control everything about your pecker or pussy. They will not be satisfied with less than complete control. The very people who say, "Get the Government off our backs!" are the same people who say, "Get the Government on our beds!"; they wish to control your pecker and your uterus (whichever you may have, assuming you can't have both but do indeed have one or the other). What happens to your pecker and your uterus ought to be, to my way of thinking, between you and your pecker or between you and your uterus; not between your pecker or uterus and some guy with a Roman collar and/or a Pecker Hat (or a god damn insane politician).

Maybe they are Professional Liars.

This all goes back before the beginning of agriculture about 13,000 years ago when we didn't understand much more than dogs do today. Yeah, some busy-body figured out that if you put a seed in the ground you got something to eat; but even that was explained supernaturally. Unlike dogs, we have to pretend that we know everything. "Oh yeah. Lightning? Sure I know what causes lightning. It's the gods fighting. Yeah. They throw thunderbolts at each other and, when they hit, they spark, y'know." If you read the Iliad, you will note that the gods had absolute, total control of everything – if a lowly human thought that he could do something without the personal blessing of one god or another, he was presumptuous and was certain to be punished. (Did the eagle fly on your right [good] or on your left [bad]. If you turned 180° you reversed your fortune.) It is the same as today if you listened to any of the evangelical religions. Idiocy has not advanced. When our dads told us that the gods made lightning we believed it and if someone said that our dads were wrong, we called them a liar and a heretic and we killed them. As knowledge was gathered, the people who gathered it were burned at the stake (any new knowledge threatens the existing power structure. We can't have that!). People who said that we were not at the center of the universe were burned at the stake. People who saw life under the microscope were burned at the stake. Even into the nineteenth century, it was common knowledge that life sprang from earth and rotting hay and most everything else spontaneously. Mice and rats just popped up out of the fields. People who believed otherwise were considered stupid and heretics. Everybody likes a good story. Most of us resist facts that contradict a good story. Most people still don't believe in evolution! Wow! We don't have poor education in the United States of America, we don't have any education.

Chapter Four

Illustrious Immigration

Ah dint come here from nuther place
Bin settin' here since god give grace
Ahm the one who built this here thing
Mah blacks helped wile I'sn the porch swing
Now's I got it all right nigh done
Them wetback's sayin' gimme one
Tell me why I should give them space
When they just want to take my place?

What do we know for sure?

Immigration is the Quemoy and Matsu, the Missile Gap, the Communism, the "tough on crime", and the Terrorism of the 2008 election cycle (Overtaken by the Depression Cycle). Call it the epicycle. Crank it up baby, let's not talk about issues. Let's talk about this old, old cinder (dating at least back to 1894 when George Pullman owner of the Pullman Palace Car Company imported Mexicans to break the Pullman Strike) this cold cinder, which we will rediscover whenever we need a red herring. Step right up folks. Extra, extra, read all about it. Mexicans are invading our country rather than starve to death. We used to call 'em Wetbacks but that is no longer politically correct. Now they are "Illegal Aliens" something like ET, Alf, Jabba the Hutt, or Predator but not quite so nice or from so far away and they don't speak English as well as Chewbacca; maybe they need a Babel Fish. But, what the hell, for voters who don't know that Kansas is a state instead of a stopover on the way to Oz and don't know who's buried in Jimmy Hoffa's tomb or what "in like Flynn" means, it's all the same. We are being invaded by Aliens; Illegal Aliens. Who, by the way, like Reagan's black bucks, are living off of our welfare money which, as we've been told, is most of our taxes. Not only are they living off of our welfare but they are simultaneously taking all of our jobs and occupying all of our schools and emergency rooms!

What in the hell is going on? The news and the politicians make no sense nor do we expect them to nor do they intend to (sense was tried and the ratings were low, let's stick to cleavage, banter, and "OH! MY GOD! There's a War on Christmas"). We can figure it out for ourselves as we must. What do we know for sure? Who benefits? Follow the money.

Obviously, the immigrants benefit. (They send back home about $20-billion per year; about $2000 each.) They are here by the millions we are repeatedly told (between 7- and 20-million; est. about 12-million – increasing the U.S. labor force by about ten-percent – 10%); if they did not benefit, word would get back home in a minute and the flow of immigrants crossing the border would stop pronto. So, we know for sure, that it is better to wash dishes or cut lawns in the United States and live five to an apartment than it is to not work in Mexico and other points south; Guatemala, Belize, Honduras, El Salvador, Nicaragua, Costa Rica, and Panama. Wow! How did things get so bad down there and what would it take to fix 'em?

Who else benefits?

Obviously the people, who hire the immigrants at substandard wages, benefit. Often, though not always, these are small building, road, and roofing contractors, mom and pop restaurants, and landscapers; although large firms (knowingly) hire "them" through contractors.

What else do we know for sure?

If it were only the immigrants and small business owners who benefited from the influx of illegal immigrants the flow would have been stopped permanently in the nineteenth century. No politician gives a shit about illegal immigrants or small businesses. (How do I know that for sure? I live it everyday; we are nothing but a vein for tax Dracula. When they drive one sucker to go bust they just say, "Next! Next Sucker! Who's Next! Step right up, bare your throat!") Nope, many big guys benefit, for sure. How? When there is a surplus of 12-million workers (10%, remember) who will do anything for any pay, there is a huge downward pressure on wages and an effective force for breaking unions. Who benefits the most? Whoever is the largest employer in the United States. Who is the next largest beneficiary? Whoever is the second largest employer in the United States of America. Don't ever forget who owns the government. The big guys do. They are the boss and their government employees (Representatives, Senators, and Presidents) will do whatever they are told. And they are told to talk about the "immigration crisis" and do nothing effective to stop it. Let's give Boeing trillions-of-dollars to build the Chinese Wall, the Maginot Line, Hadrian's Wall, and the Berlin Wall along the border. It makes it look like we are taking firm action. It cannot work. It is not intended to work. It will not work. That, we know for sure.

Wait a minute! You're saying that "they" "arranged" to have all those economies fail and force all those Latinos into poverty so that they would then be compelled to migrate to the United States? That's nutty! That would require a vast conspiracy and tremendous skill, power, and money to bring it off. That would be like all of the episodes of Mission Impossible played at once. Boy! Talk about whacko conspiracy theories, you got a plum there buddy. You can't even show that "they", the big wheels, the powers that be, the industrial giants would want to do it much less being able to show that they could or, finally, to show that they did. I don't even believe that those little ag nations would know if they were poor. Actually, they are not "poor" they are well off living in their little agrarian societies.

You're right! That is way too complicated to set out like a Boolean Logician to lay out a step by step fool-proof argument that, say, Nelson Rockefeller, Andrew Carnegie, Warren Buffett, and/or Bill Gates planned and carried out such a conspiracy. We can't show that they did (these things, when they are done, are done in secret). But we do know some things for sure. We can show that massive Latino immigration has created a desirable effect for United States Rich (USR). We can show that the USR would like to drive down labor costs to a low level and that no level is low enough for them. We can show that we have the will and power to destroy those Central American economies. And, finally, we can show "we", the United States, you and I, did destroy their economies with no reportage, no apologies and no regrets. And, yes, the Middle Americans really don't have a lot of choice but to starve or come to the United States of America like my great-grandparents did (from the Netherlands) (And your ancestors did from someplace - even you Amerindians).

Those, Mexico, Guatemala, Belize, Honduras, El Salvador, Nicaragua, Costa Rica, and Panama economies are in ruin:

Numbers are boring; I'll try to make it as painless as possible.

This is the Percentage of the population living below national poverty line (for a family of four in the United States that's about $20,650, for a single person $10,210): Honduras 74.8; Nicaragua 69.3; Guatemala 60.2; El Salvador 47.5; Mexico 35.5; Belize 33.5; Panama 33; Costa Rica 18; and United States (#13 from best) 12.6. (The three main sources are: CIA World Factbook; "Anuario estadístico de América Latina y el Caribe, 2006"; U.S. Census Bureau)

So, the numbers would seem to say that these economies should be in the E.R (Emergency Room): three fourths (three out of four) Hondurans are living in poverty, even among the better ones - Mexico, Belize, and Panama - one out of three are living in poverty; yes, there is an incentive to seek a better life elsewhere. Note that the United States has nothing to be proud of with one out of eight (12+%) living in poverty.

List of countries by GDP Purchasing power parity (PPP) (This is the final value of all goods and services produced within the nation divided by the average population of that nation [GDP/Population]. This does not mean that the average individual has that purchasing power as much of that money goes to institutions and, also, individuals have many subtle and hidden expenses before the money actually reaches them and there is a huge income disparity.) Six of the nine countries were listed by both the Central Intelligence Agency (CIA) and the International Monetary Fund (IMF); all of the six duplicate listings were quite close to each other so I used an average. Here they are (in U.S dollars): United States of America 43,511; Costa Rica 12,500; Mexico 11,035; Panama 8,396; Belize 8,117; El Salvador 5,250; Guatemala 5,000; Honduras 3,150; and Nicaragua 3,100.

The absolute value of these numbers is not too useful e.g. the average U.S. citizen earns no where near $43,511 (disposable income is more like one fourth of the listed amount, remember we are averaging in Bill Gates and Warren Buffett). However they are useful for comparisons; e.g. the average Costa Rican or Mexican (the luckiest two of that group of Latinos) earns about one-fourth the average U.S. citizen. The average citizen of the remainder of those countries earns about one-fifth to one-fourteenth of the average U.S. citizen. (And the earnings are not distributed equitably! There there are much huger inequalities than in the United States of America)

List of the percentage of the population living on less than $2 per day and $1/day: United States of America not listed; Costa Rica 7.5, 2.2; Mexico 20.4, 4.4; Panama 17.1, 6.5; Belize not listed; Guatemala 31.9, 13.5; El Salvador 40.6, 19; Honduras 44, 20.7; and Nicaragua 79.9, 45.1. Got that! Damn near eighty percent – four fifths; four out of five; eight out of ten – of Nicaraguans live on less than $2.00 per DAY! I'd cross the burning desert and climb the funny-fence to come to America too.

For Mexico alone that is about 22-million people living on less than $2 per day and about 5-million living on less than $1 per day. I'd put my stuff in a wagon and head north too. Do or die. Choice is limited. Guatemala and Nicaragua add about another 8.5-million living on less than $2 per day and 4.25-million living on less than $1 per day. Ouch! They can't even afford a wagon. It's a pretty desperate situation; of course, they are going to struggle to find a better life.

List of the ratio of the income of richest 10% to

the poorest 10%: United States of America 15.9; Costa Rica 30; Mexico 24.6; Panama 54.7; Belize not listed; Guatemala 48.2; El Salvador 57.5; Honduras 34.2; and Nicaragua 15.5.

So, in the United States, Peter making $20,000 might look at his rich cousin, Paul, making $318,000 whereas, in Mexico, Pedro might make $5,000 and Paulo across the tracks might make $123,000, in Guatemala $2,500 vs. $121,000. Disparity reeks. The United States of America is by no means the best country in this regard. Nevertheless, it is, numerically, two to four times better than our neighbors to the immediate south.

These are some of the economic and, yes, social factors which are driving the peoples of the Central Americas to come to the United States. These factors are powerful and almost overwhelming. I don't and can't blame them for seeking a better life in more northern America. I didn't go into the factors which force them to do it illegally but they are absolute. There is no reasonable chance for them to get visas. They cannot be legal immigrants! They **MUST** be illegal immigrants! You can bitch if you want but you might as well howl at the moon like your mother did. If you are not willing to work to fix the problem; shut your fucking mouth.

The USR (US Rich) would like to drive down labor costs and no level is low enough for them. Does anyone really doubt this? I should remove the "US" and I should remove the "Rich"; we all strive for advantage over our peers and our rivals. The only differences among us are our successes and our ruthlessnesses; we all try. I have seen the most scurvy gutter rats push humorlessly for gain over their fellow; don't most or all herd, pack, and pride animals strive for dominance? If one is humane it may limit ones success; I have no solid evidence to back this up but seventy years of observation and experiment has indicated that the considerate do not end up at the top of the heap; perhaps I should have said "at the pinnacle of success" or "triumphing in their chosen profession". Even scientists, the ultimate in objective evaluation, edge, hedge, nibble, and quibble to be firstest and mostest. Examples abound.

Success, particularly financial success, does not often seem to limit ones avariciousness or to soften one's heart. Seldom does one hear, "well, I'm rich enough, time to slack off and let someone else have some". If one is not the richest man in the world, then one is still not rich enough. Ponder this: Bill Gates, when he was the richest man in the world, lobbied his government to allow more, cheaper programmers into the country to reduce his labor costs! Failing this, he set up operations in Canada which allowed more, cheaper foreign programmers in. This was at a time when he had a virtual de facto monopoly for his products and was gouging his customers out of billions of dollars; there were literally millions of brilliant, highly qualified programmers who were available, U.S. citizens; the employees he had were already vastly underpaid compared to other professions; all of his employees had to sign the Slave Contract; and he was taking-in billions-of-dollars. His cutthroat business methods are legendary. There is no limit on greed. Further, he spent vast sums to have National Public Radio (NPR) pimp for him to make him sound like a nice boy.

The greed of man is boundless. The greedy rich are pitiless. The USR (US Rich) would like to drive down labor costs to a low level and no level is low enough for them. That is established.

Do we have the will to destroy the economies of the states to our immediate south? This is from: CIA and Assassinations: The Guatemala 1954 Documents

By Kate Doyle and Peter Kornbluh:

> *"Arbenz was elected President of Guatemala in 1950 to continue a process of socio- economic reforms that the CIA disdainfully refers to in its memoranda as "an intensely nationalistic program of progress colored by the touchy, anti-foreign inferiority complex of the 'Banana Republic.'" The first CIA effort to overthrow the Guatemalan president--a CIA collaboration with Nicaraguan dictator Anastacio Somoza to support a disgruntled general named*

Carlos Castillo Armas and codenamed Operation PBFORTUNE--was authorized by President Truman in 1952. As early as February of that year, CIA Headquarters began generating memos with subject titles such as "Guatemalan Communist Personel (sic) to be disposed of during Military Operations," outlining categories of persons to be neutralized "through Executive Action"--murder--or through imprisonment and exile. The "A" list of those to be assassinated contained 58 names--all of which the CIA has excised from the declassified documents." (In other words, even after forty years they refuse to open their files or to confess to their crimes.)

"PBSUCCESS, authorized by President Eisenhower in August 1953, carried a $2.7 million budget for "pychological (sic) warfare and political action" and "subversion," among the other components of a small paramilitary war. But, according to the CIA's own internal study of the agency's so-called "K program," up until the day Arbenz resigned on June 27, 1954, "the option of assassination was still being considered." While the power of the CIA's psychological-war, codenamed "Operation Sherwood," against Arbenz rendered that option unnecessary, the last stage of PBSUCCESS called for "roll-up of Communists and collaborators." Although Arbenz and his top aides were able to flee the country, after the CIA installed Castillo Armas in power, hundreds of Guatemalans were rounded up and killed. Between 1954 and 1990, human rights groups estimate, the repressive operatives of sucessive military regimes murdered more than 100,000 civilians."

My employees withheld this information from me for over forty years because they consider me too stupid and unpatriotic to understand why they would murder a duly, freely elected republican president and install a criminal regime. But we know why they murdered over 100,000 people; wait for it – wait for it – so I could have twenty-cent bananas. Yup, we did it so that our fruit importing companies wouldn't lose any business or have to pay any significant labor costs. "Come, Mister tally man, tally me banana / Daylight come and me wan' go home / It's six foot, seven foot, eight foot BUNCH! / Daylight come and me wan' go home". (Harry Belafonte's take on a Jamaican folk boat song.) It's a sad, sad song.

In the next fifty or sixty years there has been one brutal, gangster regime after another thanks to me and my employees. We have killed lots and lots more than a mere hundred-thousand using our trained death squads and through the more prosaic starvation and sickness. Our compliant Corporate Press and other media played this as a great victory over the Red Atheistic Menace. Fake, propagandist "newsreels" were produced and played at almost every theater between feature films (I remember seeing several). Our hero! We stopped the spread of Atheistic Communism and installed a pro-American Christian murderer. All the Moneyed Religions applauded and no one has ever apologized.

What we did in Guatemala we did also in most of the other Central American countries. To me it is exceedingly sad that when they had good governments who were improving almost every aspect of their lives and economies – you name it; increased literacy, improved health care, more diverse economies, more press freedom, etc. – we sent in "Freedom Fighters" and the like murderers and monsters to destroy whatever progress was being made. Oh! We are so good at that. And when we commit major crimes of this sort we keep it secret in the name of "National Security".

So, yes, we have the will, the means, and the power to destroy their economies and, in fact, did. But is there more? Yes, they were largely agrarian societies.

One of their subsistence crops which they developed and we copied and improved is maize which, of course, we know as corn. Corn is our most subsidized crop. Much has been written about how we dumped corn and damaged Middle Americans' economies. For example:

William Bunker; Science, The World; Republican Libertarian Constitutionalist Syndicalist

> *"Farm subsidies let the state tell farmers how much of what food to grow. ...*
>
> *"Unfortunately, this subsidy, which is repeated in Europe, has the effect of flooding the market with corn and artificially reducing the price of corn and all crops in the 3rd world. ... The results are that 3rd world farmers are sunk deeper into poverty since their labor's value is reduced, depressing their economies and forcing them to rely on imported food for much of their sustenance, lending itself to malnutrition, and in some areas, illegal farming."*

Another example: Open Source; Shows, Aired | David, April 13th, 2006 with Christopher Lydon (Christian Broadcaster) The Children of the Corn Subsidies:

> *"In our recent , our guests noted that thousands of illegal Mexican immigrants are crossing into the U.S. because following the NAFTA [North American Free Trade Agreement - Canada, Mexico, & U.S.A] agreement cheap — read subsidized — American corn has flooded the Mexican market. These one-time farmers just can't compete against U.S. corn on their soil, so they often end up picking fruit on ours.*
>
> *"It's one of many unintended consequences that follow from cheap corn, and it got us talking that night in the control room. We realized that corn (or corn subsidies) is one of those topics that often comes up in odd contexts. When you think you're talking about illegal immigration, or diabetes, or energy policy, or environmental*

degradation, or presidential politics, it turns out that you're also, and often inevitably, talking about corn..."

There have been lots of stories like the ones above; I expected to agree with them. When I checked the numbers here's what I came up with: In Iowa (the state with the largest corn subsidy) from 1995 to 2005 the subsidy was $9.9-billion, that's $990-million per year average; Iowa corn production in 2005 was 2.2-billion bushels; $0.45 subsidy per bushel; 56 pounds per bushel; $0.008 subsidy per pound (less than a penny per pound); $2.50 price per pound: 0.3% subsidy (less than one-third-of-one-percent). I can't believe that that is enough to bankrupt Mexican farmers and drive them north – but I could be wrong. NAFTA was passed in 1993. From Wikipedia: "Trade has increased dramatically among the three nations since NAFTA. In the period of 1993–2004, total trade between the United States and its NAFTA partners increased 129.3% (110.1% with Canada and 100.9% with Mexico), yet total trade between the United States and non-NAFTA partners increased 123.8% in the same period, a roughly similar figure."

But Central American (Mexican) immigration began way before 1993! So certainly, NAFTA didn't start it. The argument that NAFTA increased Central American immigration is very weak. If you are a subsistence farmer, primarily living off the produce from a small farm, then what happens in the global market is irrelevant to you. Neither NAFTA nor subsidized corn is the cause of the massive immigration from Central America.

We have to lay the biblical exodus from Central America at the feet of poverty caused by gangster governments in turn caused by our foreign policies.

(However, this does not exonerate our incredibly stupid farm program – analyzed elsewhere.) It is still possible that our super efficient farming methods reduced the price of corn to the point that we could be accused of "dumping" corn & other agricultural products. That possibility may, in fact, have helped to destroy their economies. But, alternatively, importing cheap foodstuffs from the United States may have improved their living standards – that seems most likely to me. I'm for free trade and, if someone can produce corn more cheaply than I can, I'll find something else to do. Apropos to that argument are some stories like the following:

Press conference announcing the biofuels study results by the American Meat Institute, Washington, D.C. "A major new study officially issued May 17 conservatively estimates that increased corn prices driven by rapidly expanding U.S. ethanol production already have increased U.S. retail food prices by $14 billion annually.

"Further, the study finds that the increase in U.S. retail food prices could reach $20 billion annually under a scenario in which crude oil prices range from $65 to $70 per barrel and U.S. corn prices reach $4.42 per bushel, compared to the $2 per bushel that existed in mid-August 2006."

And:

COMMENTARY February 20, 2007; 2105 First Avenue South, Minneapolis, Minnesota 55404, USA; Who's Afraid of the High Price of Corn? By Jim Harkness; "Listen closely, and you can hear a growing roar of worry about the high price of corn, increasing from $2.60 a bushel last year to near $4 a bushel now. ...

"For decades corn has been ridiculously cheap. ... And multinational grain companies exported our cheap corn to gain footholds in other markets around the world, often driving farmers in poor countries out of business."

And:

Cost of Corn Soars, Forcing Mexico to Set Price Limits; By JAMES C. McKINLEY Jr.; January 19, 2007; MEXICO CITY, Jan. 18 — "Facing public outrage over the soaring price of tortillas, President Felipe Calderón abandoned his free-trade principles on Thursday and forced producers to sign an agreement fixing prices for corn products. ...

"Skyrocketing prices for corn on the world market have pushed up the price of the humble tortilla, the mainstay of the Mexican diet, by nearly a third in the past three weeks, to 35 cents a pound in Mexico City and even higher in other parts of the country.

"Half of the country's 107 million people live on $4 a day or less, and many of them survive largely on tortillas and beans. The price increases have riled the public to such an extent that it has created a political storm that threatens to swamp Mr. Calderón's fresh presidency.

...

"Last week, the president tried to contain the crisis by allowing more corn imports from the United States and ordering an investigation into whether corn distributors were colluding to manipulate prices. But the public outcry continued, and the central bank warned that the rise in corn prices would push the price of other staples up and feed inflation.

"On Thursday morning, Mr. Calderón, a fierce advocate of free trade in last year's campaign, let the hammer fall. He announced that he had reached an agreement with the major businesses involved in corn products to stabilize the price of tortillas at a maximum of about 35 cents a pound.

"He also fixed the price of cornmeal sold to mom-and-pop tortilla shops at 14 cents a pound and announced that government-owned shops in rural areas would sell tortillas at the same price, far below the market rate."

So there you have it. Is cheap corn destroying Mexico's economy? I don't think so. Is cheap corn forcing Mexicans to flee northward? I don't think so. Is cheap corn "bad" for Mexicans? I don't think so.)

So, we know for sure "we", the United States, you and I, did destroy their economies with no reportage, no apologies and no regrets but we did NOT do it by cheap food or free trade. We did it by murdering moderate, modern rulers and by reinforcing repressive, regressive, monsters. It's the American Way.

We know for sure that "they" really don't have a lot of choice but to starve or come to the United States of America like our great-grandparents did from wherever.

And, lastly, back to the beginning with a footnote. Mexico fought the Spanish Empire for independence in 1821 as we had fought the British Empire for our independence in 1775-1783. After the war of independence, Mexico was all of what is now Mexico, Texas, New Mexico, Arizona, Utah, Nevada, California, half of Colorado, and bits of Oklahoma, Kansas, and Wyoming. Wow! But, surprise!, the war of independence virtually bankrupted them (remember, wars do do that). Mexico allowed a few hundred American families to settle in the Texas part of their territory. Give 'em an inch and they'll take a mile. Americans swarmed in like locusts. The Americans brought their slaves and religious freedom with them. Mexico was a "free" – non-slave since 1829 – country though a Roman Catholic theocracy. We tried to buy Texas but the Mexicans were not as naïve as the Indians who sold Manhattan or Napoleon who sold the Louisiana Territory (Seward's folly had not happened yet then). Santa Anna wouldn't sell. Texans declared their independence. You remember the Alamo where they kicked our ass. Texas made a Declaration of Independence in 1836, captured Santa Anna, and made him sign a Concession recognizing Texas sovereignty (independence). After Santa Anna was released, Mexico said, Go To Hell, Santa Anna was under duress. Texas was admitted as a U.S. state in 1845. Mexico said, That does it! The United States tried to buy the northern states of Mexico (What is now California etc.). The Mexican government had the jumping-bean-jitters; e.g. in 1846 the government changed hands six times. We tried to negotiate for land but it was a Mexican stand-off, they wouldn't deal with us.

In 1846 Congress declared war on Mexico for President Polk (in those days, it was Congress that declared war). (Abe Lincoln and John Q. Adams voted nay.) We conquered California in late 1846 and pushed on into Mexico. Santa Anna (returning from exile in Cuba) promised the Americans that he would sell New Mexico if they let him pass. He lied. Then he promised the Mexican government that if they appointed him general he would fight the Americans. He lied. He took over the Mexican government. Robert E. Lee and Ulysses S. Grant fought side by side under General Winfield Scott capturing Mexico City in 1848. We took all of the territories north of the Rio Grande (more than 1.2-million Sq. Mi.) but paid to Mexico US $15,000,000. We had also gotten the Oregon territory in 1846 from Britain (the United Kingdom). (Ulysses S. Grant said that our Civil War was God's punishment on us for our war against Mexico; he thought it that unjust!)

So, we took 54% of Mexico far and skwar. We put a gun to their head and said, "Sign". It's the American Way. So what has all this to do with Illegal Mexican Immigration? Well, if those were Germans down there, we'd be fighting a war every twenty years to keep the land that we took by force. Aww! Gee! That's not fair! Sure it is. O.K. I know it is racist to ascribe characteristics to any ethnic or nationality but, goodness, it also saves a lot of research and thinking. So, I will say that the Mexicans are entrepreneurial, hard working, peaceful, friendly, reliable, and, and, O.K. so they like to eat Jalapeno peppers by the handful. Nobody's perfect. So they come up here to work – is that so bad? They do the work Americans don't like to do – is that so bad. They work for half as much as we do – well, maybe that is bad – but do they have any choice? That's why I don't mess with "good" or "bad". Why don't we count our blessings; they could be coming up here with guns to get their land back? Observe how brave they are: coming into a strange country not speaking the language; not having money; not having a job; knowing that they are disliked and liable to be hunted down; knowing that if they disappear no one will know or care (other than mommy thousands of kilometers away and broke); and all to give some small help to their families! God damn! Give 'em a break already!

O.K. Houston, we have a problem! The Mexicans are invading. An "Alien" invasion; War of the Worlds. Millions of aliens are already here and are invading our bodies. I go along with you, we have a problem. Shouldn't we stop lying about it?

Here are some of the lies. "A nation without secure borders is no nation at all." - Ron Paul. Sure it is Ronnie. For a couple of hundred years we were oh so proud that we had the world's longest undefended border (with Canada). Weren't we a nation when we kicked the shit out of the Huns; twice? Now we are talking about building a fence up there too. It's called insanity. It's the American way. "What part of 'illegal' don't you understand?" Well, to tell you the truth, not much. The "ill" maybe. The "gal" maybe. The "e", of course is the base of the natural logarithms; as we all know. What I do understand when you ask "What part of 'illegal' don't you understand?" (Referring to "illegal" immigrants) is that you are a spoiled, rich city kid who doesn't know anything. You have never talked, i.e. communicated, with anyone outside of your "class". You're a country club type with no humanity or humility. You think that the American Enterprise Institute is the American Way instead of just another Institution whose inmates should be institutionalized. "Issue ... a national special card that indicates a person's name, date, birth date, biographic information..." - Mitt Romney (Are you any relation to Walter Mitty?) C'mon, Mitty! They all have cards. Cards are cheap. (Except the St. Louis Cards.) When I was ten, I fixed my birth certificate so that I could get a twelve-year-old work permit; when I was sixteen, I fixed my birth certificate so that I could get an eighteen-year-old beer permit (eighteen was the legal beer age in Wisconsin). This I did with just bleach and an ink pen; imagine what you can do with a good drawing program. But maybe Mitty wants a computer chip implanted everyone's brain; that should do it Mitty, now they can't cross our border and they can't cross you; now you've got 'em. Even a bitty chip can be easily forged. "We need a tamper-proof ID card." - Rudolph W. Giuliani. Now we know how your nose got red Rudolph. If we can't have a tamper-proof voting machine, I doubt that we can have a tamper-proof ID card. Maybe you meant Tampax proof. But, maybe not, with all the women you've had, I'm sure you know Tampax. "'Amnesty' didn't mean rewarding illegal behavior" (Jan 2008) – John McCain No amnesty! Well, John, why won't you give the Mexicans amnesty when you are so anxious to give the telecommunications companies' executives amnesty (backdated legal immunity) for spying on us? Oh! I forgot; Mexicans are poor and telecommunication executives are rich. Mexicans committed a small, victimless crime trying to better themselves; telecommunications executives committed a major crime against U.S. Citizens when they, the telecommunication executives, were trying to undermine our Constitution.

So, now I'll tell you what we are going to do about "immigration" and why we are going to do it. Then I'll give my opinion of what we should do and why we should do it.

But first here's some more brown stuff from some bulls (if you're a spoiled rich city kid, you may never have seen it splatter on the ground; here's what it looks like):

"Finish border fence; maintain border patrol of 20,000 agents." - Rudolph W. Giuliani

"Finish border fence by 2010; deploy 23,000 more patrol agents." - Mike Huckabee

"Secure our borders." - John McCain

"We must secure our borders now." - Ron Paul

"Finish building border fence." - Mitt Romney

"...Strengthening our borders." - Hillary Clinton

"...doubling the number of border patrol agents" - John Edwards

"...secure our borders." - Barack Obama

"...secure our borders." – George W. Bush

Well, at least idiocy is bipartisan. Very interesting Sherlock; here's what we've done so far:

As I write this, Boeing is building a 28 mile

demonstration "virtual fence". It was supposed to have been done a year or so ago; but you know how those things go. You might as well milk the damn contract, ride the clock. Twenty-eight miles of very funny fence to show us how it should be done. So far it has cost $67-million dollars but it ain't done. The Mexican-U.S. border, I'm told, is about 2000-miles and that, presumably, is as the crow flies (or a bee-line, if you prefer). If you follow the river, the border may wander another few hundred, or maybe a thousand, miles. But at 2000-miles, the cost would be almost 5-billion dollars. Now remember Boeing's cost overrun for the space station was 26%; for "Star Wars" National Missile Defense (still not operational) the overrun was maybe 500% (dizzying, misleading information from all involved). This privatization stuff is wonderful; Boeing doesn't get a "contract" like us po-white-trash, Boeing gets a blank check – actually as many blank checks as needed. This is fine because we know, with this honorable privatization stuff, they won't screw us. When I was doing project engineering, we project engineers couldn't be off by more than + or – 10% or we would have some mighty explaining to do and forget about any raise. Boston's Big Dig project was overrun by 484%; ah, this privatization stuff is wonderful; that was another big, highly qualified engineering firm (Bechtel) and the Big Dig started falling apart before it was finished. So, maybe the very funny fence will cost 5-billion-dollars and maybe it will cost 5-trillion-dollars. As a man who had an engineering company that didn't get paid for anything short of perfection, yes, I am envious. If that's the politics of envy so be it, I'm envious. Get a girl pregnant with a cross-eyed, furry imbecile, take no responsibility for the precious child and have the girls father pay you for your semen, well, that's wonderful but it's not how it worked in my neighborhood; so, yes, I am envious.

What's the difference what it costs; it's not going to work anyway. They stick some high-tech cameras and radar and motion detectors up on hundred foot towers. Oh, but they "protect" it with a chain-link fence at a six-foot radius all around it. Wow! Can't go wrong with that.

Hundred feet tall. That's a third of a football field. When I was about ten years old we (my brothers and I) made sling shots, not like David's swinging basket type; we cut a "Y" from one of the hickory trees, cut a piece of leather belting for the saddle, cut some strips from an old inner tube (they were elastic in those days, today I understand kids use surgical tubing); with a pocket knife you could make one in an hour; total cost: nuthin. We found round stones along the railroad track. We could knock those glass insulator things off the telephone poles pretty regular. I know it wasn't nice but I think the statute of limitations has done run out so I can admit it now. One time, to my shock and shame, I killed a robin at about 200-feet. My oldest brother could kill a sputze on top of the barn from 300-feet with a twenty-two without putting a hole in the roof. Kids'll have fun with those million-dollar cameras. I wish I was still young and lived near the Rio Grande. God, that would be fun. You could see the dicks coming from a mile away and you could just disappear into the mud. I know no adult could ever catch me along the Fox River when I did something bad. They could think that they had me surrounded and I wouldn't be there. But we will build it. Full speed ahead, damn the taxpayers!

The Customs and Border Protection (CBP) is building "regular" fences too. "Regular" being any kinky kooky kind of design. They've tried everything. Nothing works and nothing is going to work. All those clever designs have at least three things in common: 1. They're all very expensive. 2. None works. 3. They's ugly, ugly, ugly. A big purple nose wart on Marilyn Monroe. That ugly's important as I say in a minute. Know how long it takes to dig under a fence with a stick? Maybe a half hour. Ya, they can do things to prevent that. But every fence is vulnerable to one thing or another (fence designers and builders ain't smart; kids is). I snuck into everything when I was a kid. Things that experts designed to prevent sneak-ins. Movie theaters regularly. Circus every time it came to town. One time, I was about ten, my brother and I snuck into this side-show tent not knowing what it was. If they meant to keep us out, that's reason enough, we had to go in. Bunch of drunks inside. Carnival bouncer tried to chase us out. Drunks wouldn't let 'em. Drunks made room up in the front bench. Pretty soon these old wimmin, old to us, came out and took their clothes off. Well, that's passing strange, way past. Shaking their pendulous boobs in our faces; doing their dances playing to us. A little traumatic to a pre-puberty kid.

Neighbor, one of the mill owners, had this nice summer house overlooking the Fox River; they had it all locked up; they had a nice apple orchard, all fenced-in. That was a nice house inside; big walk-in fireplace, furniture all covered funny, spooky with cloths. Big house. We didn't "break" in. I don't even remember how we got in (lotsa ways in, can't block 'em all), but we went in to change clothes anytime we went swimming in that area; we never left a trace; didn't break nor take nothing; no one would ever know that we had been guests. And that fenced-in apple orchard; they never used the apples; let 'em rot on the ground. We used some; we had our own orchard; but stolen apples are a bunch sweeter than home apples – but you already knew that. We used to go through the fence – through, under, or over, I don't even remember how – crawl along on our bellies like we was commandoes; yellow jackets buzzing, eating the dropped and rotting fruit; fill our pockets, maybe a bag, with apples; go down by the river, fire up and roast 'em. They was good. That I don't remember how we got into those places means that it was easy, not part of the adventure. (One time, made a fire in a hollow tree. Could not get it out. Tried. Smoke at the end of ten yard branches. Carpenter ant streams squirting out everywhere. All the trunk, bole, gone. Circle of branches around on the ground. Fire department came. We could have been in trouble if we were visible.) Sure that fence they's abuildin' along the Rio Grande would confound those dumb Washington clucks, but it wouldn't stop for a minute some smart Mexican kid. Or even a dumb Mexican kid – they're not spoiled rich city kids. I should quit talking about this; it's so obvious; it just irks me that they's dumpin' my money on that nonsense.

Here's another thing: I don't know the Rio Grande but I know a lot of rivers. (We used to canoe a lot when we lived in Ohio and Alabama. Made an aluminum canoe, canoed all over; finally got stolen in Michigan City, IN.) There's gotta be a crik (spoiled rich city kids call 'em Creeks) every half-mile or so dumping into the Rio Grande. Whatcha gonna do about them? I've seen criks fenced over to keep cows in or out (depending upon your perspective); ain't easy. Cows always getting out. Extend the fence down to the ground in a crik; makes a dam; break the whole damn fence down. Don't extend the fence down, even cows get out. Whatcha gonna do?

Here's another thing. Any river I've seen, them mill owners build a great big house up on the bank. Now you gonna run a fence between their house and the river. Unh, unh. Remember I said those fences were ugly; purple nose wart. Already, lawsuits fighting eminent domain are a major cost for the little pieces of fence already done. I understand that's a purty river that Rio Grande. I used to do quite a bit of work down in the oil patch – the Permian Basin – guys there would say, "Oh, you gotta go see Big Bend National Park!" But, for me, it's not a lot of fun goin' sight-seein' without my wife – even then we was married 30-years or so. Kinda like not bringing your heart to Texas. So I didn't go. Shoulda. Now it's too late. Lot's a pretty stuff along that river. Now it's too late. Good thing we saw the Grand Canyon and all the Mississippi River; maybe them spoiled rich city kids in Washington will want to build a fence along them places too. National Security, you know. Shame to spoil that Rio Grande though. Maybe we should call it the Rio Was Grande. Now it ain't so Grande no more. Makes me tear up.

Here's another thing. Them fellers up in Washington are saying, "20,000 or 23,000 more border patrol agents". They're great kidders, those Washington boys. Let's see 2000-miles; 5280 Ft. per Mi.; I make that 10.6-million feet; four agents every thousand feet, three shifts; comes to 127-thousand agents. Oh, wait, when you nab those little buggers sneakin' across the river you don't just put 'em on the western side of the highway and tell them to stick their thumbs out; you gotta put 'em in the corral; feed 'em; get a judge; find 'em guilty (it's a nice formality, makes you look like you got clean hands, legalities you know); get a paddy wagon (this ain't Boston, it's a wet-back wagon); get a driver; notify the Mexican authorities; drive south; release; go back north; repeat. (DHS Secretary, Michael Chertoff, says it'll cost $7,833 per person [he is good if he's got it down that fine; I'm surprised he didn't add the 19¢].) So, for every agent you need maybe nine white collar guys; total so far maybe a million and a quarter guys. Now, if the CBP is about as efficient as the military, for every agent in the field you need about twenty support people; now we got about 23-million jobs created that the politicians can brag about. "We's creatin' jobs. We Washington boy is creatin' jobs. But now we gotta raise taxes to pay for all those jobs we's been creatin'" They don't get any dumber then those Washington boys; they's all lawyers at base. Going by what our embassy employees cost, those 23-million guys and gals are gonna cost about half-a-million each. That's about 11-trillion per year. No problem, we got it. I see the President's asking for 8.2-billion for embassies – the Post-Dispatch put it on the second page just behind the football game so you'll never notice it.

Oh, I forgot! There's gonna be boys and girls (agents) in them little shacks along the border; get lonesome at night in the Lone Star state; we're gonna have to have a budget for condoms too [or babies or abortions; and they's more expensive].

Now I could just hear them congressional budget experts (if they ever got wind of my rant) sayin' that boy's numbers are absurd; them numbers are ludicrous. Now I have to bow down to those spoiled rich city kids workin' in them Washington towers; all that granite and hand carved maple and $5,000 suits and million dollar C.P.A.s. They must know something. Absurd those numbers are. Even ludicrous. But which way? High or low? Now I've worked with a lot of accountants in my time; and I have to admit they are super at predicting last year. They can split the penny to eight decimal places. Unfortunately for engineers, we always had to predict next year. A mite harder. We had to guarantee that the machine that we were going to design (as soon as we figure out how to design it) would make 3,600 widgets per hour. And we could design and build the machine for $60,000. Oh, plus or minus ten percent. And we had to bet our soul (and oldest kid) that we would be correct. Now, the accountant would get a bonus because the machine saved $200,000 per year; and them widgets, bein' cheaper and better, would "jump off the shelf" so, of course, the salesman would get a big commission. And the engineer would get his ass chewed because it only produced 3,590 widgets per hour (downtime for lunch, you know, forgot to consider it). I have done a lot of estimates and cost projections in my time and I can tell you that those numbers are neither high nor low. I've done blue sky and black water projections. But this is a guess, not a projection.

Here's the nub of it; they're not going to spend 5-trillion or even 5-billion to build that wall. Nor are they going to spend 11-trillion per year to try to make it work. That's too much money for the first ten or so years. They'll spend maybe $500-million to build the wall over maybe seven or eight years. And it will cost maybe a couple hundred million to "operate" it every year. And, like the war on drugs, every couple of months there will be a report issued. Period. The report will one time say crossings are down therefore our plan is working and it will work that much better if you give us more money – we still got a few leaks. The next time the report will say, Hey! Crossings are up; better give us more money! Now, here's the rub of it; if we spend as much as my estimate, it still wouldn't work! I'd like to use the metaphor of a childhood game we used to play called Tom-Tom-Pull-Away; it was a tackle game with players running between goals and players in the middle tackling them. But the description wouldn't be worth the candle (see, these old metaphors don't work either; it wouldn't be worth the effort [or the electric light bill]). The odds are high that you know a little bit about football (even Nixon did), so I'll use that analogy. Football you've got a 50 yd. wide field with eleven guys trying to move in one direction and eleven guys trying to tackle them. (~4.5 yds. wide per player) Simple. The reality, the workability of the game is that often the guys trying to move do. Now imagine a 3.5-million yd. wide field with 30,000 guys (10,000 per shift with no weekends and no vacations off, forget about sick days) (352 yds. wide per player) trying to tackle 100,000 guys moving through. Imagine that the tacklers are coached by George W. Bush and the runners are coached by Vince Lombardi. It's a sick joke; Charles Addams would have used it. But no one will laugh unless you hate America; this is very serious you know, National Security you know perfectly well we're keeping you safe. Certainly the runners could send a sacrificial goat through a couple of hundred yards upstream (like drawing off the piranhas); when the tacklers are chasing the wild goose, the real runners will scurry through downstream. The goat gets paid and is reusable; he could make a nice living.

I wrote this chapter in about February 2008; now it's April 23, 2008 and Homeland Security Secretary Michael Chertoff says that he is going to "waive" all of the laws (that he doesn't like) that are 'hindering' the building of the funny fence. I just love it! Nixon said that when the President does it, 'it' is not illegal – he effectively "waived" all the laws of these United States. Now, hallelujah! George W. Bush has effectively said that when the Executive Branch of the government – this once government of the United States of America – that 'it' is not illegal. It follows as the horse the cart that the Right Honorable Mickey Mouse Chertoff can "waive" any damn law that displeases him. Hallelujah! Hallelujah! Hallelujah! Sin again!

Hadrian's Wall was built; sentries continuously marched on top; garrisons, whose principle occupations were drinking, gambling, and whoring, were stationed all along its length; yet, whenever the Picts decided to pillage a village to the south, they were free to do so.

But that's what we are going to do. We are going to build a fence. It's the American way. The rich will get their cheap labor. We will be "protecting" America from the "Terrorists", the Communists, the Vietnamese, the Iraqis, the Iranians, the Taliban, the Mermaids, the Trojans, the Islamists, El Quida, the Spartans, the Pagans, etc. etc. You won't object unless you hate America. We spent billions and 40 years building the VTOL and it never worked; we spent billions and many years building the space station and it was pointless; we spent hundreds of billions over thirty or forty years on "Star Wars" National Missile Defense and it doesn't work and scientists say it will never work and, if it does work, it will be useless; we spent trillions on the Viet Nam war and it was a tragedy (thank god the Christ-like Vietnamese seem to have forgiven us); we spent trillions on the Iraq War, Cheney didn't get his oil and we fucked up the whole region. It's the American way. But you won't say that unless you hate America; if you love America, you will encourage us to go on and on wasting money and doing stupid things. So, we will spend trillions on our little ye olden golden fence. It can't work; if it does, immigrants will go around it and we will extend the fence into the Pacific and into the Gulf and when that doesn't work we will extend the fence up both coasts; and when that doesn't work we will launch a million coast guard Cigarette boats; and when that doesn't work; we'll make the immigrants heroes like we did with the Cuban boat people and declare victory, welcome them and give them money.

O.K. that's what we will do. Here's what we should do but we won't because it just might work if we would give it a try. But we won't. It's not the American way.

Early in this chapter I gave you a rundown on the Mexican (and Central American) economy (ies). The rich have about 50 times more income than the poor; and in addition the richest also own virtually all productive property and arable land. The rich are condemning vast numbers of poor to horrible lives and miserable early deaths but you can't say anything against them or you will be pilloried. This is a crime against humanity. You can't pull yourself up by your bootstraps if you don't have boots. We could stop those crimes if we wanted to. Stopping that horrible misapplication and unbalance of wealth would also instantly stop the emigration from those countries and, thus, the illegal immigration to this country. Period. We must assiduously avoid the sins of the McNamara World Bank where the money shipped to poor countries was given exclusively to the richest and ended up in New York banks within a week leaving the poor to pay-off the debt. We cannot give money to the rich like we usually do; Supply-side economics and Trickle-Down Economics are cruel, deliberate lies and do not work; cannot work. If there is a hell, Supply-Siders and Trickle-Downers are going there as Satan's best friends as discussed elsewhere.

Mexico's Gross Domestic Product (GDP) is about $1.2-trillion. For the moment let's just tend to the population living on under $2 per day: 20.4%; Mexico's population = 103-million souls; thus 21-million living on under $2 per day. Say we took the $100-million that the funny fence will cost us per year and distribute it to those 21-million people; we could increase their income by over 300-percent (earning four times as much); that would do a lot to diminish illegal immigrants into the U.S. (A hell of a lot more than the stupid, funny fence.)

Better yet we could use that money to make micro-loans to those people. Micro-loans have been proven phenomenally successful everywhere that they have been tried. And the lender actually makes money on the deal. Borrowers might use the money to buy seeds, fertilizer, supplies for any business, or a little piece of land. Mexicans seem to me to be very entrepreneurial. (If you are interested in doing a little do-gooder deedys yourself, Google Kiva, Grameen Bank, Namaste Direct, FINCA Village Banking, Unitus, or Accion.) Anyway we could stop the illegal immigration any time we wanted if we cared to withstand the wrath of self-styled, pro-slavery Reaganites.

We could. But we won't. It is not the American way. Mores the pity; it is passing pity. Shame on us. Shame on me. Shame on you. It is passing shame.

Chapter Five

Picking Up the Tab

There's a lot of confusion out there about taxes. Why taxes? Who pays the most? What is the purpose of taxes? You may be surprised to learn that taxes do have a purpose. A purpose other than stompin' on the poor. There is a lot of misdirection about the purpose of taxes. Some people who ought to know better – and I firmly believe that they do know better – actually claim that the purpose of taxes is to pay for essential government services. Granting those people the benefit of the doubt; and granting that maybe five or ten percent of our taxes are put to that nefarious use; it is possible that all of them are not lying all of the time. Occasionally, they may just be misinformed and not outright lying.

There are two primary purposes of taxes. Well, there can't be two primary purposes; one purpose must be secondary. So, the Primary purpose of taxes is the same as the Primary Purpose of business, it is to pay off the investors. Every year, but particularly in election years, billions of dollars are invested in good government. Politicians don't come cheap, competition is steep; there is a big entry level wall and a moat too. An investment in good government has a yield approximately two-thousand times the yield of any other investment. For every dollar spent buying a politician or judge you can expect a return of between $200 and $1200. If you look at just the low end, that $200 return represents 20,000% return; since the return often takes place in just one or two months it can be an annualized return of 240,000%.

Fortunately this is a high stakes game. There are entry barriers that eliminate the undesirables. You can buy a local politician; say an alderman, selectman, or a councilman for a few hundred dollars or maybe just a glass of beer and a comfort lady. If you want the blacktop contract, the electrical or plumbing work, or even the food service concession for the school, city hall, or ballpark you may be able to outbid/outmaneuver your competitors for just a few thousand dollars. But to buy-in effectively at the federal level takes hundreds of thousands of dollars. You can contribute $25 or $100 or even $1000 to senate, house, or presidential candidates but that is like peeing in the ocean to influence the stone gentlemen on Easter Island; you will have limited success.

Fortunately, the Constitution protects "free speech" so you can buy congressmen, senators, and much more. *Amendment 1 - Freedom of Religion, Press, Expression. Ratified 12/15/1791. Congress shall make no law respecting an establishment of religion, or prohibiting the free exercise thereof; or abridging the freedom of speech, or of the press; or the right of the people peaceably to assemble, and to petition the Government for a redress of grievances.*

For some reason the Supreme Court glommed onto the "or abridging the freedom of speech" phrase here. And the gentlemen and gentleladies of the Supreme Court know how to read and, if they don't know how to read, someone can read it to them. But you can read to a horse from paper but you can't make him think. Since the money flingers buy lawmakers and law-signers from "both sides of the aisle" money invested in law grinders, clearly is not about "better government" or "insuring my ideology" it is about business investment. I didn't read the arguments in the case (nor does anyone need to unless the comics are on strike) but, I'm sure, no one would be such a flagrant liar or idiot as to claim that buying politicians has anything to do with "free speech". It is far from free.

I have huge respect for the Supreme Court just as I have respect for someone holding a gun to my head in a dark, deserted alley (the Justices control more guns than the average general). Unfortunately, putting a robe and a powdered wig (they still use powdered wigs don't they as in Bleak House and Notre Dame?) on a numbskull and letting him sit behind a hand-carved desk, does not instill wisdom. Hugo's judge for the humpback was deaf and, when often distracted, blind. Hasn't been much improvement since then. When, in the 2000 presidential election, the members of the Supreme Court said "to stop counting the votes, we want to appoint the president", I realized that they had not read the constitution or they did not comprehend it or, yet, they did not respect it – most likely the latter. They are ward-heelers of the meanest sort who see and use the law as a means of tormenting those with whom they disagree politically or religiously or who do not come up to their social standards. Inquisition and Salam Witch Judges were also quite dignified and wore the trappings of authority and the power of the sword; I don't recall if the scales were balanced or not; nor do I know what they were weighing. The lower the judge, the higher his dignity. I am surprised that the Supreme Court judges do not wear ermine trimmed robes – or do they?

Had they, our honorable servants on the Supreme Court, the sagacity of the average bus-boy, they would have seen immediately that purchasing politicians has nothing to do with religion, speech, press, assembly, or petition; it has to do with commerce. No one with any humble religion (if such exist) would tolerate purchasing politicians. No one who trusted free speech would sanction such purchases. Such bargains are the enemies of any self-respecting journalist (if such exist). Such commerce is quite the opposite of assembly since it is always done in as much secrecy as can be mustered. And, finally, one who does buy the government, does not intend to petition the government for redress of grievances; one does not petition one's paid agents, one directs and the agents obey, or else. The applicable Constitutional clause, if any clause is to be applied is ***"Section 8 - Powers of Congress:*** *No Preference shall be given by any Regulation of Commerce or Revenue to the Ports of one State over those of another: nor shall Vessels bound to, or from, one State, be obliged to enter, clear, or pay Duties in another."* Since Presidents, Senators, and Congressmen are clearly vessels (an obvious eighteenth century misspelling of "vassal"), it is clear that they are commodities which can be bought and sold and, as such, political purchases (sometimes erroneously euphemistically referred to as "donations" or "contributions") are perfectly allowable within Constitution or, more legally, are protected by the Commerce Clause of Section 8 of the Constitution.

My intention, when I began writing this chapter, was to begin concentrating on the 'earmarks' and show how they were really slavery because 'they' (our employees in Washington D.C) take our money and give it to another private person (or corporation). And, then, I would show how the Farm Program was similar. And, then, expand to show how almost all Government expenditures were similar – giving your and my money to another private person which is the essence of slavery; the recipients earn their daily bread by the sweat of our brow.

And it would have been no problem, I believe, to demonstrate that it was quid pro quo, a dollar for a doughnut hole. If you paid $100,000.00 to buy a congressman or a president, you didn't just get to sleep in Lincoln's bed, you also got the $20-billion contract.

But I have been preempted. The news lately (today is 5-14-8) has been, if not dominated, then suffused with articles about the abuse of 'earmarks' and the abuse of the Farm Program and even more generally about the abuse of taxes (now it is 4-28-9 and we [congress + President] have just passed the 2009 budget with more earmarks than all the pillows in this kingdom). 'Earmarks' at first were hotly defended by the worst perpetrators, then less so and less so until, finally, denial. "I don't do it!" "Me neither!" The battle may not be on hold (Joshua may have lowered his arms), but I get no joy chasing the enemy and striking at his back or shooting an arrow at his horse's rump or walking over the battlefield killing wounded enemy. Let us find a new enemy to fight and, unlike the cowardly neocons, a real enemy and engage him personally and in his face.

I shall take a new tack, ladies and gentlemen of the jury. I shall determine who pays what. Not just the income tax wherefore the payers, I presume, are well known and can be easily determined and quantified. Which 'class' pays how much of which tax. Who pays the excise taxes – liquor, gasoline, telephone, luxury, etc? Who pays city, county, state taxes – personal property, real estate, sales, state and local income. Who really pays what percentage; who is really taxed? Stay tuned.

I expect to be surprised. If everything turns out as I now expect or if it turns out to be as the Professional Liars – the guppies in the think tanks – claim, then I shall not find that to be a sufficiently interesting to present to myself and to you and I will delete this chapter. So, if you are reading this, I have been surprised.

I hate to waste your time on some of this very basic stuff but, by god, it just doesn't seem to be believed even though it is most obvious.

First tax axiom: only humans pay taxes (that's on earth – I don't know about other planets). Pencils do not pay taxes. Dogs do not pay taxes. Horses do not pay taxes. Automobiles do not pay taxes. Houses do not pay taxes. Corporations do not pay taxes. Got that? Did I slip it in on you when you weren't looking? If you already know that, go to the next paragraph. We, my wife and I and some of the kids, own a little restaurant, (I almost called this book *Rest or Rant*. Or *Rest Au Rant* [Au, as you know, is the chemical symbol for gold.]) the Soulard Coffee Garden Café (legally, Coffee Garden, Inc.). We collect sales taxes, we or Coffee Garden, Inc. do not pay them, the customer pays them. That, presumably, you knew. Suppose we become profitable some day; Coffee Garden, Inc. will pay profits tax. NO, no no no NO. We will write and sign the check and send it into our government. But we will not be paying those profits taxes nor will Coffee Garden, Inc.; they will be included in our prices. The CUSTOMER will pay our profits taxes! The CUSTOMER. The CUSTOMER, the retail CUSTOMER, pays all corporate profit taxes. They, those pesky profits taxes, MUST be passed through to the CUSTOMER just like any other cost. Just like the cost of eggs or flour or labor or gas or rent. The owners, the investors, the stock holders, do not pay them. Only money coming into the company on a regular basis can pay those taxes (or any other regular expense); only the CUSTOMERS bring money into the company on a regular basis. Yes, yes, yes. The CUSTOMER pays the profits taxes. Don't let the Professional Liars bullshit you otherwise!

Second tax axiom: everybody in the United States (god, please don't find an exception and tell me I should have said "most"; there might be some hermit living in a cave eating roots and berries who, god forbid, pays no real estate taxes.), everybody, except the homeless, pays real estate taxes. We pay them, real estate taxes, whether we rent or own our domiciles and, equally important, we pay them, the real-estate-taxes, when we purchase products which were produced in a plant or sold in a store which pays real estate taxes (remember already, corporations pay no taxes). So, even the homeless, if they purchase anything produced in a plant which pays real estate taxes or from a store which pays real estate taxes, even the homeless will and do pay real estate taxes. Even your friendly corner wino pays real estate taxes so he is your equal (at least in that). *Well, renters don't pay real estate taxes!* Oh! Yes they do! What landlord would be so stupid as to not pass on his mortgage cost, his new carpet cost, his new paint job cost, his gas cost, his insurance cost, his electricity cost, and, yes, his real estate tax cost. And so do manufacturing plants. And so do wholesalers. And so do retailers. The CUSTOMER pays the real estate taxes.

Second tax axiom, first corollary: real estate is a sub-category of wealth. We will ask why is there almost universal taxes on this class of wealth while other classes of wealth escape all or almost all taxes? And we will answer our own question and note that almost no one else is asking it.

Third tax axiom: Everybody (almost everybody) pay excise taxes. Here there might be Huck Finn floating down the River with Jim, fishing and scratching, and not paying excise taxes. Some examples of excise taxes (also called franchise, duty, and other names – including some four letter names) are on tobacco products, alcoholic beverages, petroleum products, some luxury items, utility bills, including telephone. It is easier to give examples than it is to define excise taxes. The term 'excise taxes' pretty much covers taxes on everything except income, wealth and property (property being a sub-class of wealth).

Fourth tax axiom: A tax is a tax is a tax. A rose by any other name... A fart by any other name... Local, city, county, state, federal; a tax is a tax. I apologize for stating the obvious but the Professional Liars, the guppies in the think tanks, are often segregating taxes and saying things like, "Oh! My god! The rich are paying way more than their share of income taxes (or, cruel horrors, the death tax). What is their total share of taxes, Buster? A tax is a tax, Asshole. What is their total tax rate, Prick? How much money do they have left after taxes, Liar? (The guppies love inequality. It makes them lots of money. They get paid a bunch to promote and honor inequality; and they have no shame.)

How are we going to proceed here without getting bogged down in millions of calculations and estimates and fifty state tax codes and ten-thousand municipal tax codes, and twenty-thousand taxes within each taxing authority? Without boring the shit out of you while we use 500 words to describe West Virginia's tobacco tax. Or Hawaii's GET (General Excise Tax)

Sorry, but we are going to have to use some estimates and simplifications. As I may have mentioned elsewhere I'm almost three quarters of a century old, I've lived in eleven states and maybe twenty cities all over the country, all four corners, and north, south, east, west, and the middle belly and I've visited most of the other states and several other countries. That doesn't necessarily make me an expert on taxation, but, at least, I've seen a little and know what a tax is and what a tax is not and when it walks like a duck but doesn't shit like a duck. I have also worked at several levels – from janitor to president – in little companies and big ones including DuPont, Central Foundry, Wolverine Tube (Calumet and Hecla), U.S. Steel, Chrysler, plus a dozen others. If that's bragging, that's enough. If that's complaining, that's too much.

Maybe a little more. I had a 'friend' who was the comptroller at a Dow 500 company. At his house, he and I were drinkin' and chewin' and he picked up a financial quiz that had been in one of his 'trade' professional magazines and administered it to me figuring you-know-what. Well, he didn't get you-know-what, I trounced him good and he got really pissed. So, yes, I am well read.

I am not going to do this in the abstract or it won't be any fun at all. I am going to compare real people making different amounts of money. I can't compare by equal increments like $30,000, $40,000, $50,000, and $60,000 or we will have a government project here. So I will go up by orders of magnitude of earnings - $10,000, $100,000, $1,000,000, $10,000,000, $100,000,000, $1,000,000,000. I may have lied back there, I am not going to use 'real' people, I am going to use made-up but, hopefully, realistic people or, at least, realistic amounts (dollars).

I don't know, what do you think? I can only think of three things that any government can tax: income, wealth, and purchases (purchases are, of course, the obverse side of the sales coin). If that is correct, it makes our task a little easier. Only three categories instead of the hundreds that the politicians have learned to use to hide their nefarious tricks.

INCOME such as: wages, salary, interest, dividends, gifts, inheritance, rents, commissions, franchises, sales, etc.

WEALTH such as: real estate, stocks, bonds, loans, mortgages, businesses, property, patents, copyrights, savings, metals, wheat, sow-bellies and other commodities, etc.

PURCHASES such as: various retail consumer goods (food, clothing, fuel, rents, etc.); the different classes of wealth (stock, bonds, capital goods, real estate and other property) when changing hands at sale, intangibles (insurance, annuities, etc.).

Our purpose is to determine what and how much taxes people DO pay, not how much they SHOULD pay. The latter, the 'should', is too complicated, opinionated, and not our business. The 'do' is plenty complicated all by itself.

We are going to dance. Let us: attend to the Aesopian allemande.

$10,000!

Here's Al and Annie, usually hopelessly homeless.

January, last year they found an abandoned American car off Acorn Street in the parking lot of the defunct Acme Apples wholesalers' warehouse, by the A and A railroad track. They lived in that car. They could lock three doors from the inside; the fourth door had been damaged in an accident and could not be opened anyway. They were fairly secure when they were in the car but they couldn't lock it when they were away. Any time that they bought anything, clothes or non-perishable food, it would disappear when they were away from the car.

Annie worked three months last year at the All-Night Motel as a maid. She was paid $6 per hour. She had to write down that she worked five hours per day, seven days per week and sign the punch card; but she actually had to work until the job was done which usually took eight or nine hours per day. She had to wear a crisp uniform which her friend Amanda let her keep at her apartment (she would sneak showers at her job). She had to buy and keep her own uniforms. But she liked the job because she could chat with the other maids while they all worked. The boss only came around a few times each shift so she could work plenty independently.

One day a man came and cornered her alone in the laundry and shoved a clipboard in front of her and said she had to sign it. She hesitated but he was very authoritative and she was afraid not to sign. The other maids, later, said that they had not signed. Two days later, Annie forgot to empty an ash tray and she was fired for poor performance (it was funny, she thought, because it was on a non-smoking floor). She never knew that the man with the clipboard was the company attorney pretending to be a union organizer – and Annie had signed. Good bye Annie. Annie was stuck with two uniforms which she could not sell or use anywhere else. She could not get unemployment compensation because she had been fired for cause; for poor performance. Jobs were scarce. She kept looking but, well, jobs were scarce. Every interview was a major preparatory event.

Al worked for a rehabber/landlord, Mr. Arnold. Every day was something different – cutting lawns, shoveling sidewalks, unplugging toilets, painting, installing carpets. Al wasn't great but he worked pretty hard and Mr. Arnold was a fair man. Al was on salary and Mr. Arnold paid him $143 per week at the beginning of the year and $144 per week toward the end of the year. No one kept track of the time. Taxes were withheld from his check. He didn't know how to file for a refund.

In July, Al was painting in one of the apartment buildings, 44 Aloof Avenue, and he noticed that on one side of the hall there was a three room apartment but on the other side of the hall there was only a two room apartment. The third room on that side was not connected to that apartment; and it was empty except for some trash and painting supplies.

Al was a sly fox. "Say, Mr. Arnold," he said, "I notice you got a empty room at 44 Aloof. Seems a waste. Whatcha gonna do with that empty space. Seems a waste."

"Yeah," said Mr. Arnold, "I was going to connect that to 102 like we done to 101 but ain't got there yet. I'll put it on the schedule sometime next year."

"Next year!" Said Al. "Next year, why you could put number 103 on the door and rent it now!"

"Can't." Said Mr. Arnold, "no kitchen, no bathroom; hardly as big as a shoe closet. Couldn't rent it thataway."

"How much you want? We got a coin washer and dryer in the basement; already a sink there; wouldn't run morn a hunnert to put in a shower head and curtain or maybe even a stall in the basement. How much you want?" Asked Al.

"Whatdya mean?" Asked Mr. Arnold.

"Maybe I know someone who'd rent it, maybe I don't".

Mr. Arnold stared at him for quite a while and then slowly started to just barely nod his head. "I get $500 for 101 and $400 for 102. I suppose I could let 103 go for $100."

"I'll see what I can do," said Al, "bettern where he's stayin' now."

So, in the middle of July, Al and Annie were no longer homeless. They loved apt. 103 at 44 Aloof Avenue.

They had their own mailbox; actual home address all their own; and Al got paid, to boot, to put up the mail box. And Al got paid for painting the apartment just the way they wanted it. Secure at last! With a hot plate, it was the Taj Mahal, the Ritz, Shangri-La. They took the back seat out of the American car where they were staying and that gave them a start on the necessary furniture. Rent-2-Hav was wonderful; you could get a hot plate and just pay monthly rent for it and, sure enough, in a year or two it would be yours. They even got a T.V. with rabbit ears! They were in paradise. Now that they had a joint to stay in, they bought a joint to celebrate. They were pretty damn sure that now Annie would be able to get another job too. Things were looking up for Al and Annie!

So where does their $10,000 go, annualized.

Rent, $1200. Utilities, $1000. Transportation, $500. Clothes (mostly Good Will, Salvation Army), $300. Furniture (most from the alleys), $500. Miscellaneous, $500. Food, $6000 ($2.74 per meal).

We have to say right here that, even with an army of accountants, it would be absolutely impossible to calculate to the penny how much taxes Al and Annie pay on the $10,000 income. Here's one 'sort of' reason why: Take food for example; Annie goes down to Krogers or some local store and buys a pound of hamburger for, say $2.50. Most states don't have a sales tax on food, so there is not a direct PURCHASE tax that Annie pays when she buys hamburger. Is hamburger a low profit item or a high profit item? (You'd have to determine that for every item she purchased.) Included in that $2.50 is the profits tax; what bracket does this sale put Kroger's in; anywhere from 15% to 39%? How much of the $2.50 is profit to be taxed? The profit tax that Annie pays is a tax on PURCHASES. Another part of that $2.50, Kroger uses to pay their real estate tax (often included in rental costs). The real estate tax that Annie pays is a tax on WEALTH. Kroger has a butcher in back who cuts chunks from the side of beef or the top round, depending upon how Kroger purchased it, and tosses those chunks into a grinder, and then he packages it, etc. until it appears magically in the meat counter. Kroger pays him wages and withholds from his pay check his income taxes. The portion of those income taxes that Annie pays when she buys the burger is a tax on INCOME. O.K., Kroger purchases the slab of beef or the top round from some other business (a butcher or slaughter house). Part of the money that Kroger pays to them, the butcher, covers the butcher's payments of real estate taxes, part for their profits tax, and part for their employees income tax; WEALTH, PURCHASES, and INCOME. In addition, Kroger purchases some meat from one butcher and other meat from a slaughter house. The slaughter house purchases their steers from a feed lot. They pay all three types of taxes and pass them on. The feed lot buys from a rancher. They pay all three types of taxes and pass them on. The rancher (do you want me to stop now) purchases supplies, etc. etc. O.K., I'll stop. You get the idea. It's like figuring out where on earth every drop of rain water landed by observing a bucket of ocean water.

O.K., although we can't know exactly how much, the important thing to recognize is that Al and Annie do pay all three types of tax, INCOME, WEALTH, and PURCHASES, all three types of taxes whenever she buys something. So we will have to make educated calculations as to how much. To ignore that she does indeed pay those taxes, hidden though they may be, would be terribly dishonest as well as totally inaccurate.

I have made the whole thing seem so complicated that you might think that I have 'painted myself into a corner'. Not so. The wonder of computers' spread sheets (Excel in this case) is that to get a good estimate of all the taxes that Al and Annie pay will take me maybe a half hour to set up; and then I can just plug-in the figures for everyone talked about below and get fairly quick and accurate estimates.

Thank goodness for the internet! My main data sources are the IRS (eight statistical studies and Corporation Income Tax Returns), the National Association of Homebuilders (Property Values and Real Estate Taxes), and the Kroger Co. (and other corporations) annual reports (can you believe that they don't do P&Ls anymore? They do things like "Statement of Earnings, Operating Statistics, or Statement of

Operations" these don't follow a format and are basically evasions of reporting; the C.P.A.s are probably from some ivy college and never learned how to do P&Ls.). For some of the household budget figures I used National Center for Children in Poverty and other sources.

How much detail must I show? Do you trust me enough that I can just jump to results? If I show all the detail and all of the calculations, I will bore you to death. I'll show some detail but not all the calculations. Taxes paid are in dollars.

Tax on>>:	Wealth	Purch.	Income	TOTAL
Rent, $1200	96	0	0	96
Utilities, $1000	150	20	40	210
Transprtn., $500	50	77	40	172
Clothes, $300	36	18	36	96
Furniture, $500	60	30	60	160
Misc., $500	60	30	60	160
Food, $6000	10	52	352	461
Income Tax	0	0	900	900
TOTAL	462	227	1488	2177
% of income pd	4.6%	2.3%	14.9%	21.8%
% of wealth pd	∞	∞	∞	∞

Income remaining after expenses and taxes: NONE
Wealth remaining after expenses and taxes: NONE

So Al and Annie pay about 21.8% of their income in taxes of one kind or another. True, almost half of these are hidden taxes and we did not fully account for the multiplier effect, but 21.8% is still a substantial portion of their income; it is more than one fifth, one dollar out of every five dollars.

The percent of their wealth paid in taxes is infinite or undefined. Al and Annie have no wealth. They, in fact, have a negative net worth. They have two contracts with Rent-2-Hav – those pesky unfunded liabilities – that are of greater value – negative value – than the goods (the hot plate and the T.V.) that they bought are worth (by a factor of three or four). Then there's the matter of the credit card that Al unwittingly used; he charged one meal for $6.57 eighteen months ago that is now worth $786.32 and growing like the plant in The Little House of Horrors

(Feed Me! Feed Me!). And two years ago Annie neglected to file her 1040; the I.R.S. breath is getting hotter and hotter. They don't even remember taking one spade full of earth out of the ground and now the hole is deep enough for two graves. Even if they splurged on a hit of L.S.D. and had an I.Q. blossoming of ten or twenty points, it would take great effort and luck to dig out of that hole that they are in. Good luck Al and Annie; my heart goes out to you. The Gendarmes are on your back.

Let us Break into Begin the Beguine:
$100,000!

Bob is an accountant. Three years ago he picked up his C.P.A. in night school; he had to drive over to Beaverville three nights a week to the community college for two years but it is paying off. He works for Bartlett Construction which has contacts with several of the large manufacturing firms in the county. Contacts were not contracts; every contract is a bid job but they usually know; Bartlett knows, that they are the only bidder for the job. Six months ago he, Bob, started to make all of the workmen keep more complete time cards and he trained Brad, his accounts receivable guy, to carefully compare the time cards to the wording in the bids and charge every deviation as an add-on-change-order. He has increased the "take" on the bids by an average of 20% and he makes sure that Mr. Bartlett knows about every one. He talked Mr. Bartlett into making some "noticeable" contributions to some of the city and county aldermen and executives and then to get into blacktopping some city and county roads, and paving concrete roads and tennis courts and the like. The contracts poured in. They were profitable, very profitable. Bob received his first bonus last year.

Bob dated Betty a few times back when they were going to Buchanan High. They were both "B"-list kids and they knew it and were fine with it. Betty had a scare when she "missed her period" but it was just the flu or something (she didn't tell Bob that it might, just maybe, could have also been one or two other guys). Bob played left guard on the football team and the coach actually had a play where Bob pulled and carried the ball a few times. But he was not in the back-field and was not quite good enough for college football. He had a knack for algebra but that was it. He took no college prep courses; he always knew he wasn't headed there. He took woodworking, theater, shop, art, chorus, and anything else that guaranteed him a good grade for showing up and pretending interest. Then, to his surprise, Bremen Community College over in Beaverville offered him, not exactly a scholarship, but a "study job". Bob didn't even know that they had a football team. Bob had to answer the phone three nights a week in the coach's office and he was well paid for his time. So, he went to college after all. The coach provided tutors for him if he was having any difficulties and the professors placed him next to a smart kid when taking tests. Much to his surprise, he found himself with a mortar board on his head and an inlaid, fancy degree in his hand; and then on his wall. Bartlett Construction was looking and Bob was looking and they saw each other. And presto, a job and man were found and a job filled.

Sure, Betty took chorus and art but she also took Latin and German along with mid-level math and science. Bob had a better grade-point-average but they were "gimme grades". Betty had to work for hers. Sometimes Bob felt that she was "putting on airs" – whatever that meant. They thought that they parted-ways when Betty took nursing at the Bremen Community College; but then Bob showed up. She did pretty well there over in Beaverville about twenty miles toward Columbia. She and Bob would "hook up" in the modern parlance. Sometimes they talked of marriage if things didn't work out with Tom, Dick, or Harry (for her) or Mary, Sally, or Marsha (for him). So it wasn't a "bodice ripper", they just got along and rather than drifting apart they drifted together. The "hook ups" were good and, what the hell, the clock was ticking. So Betty came back to work at St. Boniface Hospital and, well, all of a sudden without knowing why or how they were making the trek down the aisle wondering all the while "what in the hell am I doing?" But it was done. They both liked it. Both were happy. And, surprise, it kept getting better.

Bob was making $65,000 including a bonus from a plan that Bob had sold to Mr. Bartlett; the bonus technically applied to everyone but, somehow, only Bob qualified for any significant bonus. Bob took it. Betty pulled down $35,000 but she had to do the night shift most of the time. They talked of having kids but didn't see how they could do it. Some people had half-a-dozen kids on a lot less but Bob and Betty didn't see how they could do it. Bob and Betty both felt trapped in their jobs. Sure, they were doing a lot better than they had any right to expect but what could they do to make a quantum jump? Break loose from the hum-drum to the hum-dinger. They were both stuck. Maybe they should have done something different? Bob considered starting his own construction company but he knew he didn't know anything about the millwrights, plumbers, electricians, the heavy-equipment operators, of any of the actual work. So he felt stuck and so did Betty. Not stuck in a bad-place but stuck in a mediocre-limited-future-place.

They both looked at that $100,000 that they were making (without the expense of kids) and marveled at how much it was. And, yet, how it wasn't enough. Shit, he was making a lot more than a lot of other college kids! He and Betty could remember when $50,000 seemed like a fortune. Where did it all go? I mean, you had to have a little fun. What would life be like if you didn't go to a bowl game a few times in your life? Everybody should do the Indy 500, shouldn't they? Certainly Friday night at the Beef House with a nice little bottle of wine wasn't too much to ask; it was part of his job to socialize with the "powers that be". He had to join the Baron Country Club to keep those government contracts coming; that's where the movers and shakers were; that's where you had to be! You can't give up everything for Christ's sake! It wasn't like they were spendthrifts or anything. A little golf wasn't that expensive. They were saving toward retirement; Bartlett's had a Profit Sharing Plan that Bob had devised. It was worth around $10,000 already; that's not chicken feed, for Christ's sake!

Two years ago, Betty had borrowed some Boeing

stock from her uncle. The stock remained in her uncle's name but the bank was given power-of-attorney so that Bob and Betty could borrow against it to buy their first house. They never would have bought one of the houses on a corner lot if they had known that they were going to have to pay to put the sidewalk in; twice as much sidewalk on a corner lot; Bartlett Construction did "do them a deal" but still.... After two years of payments, their equity was $2400 if the house was still worth what they paid. They were making payments on two cars and on the house. Damn! How do you get ahead? When they gave the bank their personal financial statement at the end of last year they showed that their net worth was $50,000. Ha! Reality bites. If they had to liquidate; if they sold everything at auction, and then paid off all of their creditors they would be damn lucky to walk away with their underwear on and Bob and Betty might have to sell their asses as well.

The knowledge that had begun to rankle Bob was gained because he, a few years past, had started, as a favor, to "do" some of the tax returns of his "friends" at the Baron Country Club. The other members were each and all better tax positioned than he was. None, save himself, was an "employee". Each owned or was principal, partner, shareholder, or high executive in their organization! As such, most of their expenses were deductible for tax purposes. Bob's Country Club fees were not a "business expense" for him; they were for everyone else. Most of their meals were "business expenses" taken with clients, vendors, or associates. Likewise their vehicles. So too their second homes; their first homes had 'offices' that took up half the house. It was a sweet deal but not for Bob. Not that Bob didn't take care of himself tax-wise; he knew the red-flag country pretty well and walked it to the edge. Still, yes, he was envious.

It cost money to live. Where the hell does it all go! Housing: $37,200. Food: $10,920. Transportation: $7,800. Clothes: $960. Utilities: $2,400. Furniture: $960. Other: $8560. Medical: $7,200. Income tax: $13,094

Tax on>>:	Wealth	Purch.	Income	TOTAL
Housing, $37200	6500	0	0	6500

Food, $10920	17	94	641	752
Transprtn., $7800	780	624	1206	2610
Clothes, $960	115	58	115	288
Utilities, $2400	360	96	48	504
Furniture, $960	115	58	115	288
Other, $8560	1027	514	1027	2568
Medical, $7200	864	432	864	2160
Incm tax, $13,094	0	0	13094	13094
TOTAL	9778	1876	17110	28764
% of income pd	9.8%	1.9%	17.1%	28.8%
% of wealth pd	19.6%	3.8%	34.2%	57.5%

Income remaining after expenses and taxes: Virtually none

Wealth remaining after expenses and taxes: Maybe $50,000 tops

So Bob and Betty pay about 28.8% of their income in taxes of one kind or another. 28.8% is a substantial portion of their income; it is almost one third - three months and three weeks of work. Their wealth does not increase and they are probably slipping backwards. Any financial advisor will tell them to save for retirement. That advice is the path to ulcers (you must but you can't).

If, in fact, Bob and Betty have a net worth of $50,000, they pay almost 20% of their wealth directly in wealth tax but they also pay almost 60% of their wealth in total taxes. But they do not have a net worth anywhere near $50,000; so the tax on their wealth is almost infinite. It is a barrier, a wall, a moat deliberately put up to keep working people "in their place". It is an almost insurmountable entry barrier to getting out of the rut. It was put there by despots, monarchs, kings, tsars, queens, and it is happily kept there by the rich and the super-rich and their Professional Liars in the Think Tanks, in the Corporate Media and in the Chattel Law Grinders. It is not liberal, it is not conservative, it is not fascist, it is not anarchist; it is pro-slavery.

Good luck Bob and Betty! Work hard, save your money and you may have enough money when your phantom takes flight to buy a bedtime chamber and dig a hole to plant it.

Next let us cavort to the Carnival City carioca.

$1,000,000!

When Charles was rambunctious green, he was going to be something else – fireman, policeman, or astronaut – but it was never to be: there were Doctors in the family; including Daddy; and that settled the matter. He came out of his mother's womb into a hallway with many doors – fireman, etc. – but only one door at the end. M.D.! All of the other doors were closed as he looked into them. His parents were good at gently but firmly closing the doors. He was Ivy Cultured. Ballroom dance lessons, piano, many theatrical stage plays. Everyone, all cultured (respectable, worth-while) people did those things; they knew history, dance, music, drama, biology; you could tell the difference. "Where did, 'From high good fortune in the blood blossoms the quenchless agony.' come from Charles? Right Charles! Correct Charles! I told you he would know that didn't I George. My, he is so clever. You are so clever Charles! You know there are 'people' out there who simply don't understand these things. They simply have no interest in knowledge, civility, or culture. Thank goodness we don't have to have anything to do with them."

So Charles received a scholarship to Cambridge Class Ivy Tower University. Not, certainly, a 'needs' scholarship, no, a Merit Scholarship; everyone wanted him. Charles had no 'needs'. He was, of course, a member of the secret Clawson Club – some people called it a fraternity but that is because they simply did not understand; these were the future world shapers; of the new world order; the ones who would bring democracy and progress to the backward people of the world whether they wanted it or not. (You may remember that they had that little trouble with some of the town girls, it was kept from the papers and quietly settled. The Boys, of course, were given a firm talking to; and no alcohol for a month; although no one would need to check.) Charles was athletic; he joined crew and was coxswain for a semester until it bored him. Friends of Charles' parents introduced him to Cherish. She was beautiful, cultured, intelligent. She was studying Social Science, not to work in the undesirable neighborhoods certainly, but maybe where she could really do some real good like fund raising. They both graduated, of course, with honors. Charles became a Hematologist. Cherish became a fund raiser for worthwhile causes and, of course, the Correct Political Party (the one that hates those mobsters in unions). They knew all the right people. The names of both their parents were engraved on the donor board at the Chesapeake Art Museum and their conservative church paid them special homage.

In two years, Charles was on the board of the Charity Christian Hospital (although his Christianity was quietly questioned by some jealous wood-bees who simply were not competitive; they couldn't hold to the standards.) Cherish was on the board of several Charitable Foundations whose charters earnestly promised to do much good (to at least cure some major plague, if not to actually save the world in short order). Cherish received inquiries from the White House for some sub-cabinet posts but her husband's career was too important for her to accept.

Oh yes, indeed! They were married. Everyone knew they would be. A small, intimate wedding with only 750 guests. He had several special female friends whose blood he checked from time to time. She had a few valued advisors with whom she had long, lingering trysts; learning more about collecting contributions. It was a good marriage. They would have children someday. For sure.

They had an accountant to keep track of their income. They each had stock and bond portfolios since they could remember; Mommy and Daddy and Aunts and Uncles and several trusts all made contributions. Charles' salary, fees, and teaching brought in about $400,000. Cherish had several salaries plus speaking fees that netted about $300,000. Dividends and interest totaled about $300,000. The accountants kept "his" and "her" books – just in case – but there would be no problem, they had a pre-nuptial agreement. At the end of the last fiscal year, their joint net worth was $3.65-million.

The accountants drew up a budget. Charles and Cherish tried to keep to it, they really did. Housing: $50,200. Food: $16,870. Transportation: $7,000. Clothes: $1,200. Utilities: $2,900. Furniture: $1,340. Other: $10,500. Medical: $500. Income tax: $548,836. Investments: $392,546.

Tax on>>:	Wealth	Purch.	Income	TOTAL
Housing, $50200	8785	0	0	8785
Food, $16870	26	145	995	1167
Transprtn., $7000	700	560	1085	2345
Clothes, $1200	144	73	144	361
Utilities, $2900	435	116	58	609
Furniture, $1340	161	81	161	403
Other, $10500	1260	634	1260	3154
Medical, $500	60	30	60	150
Incm tax, $548836	0	0	548836	548836
Investmnts,	0	0	0	0
TOTAL	11571	1639	552599	565809
% of income Pd	1.2%	0.2%	55.3%	56.6%
% of wealth Pd	0.3%	0.0%	15.1%	15.5%

Income remaining after expenses and taxes: $360,654

Wealth remaining after expenses and taxes: $4,010,654

So Charles and Cherish pay over half of their income in taxes of one kind or another. 57% is a substantial portion of their income.

The taxes on their wealth are a rather modest 1.2% and the total taxes as a percent of their wealth is 15.5%. Their wealth increases by more than a third of a million dollars.

Now let us dance the ductia
$10,000,000!
Donald drank too much when he was in high school

and college. Donald's dad was a psychology professor; dean of the department at Dreadnaught University and he simply could not understand Donald. Donald's dear mother was a Southern Baptist preacher. She simply could not understand Donald. He was expelled from two different high schools. He would surely break Mom and Dad's hearts. So fucking smart and pissing it all away. Everybody tisk, tisked him. The pastor gave up on him. The principal of Danforth High gave up on him. ("What a shame", he said. 'So bright!" "What a loss!" Nothing original in that – that's what everyone was saying.) Three counselors gave up on him. All the advisors gave up on him.

The Dean of the Mathematics Department, Professor Daniel Dopperhause, did not give up on him. Donald was almost as good drunk as he was sober. And the Dean only laughed when Donald said that he was in love with David and intended to marry him. The Dean was only slightly surprised to learn that Donald was gay. The Dean called him a fag and a homo and Donald loved it. (Don't YOU try it! Donald is not swishy!) The dean could love anyone who could prove, to his satisfaction, that string theory was a dud. In addition Donald developed a brand new iterative paradigm to solve the Traveling Salesman Problem. The dean with Donald was like the Horse Whisperer with horses. No one else could tame him but the Dean could. (Promise not to tell anyone and I will tell you that the Dean got Donald to switch from alcohol to 'the weed' and pretty much sobered him up.) The Dean got him through English and German and composition and the other entire freshman junk. ("Donald, why learn this shit after you graduate with a "D" average; you most certainly are going to learn it someday, why not learn it before the test and graduate with an "A" average; if you get a four-point, I promise not to tell your parents.")

Another lucky break came when Donald took economics with Professor Dormantcrotch. Donald was one of those kids you noticed because he asked relevant questions that the Professor had never thought of. And the next day he, Donald, would answer them. Sure, Dormantcrotch and Dopperhause were academicians but they were not adverse to money. Money did not give them hives. (Where do you go if you want corn? You go to a cornfield, a corn crib, a corn silo, or even a can of corn. You do not go to a meat market, a police station, or even toy store. Where do you go if you want money? You go to banking, insurance, or stocks and bonds. You don't go to a playground, a damn restaurant, or even an automobile factory.) Donald developed some damned stock market algorithms which were very interesting. They, Donald and the Professors, took a year's stock market history and they tested the damned algorithms. Then they took a ten year stock history on the University's high speed computer and the damned algorithms did not fail them.

But the damned algorithms could not speed up time. It took a full year, with real money (the Professors re-mortgaged), with Donald a full partner, to test the algorithms in the real world in the real stock market. Wow! They worked!

They were not in Massachusetts or California and so Donald could not marry David. But they did cohabitate. David was a good artist and made good money. He also was very domesticated so that he and Donald had something to fuss about. Donald was not a neatnik. They were not "The Odd Couple" but they were a close second (the Odd Couple were straights [called "breeders" by gays]).

David was brought in as a partner too. And their little investment club grew and grew. The first year they did 48% return. The second, 33%. Donald's parents stopped tisk, tisking and became investors in the little club. David's parents were socialites and had friends with a little money and soon Donald and friends had to name and register their little club.

The called it the Devotional Fund in honor of Donald's mother (and to hint that they were in league with God). It was soon noticed by some of the big boys and Damein Brothers Investment Bank took them in. The little club soon carried a big club. Professors Dormantcrotch and Dopperhause took leaves of absence and joined the Devotional Fund. By some estimates, Donald was still a kid. Donald needed Dormantcrotch and Dopperhause's gravitas and shall we say 'senior conservatism' or shall we say 'damping' or 'judgment'. And the professors needed Donald's algorithms. The four of them (including David) would 'group think' and come up with new 'instruments', and 'derivatives' and then test them on the University's high speed computer. And when they worked spectacularly – as they usually did – they would sell the hell out of them and make piles and piles. Everybody trusted them so they could print "derivative" stock certificates that had only imaginary backing and sell them for whatever number they printed on the front. Then later they didn't have to print any number. Investors bought and sold them as though they actually represented something besides a piece of paper. The pieces of paper were treated like a stock or a bond which was really backed by something solid.

They could not lose. Start compounding millions then billions and billions at 30% or 40%; add fees and fees and fees and bonuses and bonuses and in a few short, spectacular years you have a fortune. Is everybody happy? They gave the derivative funds nice sounding names which didn't exactly reflect or reveal what they were really selling. The Progress Fund; The Freedom Fund; The Fortune Fund; The Apostles' Fund; they had peeked at the politicians' play book. These are honest men, but they are blowing up this balloon so fast you have to worry about them. What if...

Pray for them.

Professor Dormantcrotch, admittedly, from the first did not understand the math. But he did understand the stock market and the economy much better than the others. When he ran the historic computer simulations he was worried that the numbers flipped a bit during even light recessions. Hmmm. What the hell is this? What is wrong? He ran the simulations even further back; back through the 1920's; back through the First Depression. Then the numbers did more than flip a bit; the numbers blew up! Then he studied economic fundamentals – not just corporate stock fundamentals. Then he flipped! The economy was worse in the 2000's than it was in the 1920's! Dormantcrotch conferred with his partners and they all became concerned. But they couldn't stop now! But Dormantcrotch pulled all of the partners' money out of the funds and searched for stodgy companies. He wanted companies involved in commodities whose P.E. was steady for long periods of time even through recessions. He wanted companies whose book value was greater than their stock market value. He wanted fundamental commodities. Rather than real-estate, he liked construction; rather than construction, he liked lumber or nails; rather than lumber or nails, he liked logging or steel; rather than logging or steel, he liked forests or mines. He wanted his and their money out of the derivative funds!

Donald didn't flaunt his new-found wealth but he wasn't a monk either. They bought a fine penthouse condo with fine furnishings, wine, and catered dinner parties. The roof outside their windows was like a verdant park. What the hell, why not? If this blows up – and it is not going to – we will just make a killing at something else; something more fun. There's always pornography and you don't have to deal with these asshole stuffed shirt, empty head bankers.

We find Donald with a net worth of $50,000,000 and an annual income of $10,000,000. Nice work if you can get it. Fucking taxes! God damn government! We gotta start buyin' us some god damn Senators, maybe even a fucking President! With all the god damn wealth we are creating, we shouldn't have to pay taxes! The god damn government ought to pay us, for Christ's sake! We're keeping the economy running!

Donald and David lived frugally but well: Housing: $60,000. Food: $18,000. Transportation: $7,800. Clothes: $1,200. Utilities: $2,400. Furniture: $2,400. Other: $9,600. Medical: $14,400. Income tax: $3,178,240. Investments: $9,103,566

Tax on>>:	Wealth	Purch.	Income	TOTAL
Housing, $60K	10,500	0	0	10,500

Food, $18,000	28	155	1,062	1,245
Transprtn., $7,800	780	624	1,209	2,613
Clothes, $1200	144	73	144	361
Utilities, $2,400	360	96	48	504
Furniture, $2,400	288	145	288	721
Other, $9,600	1152	580	1152	2884
Medical, $14,400	1728	870	1728	4326
Incm tax, $3,178,240	0	0	3-M	3-M
Investmnts,	0	0	0	0
TOTAL	14,980	2,542	3-M	3-M

% of income pd	0.1%	0.0%	31.8%	32.0%
% of wealth pd	0.0%	0.0%	6.4%	6.4%

Income remaining after expenses and taxes: $3,527,720

Wealth remaining after expenses and taxes: $53,527,720

So Donald and David pay about 32% of their income in taxes of one kind or another. Almost a third is not a trivial portion of their income.

The taxes on their wealth are a rather modest 6.4% and the total taxes as a percent of their wealth is under 10% at 6.4%. And their wealth increases by over $6-million.

Now let us escape to the enchanting estampie stomp.

$100,000,000!

Emmanuel Earlcountcourt is the 10th descendant of the founder of the Earlcountcourt Powder Company. The founder, Effinghambent Earlcountcourt, was given a land grant from the French king (in disputed English territory) and money from various members of the French peerage to go to America and found a black powder manufacturing company so that France would have powder to defend itself against the peasants; they also sent with him servants who knew how to do it since he did not. Things went well for him. Ship owners, understandably, did not like shipping dangerous black powder across the wide Atlantic. He was able to purchase slaves to employ mining the nitrates and also to manufacture the black powder. There was a ready market because there were many bears and Indians to kill. Everybody needed a musket and black powder. He used agents to make sure that his competitors had mysterious explosions (mysterious explosions are expected in the manufacture of black powder). He soon had a wonderful monopoly. Whoever didn't blow up, sold to him after considering the probabilities. Emmanuel did not use slaves to manufacture the black powder; it was too dangerous. He was happy to work his slaves to death but he certainly was not going to blow-up an investment. He used wage-people, and then he did not lose investment when they blew-up.

Good luck rained upon him. The American Colonies began a stupid war against the English King George the Third and Earlcountcourt was able to sell, at very dear prices, to both sides. Then more good luck: the French Revolution "took care of" his backers and investors and Effinghambent became the sole owner of the Earlcountcourt Powder Company. He also had the good fortune to make black powder in a war-loving nation. There were perpetual wars and enemies strung over the years like pearls on a necklace. And Effinghambent and his successors did everything to encourage the number and the growth of those pearls. Wars are wonderful! No one talks about monopoly, gouging, excess profits, or war mongering if you are on the winning side and control the 'news' sources.

Effinghambent had the good judgment to hire every very, very bright chemist that he could find (they came almost at slave wages because they had nowhere else to go). These young, bright, ambitious chemists pushed him into other products and soon he had to change his name to the Earlcountcourt Chemical Company, Incorporated. Those foolish chemists hoped fruitlessly that they might be rewarded for discovering the base of a fortune.

The rest is history. Back to the present.

Emmanuel was raised by servants, was taught

by servants, mothered and fathered by servants who manifested his every wish and anticipated and satisfied every latent desire. (Servant mama's encouraged servant daughters to cooperate. The Earlcountcourts had a family history of taking good care of their bastards – either a large lump sum or, sometimes, continuous support or, rarely, continuing interest – they would actually see their bastards.) He bought his degree from one of the prestigious, eastern ivy universities. At the proper time, he was married to Elizabeth Enchancamelot whose family controlled Encompressal Petroleum Company; it seemed a good fit.

Surprise, Emmanuel was hired by the Earlcountcourt Chemical Company, Incorporated. He was put on the fast track and managed a laboratory here and a manufacturing plant there; the existing Works Manager remained on site and was given 'special assignments'. In due time, when he was of a ripe age (and his uncle died), he was elected CEO and took a seat on the board. He knew everything that there was to know about life wherein you never have to strain a muscle or a neuron, never have to pay a bill or a piper, and never have to meet anyone who is not a peer or a servant. He knew that he owned everything that he could see; he knew that he could make no errors; that workers were thieves, lazy, violent, and stupid; and that everyone knew that he was brilliant, courageous, and shrewd.

Every day of his life he had been given a $1,000 tax-free gift from a relative, friend, or foundation. His net worth at 40 years of age was $5-billion; his income (with bonuses and stock options) was $100-million. Most of his expenses were corporate and were taken care of by the company. Mansions are 'always' appraised, for real estate taxes, at a lower rate than a shanty. Did it bother him that no member of his family had ever put up one dollar or un franc; no ancestor had invested one penny of capital in the multi-billion dollar company that they now owned? Every cent of value in the Earlcountcourt Chemical Company had come from the labor of the workers. Of course it didn't bother him anymore than pygmies in Africa, slavery in America, or starvation in

New York bothered him.

Emmanuel and Elizabeth did what they pleased. There were over a dozen CPAs and corporate lawyers who structured everything. No agent in the IRS was so stupid as to challenge anything that Emmanuel and Elizabeth did. Emmanuel and Elizabeth had slept in the Lincoln bed in the White House; to challenge Emmanuel and Elizabeth was tantamount to challenging the United States; more than hell would descend upon anyone so foolish; they might as well walk into boiling quicksand. But even the CPAs had to list some expenses: Income: $100,000,000. Housing: $72,000. Food: $14,400. Transportation: $600. Clothes: $1,200. Utilities: $600. Furniture: $2,400. Other: $9,600. Medical: $0. Income tax: $1,722,206. Investments: $96,454,788.

Tax on>>:	Wealth	Purch.	Income	TOTAL
Housing, $72K	12,600	0	0	12,600
Food, $14,400	22	124	850	996
Transprtn., $600	60	48	93	201
Clothes, $1200	144	73	144	361
Utilities, $600	90	24	12	126
Furniture, $2,400	288	145	288	721
Other, $9,600	1152	580	1152	2884
Medical, $0	0	0	0	0
Incm tax, $1,722,206	0	0	1.7-M	1.7-M
Investmnts,	0	0	0	0
TOTAL	14,356	993	1.7-M	1.7-M
% of income Pd	0.0%	0.0%	1.7%	1.7%
% of wealth Pd	0.0%	0.0%	0.0%	0.0%

Income remaining after expenses and taxes: $96,454,788

Wealth remaining after expenses and taxes: $5,096,454,788

So Emmanuel and Elizabeth pay about 1.7% of their income in taxes of one kind or another. They are furious that they have to pay almost $2-million when they give so much to the United States. They provide hundreds of thousands of jobs – overpaid jobs – they provide a bulwark for the defense of the United States of America against its enemies. It is so unfair that they have to pay taxes too.

The taxes on their wealth are a vanishingly small percentage.

Now let us fan the flames with the famous flamenco.

$1,000,000,000!

Fred can still remember when, on the first day of first grade, the nun was taking roll and called out, "Frederick!". No one responded. Fred looked around with everyone else. There was no Frederick in the class. Finally the nun said, "Fred". Still no response. Fred looked around with everyone else; it's disturbing to frightened first graders to have two kids missing. Then she said, "Freddy!". And our Fred raised his hand. A boy of many names if not talents. Fred would never let a lack of talent stand in the way of good grades. But no grade was good enough for his mother. Fred was always terrified when he received a grade so low as a "B". His mother wrung his self esteem. He was certain that she would leave him in the dumpster although he did not visualize it in that way; he knew that she would not have him if he did not excel. He pushed himself to his limits but that was not nearly good enough. He was forced, absolutely forced, to "skin the cat" another way. He took his grades anyway he could. His need trumped his conscience. Take what you must to kill the pain.

Fred's father lived in the same house as Fred and his mother but was neither a husband nor a dad. Other than an unnerving disapproval, Fred had no relationship with his father. Fred never saw his parents touch or talk to each other. Fred never had a hug from mother or father. Fred would have done anything, anything to please either parent.

Fred learned to answer to "Freddy, Fred, or Frederic" but he was still somebody else. When, as a freshman in college, the TA called, "Mr. Fooenscow"; our Fred, now Frederick, knew that it was he or him and not some mystery or whim. Frederick was provided with all of the material things needed to succeed at the university. Talent is not a material thing. But Frederick would not let such a small thing as a small mind stand in the way of a large grade-point-average. No one studied longer or harder to less effect. But there are other ways to "skin a cat". Frederick learned them all. And used them all. In seven years he walked out thin lipped with an MBA and a 3.5 GPA.

In his own mind, he was qualified to run General Motors. In other people's minds, the minds that counted, he was not. Frederick was adamantly able to bulldoze barriers. Life was a series of roles to him. Nothing, no one, was going to stop him. He would succeed so high that his parents would have to see and approve. But no one would let him run the world. Well, he would have to start somewhere else, damn it, then he would show them, then he would wow them. He took the only job offered in the bowels of 50-story Family First Friendly Insurance Company. The brains were in the Actuarial and the Legal Departments. The money was in the Sales Department. Frederick quickly migrated to Sales.

Sales suited him; he suited Sales. He could wear any face, say anything, promise anything to get to the close; sign here or I will be very upset, I will lose this major contest, I might be fired, my parents will disown me, your children will be placed in an orphanage, your wife will be destitute, it costs less than a cup of coffee a day, it is guaranteed savings for your kids college, it is better than CDs, you can borrow against the cash value, you are cruel and thoughtless if you don't. In five years he entered the million-dollar club. He could sell but no one considered him for sales management. They let him train some, but no management. Still, he was layering on the honors. Then disaster hit. The father of one of his competitor salesmen, Fanny, was Head of Personnel. Fred beat Fanny in sales contests and the Head of Personnel transferred Fred to Customer Relations (the complaint department). Fred would not have been so miserable had he known that this was a "stroke of luck". Having access to the water cooler, he learned what really makes an insurance company tick. The Head of Customer Relations retired; Fred was given Head. He was astounded by how much money was really being made. He did 'back of the envelope calculations' when he learned that 36% of twenty-pay-life-insurance-policies are never cashed in. WOW! There is really money to be made in this business. Those that were cashed in were reduced to a fifth by inflation. It was better than selling Free-Spring-Water; you never have to deliver the product. You don't need a mask or a gun. Take the money and run.

Frederick's mother and father died with no real reconciliation. Fred felt very empty. But they bequeathed him a fortune far beyond his expectations.

A head-hunter contacted Fred. The Fabulous Fair Health Insurance Company was being eaten alive by ever increasing claims. They needed a savior. Fred needed five minutes to decide (he could always return to sales). Nobody thought that the Fabulous Fair Health Insurance Company could be saved so, Frederick did not know it, but he was the twentieth prospect contacted. He was required to invest heavily in the Fabulous Fair Health Insurance Company to show his personal confidence in the company. So even without the inevitable stock options, Frederick was a major stockholder in the company. He was the indisputable "head".

Suddenly, Frederick Fooenscow was President and CEO of the Fabulous Fair Health Insurance Company; a small beleaguered, failing, unknown company. He was given a small salary and large stock options (the board figured he would never collect a penny on the options, so they ladled them on). Fred took two axioms with him to his new job: 1. Sell the goddamned stuff (higher commissions, more salesmen). 2. Don't deliver what you are selling (put some goddamned clauses in the goddamned policies). Pre-existing, pre-existing, pre-existing conditions – it's a wonderful song. Were you born? Well! Then it is pre-existing. Anyway, your policy does not cover that particular procedure; everything else but not THAT one.

In a year the Fabulous Fair Health Insurance Company was back on very stable feet. In two years you could hear the roar of recovery. In three years it had branches in every major city in every state. Fred was getting raises, bonuses, and more stock options.

Claims had been cut to the core. You could buy health insurance and, as long as you didn't get sick, you were securely covered. Feeling secure is a major benefit; they were selling the sizzle not the steak. And if you are really sick, you might as well die anyway. Your policy with the Fabulous Fair Health Insurance Company certainly did not cover THAT, read the goddamn policy. The salesman did NOT tell you that! You see, the contract only covers what is written in the, guess what, the contract. You obviously misunderstood what the agent said, and (what, you have a tape recording) even if he did say it, it ain't so. Read the print, print, print. "Written only" counts. Verbal does not trump ink. READ the contract, for Christ's sake.

Frederick's prize-sales-person was Flame Flasher (she had changed her name from Frolla Frieburgstein for sales purposes). Frederick had several serious conversations with her about sales; very serious. Then they started to meet at a local coffeehouse and pretty soon over drinks they were playing footsy and then (in the current palaver) they 'hooked up'. He soon found out that she was deeply into S&M. And then into "the Lifestyle". This was, by far, the most exciting thing that had ever happened to him. Why he loved being tied up with several women tormenting him and sexually teasing him until he almost went over the edge he could not comprehend. But he did. Did he ever. Frederick and Flame Flasher flew to Reno and were done with it. It was legal. Let the games continue. To her credit, Flame Flasher had no real appreciation just how rich Frederick had become; she was not a fortune hunter she was a foremost cunter. His income (including interest, dividends, and stock options), counting everything, that very year hit just $999,000,000; she had just hit $1,000,000; she thought he was maybe at two ($Million). Neither had asked for a pre-nup. Could they grow old together? Who gives a shit? When you are having so much fun, the future is in the future, not in the moment. And his mother and father stopped haunting his dreams; he was at peace, the greatest gift that could be given.

The Fabulous Fair Health Insurance Company's Comptroller did Frederick's taxes. As best the

Comptroller could figure – here are Frederick and Flame Flasher's expenses: Housing: $72,000. Food: $24,000. Transportation: $8,400. Clothes: $2,400. Utilities: $6,000. Furniture: $2,400. Other: $10,800. Medical: $0. Income tax: $4,722,206. Investments: $990,429,588. Frederick and Flame Flasher also had $Millions of expenses to make sure that the U.S. didn't come to it's senses and adopt the sane, logical, moral "single-payer" health care insurance which would have cut off his $Billion income. But that was a business expense and did not figure in his and her taxes.

Tax on>>:	Wealth	Purch.	Income	TOTAL
Housing, $72K	12,600	0	0	12,600
Food, $24,000	37	206	1416	1660
Transprtn., $8,400	8,400	672	1302	2814
Clothes, $2,400	288	145	288	721
Utilities, $6000	900	240	120	1260
Furniture, $2,400	288	145	288	721
Other, $10,800	1296	652	1296	3244
Medical, $0	0	0	0	0
Incm tax, $4.7M	0	0	4.7M	4.7M
Investmnts,	0	0	0	0
TOTAL	16,249	2061	4.7M	4.7M
% of income Pd	0.0%	0.0%	0.5%	0.5%
% of wealth Pd	0.0%	0.0%	0.2%	0.2%

Income remaining after expenses and taxes: $990,429,588

Wealth remaining after expenses and taxes: $2,990,429,588

So Frederick and Flame Flasher pay about 0.5% of their income in taxes of one kind or another.

The tax on their wealth is a vanishingly small percentage.

Obviously, people spend their money in different ways. No single example at any given income level represents everyone at that income level. No one example can represent all individuals at any particular level. We tried to make these examples typical and middle-of-the-road. These examples are as representative as any other. And relative to each other they certainly tell a story different from what one would come to believe if one only paid attention to the Professional Liars who exclusively dominate the news.

Now let us compare the results of our little study.

In the table below we have rounded off and simplified to clarify. "A" is, of course, Al & Annie; "B" is Bob & Betty; "C" = Charles & Cherish; "D" = Donald & David; "E" = Emmanuel and Elizabeth; and "F" = Fred & Flame.

The numbers are in thousands of dollars and are rounded to the closest whole number. Thus Al and Annie's income of $10,000 is represented as 10. Charles and Cherish's Tax on Income $552,599 is represented as simply 553. Donald and David's income of $10,000,000 is put down as 10,000 and their Total Tax of $3,200,000 is listed plainly as 3,200.

	Income	Tax on Income	Tax on Wealth	Tax on Purchases	Total Tax
A	10	2	0	0	2
B	100	17	10	2	28
C	1,000	553	11	2	565
D	10,000	3,200	14	3	3,200
E	100,000	1,700	14	1	1,700
F	1,000,000	4,700	16	2	4,700

So, what does this tell us? The income increases are very orderly, each tier going up by a factor of ten; nothing else (none of the taxes) makes any sense whatsoever. The tax system clearly has not been designed by intelligent beings. It was made by lawyers. The tax code has not been created and organized by compassionate beings. It was created by lawyers. It makes no sense. No sensible person would call it fair. It was made by lawyers. (Defend yourselves; don't look to me [just the facts, Ma'am]) Because there are so many deductions, dodges, ditches, and dithers; the least honest pay the least taxes. If you were raised fearing that big 'eye in the sky', you will pay sky high. The current system rewards liars and crooks. An honest person, over his lifetime, will pay hundreds-of-thousands more dollars than a slicker.

How much money (revenue) is raised from each level? Well, damn it; there is no way to know for sure. However, the brave-hearted can estimate. We won't attempt to estimate the total revenue; we will just estimate the percent to be raised from each level.

	Income	Percent at that Income	Percent raised at each level
A	10	10	0.58
B	100	89	72.89
C	1,000	1	16.53
D	10,000	.1	9.36
E	100,000	.01	0.50
F	1,000,000	.001	0.15

As I'm sure you have heard, the Professional Liars say that the richest 20% pay 90% of the taxes. Or some such lie. That's what you would expect from Professional Liars. They lie. That's how they make their living. They will always throw a deep shadow over their lie so that you can't see what they are really saying. They will add some confusing caveat like "income taxes" or "capital gains taxes" but they will always make it seem like they are talking about ALL taxes. And I can guarantee that the chart that I show above can be picked apart in dozens of ways. Maybe, for example, the $100,000 range represents only 88% of the population – or some such thing. But, overall, the picture that I am presenting in the above chart is the correct picture. The poor and the middle class support this country. The poor and the middle class, because of their abundance, pay the most.

Now, let's look at the percentage that each income level pays in the various classes of taxes and also for the total. Again, the amount ($) numbers are in thousands.

The percentages are as shown. Thus, "A"s (Al and Annie's) tax on income is 15% and this is shown as 15.

	Income	% Tax on Income	% Tax on Wealth	% Tax on Purchases	% Total Tax
A	10	15	5	2	21
B	100	17	10	2	58
C	1,000	55	1	0	57
D	10,000	6	0	0	6
E	100,000	2	0	0	2
F	1,000,000	1	0	0	1

Surprise, surprise; when we include ALL taxes, the poor and middle-class pay far more than the rich. In fact, the discrepancy is amazing and ugly. It is clear that taxes are erected as a barrier to prevent the poor and middle-class from having a chance in life. The tax burden is crushing on the poor and middle-class. And the tax burden is fluffy and, in some cases, non-existent on the rich. In the sense of 'burdened', the rich are not taxed at all. Clearly, the Caesars won; the Tsars won; the Sun Kings of France won; the Lords of Great Britain won; the Emperors of China and Japan won; Hitler won; Stalin won; Rockefeller won; Kennedy won; the American Aristocrats won; the people lost. The rich do not hold the poor in contempt; contempt would take knowledge and effort; the rich, absolutely, do not consider the poor and, if by chance, they consider them at all it is as they would consider germs on mars. Is the struggle over? No? Do we have to use the guillotine or lead and cyanide? I hope not. But, clearly, there must be change. Change. Change.

The results of the tax system are shown below. Once again, the numbers are in thousands and are rounded to two significant numbers (that's how we engineers did it when we used to use slide-rules). For example "D"s (Donald and David's) After-Tax-Income-Remaining is $3,500,000 and is represented here as 3,500.

	Income	After Tax Income Remaining	After Tax Wealth Remaining
A	10	0	0
B	100	0	50
C	1,000	360	4,000
D	10,000	3,500	53,300
E	100,000	96,000	5,100,000
F	1,000,000	990,000	3,000,000

At the lowest income levels, from say $0 to $30,000, there is no incentive to work because of taxes. Even if someone works two or three jobs and lives with someone who does likewise, all of their money is stripped from them by taxes. They have no chance. No chance. No chance to advance. No chance to succeed. They will die young with rotten teeth because of taxes. They cannot own a car. They do not have health insurance. They can never own a house. And, because there is almost no punishment worse than taxes, there is a huge incentive to cheat; on both the part of the employer and the worker. And the rich celebrate ("we want everyone to have a productive life", is there a greater cynicism?) knowing full well that they are destroying humans at an 'ethnic cleansing rate'. If this were a Christian Nation, we would not; we could not have such an immoral tax system. If anyone who is or was rich had any conscience, any trace of decency, we would not, could not have such an unjust tax system. This is not ignorant hyperbole, I personally know several people like this; they work all the time and gain nothing except self-respect. They CANNOT get ahead no matter what they do. The stress that they live under is unimaginable by anyone who is not conversant with their efforts and condition. If there were a god (unless this god is a sadistic human hater), of course, these conditions would not exist. This tax system is staggeringly unfair. The present tax could be whacked except Gates hates.

At the next order-of-magnitude level, Bob and Betty's level; at income levels from say $50,000 to $200,000; particularly at the lower end of this range, the tax burden is likewise Promethean or Sisyphean. In the range of say $40,000 to $100,000 annual income a citizen becomes a target of economic rape by the city and state tax collectors. Those tax collectors can be ever so clever finding ways to atax the little guy.

We have a little tiny restaurant; here's what they do: about (keeps going up – hard to keep track) state sales tax 8%; about $40,000 (on receipts [revenue]). City "restaurant" tax, 2%; about $10,000 (on receipts) (for "culture" [like the symphony orchestra so that the fiddlers don't have to go to work {oh! Pardon me! Fiddling IS work! Ha! Ha ha.} You'd think that the least they could do is give us season's passes since the symphony is seldom sold-out]). Real-estate tax, $7,276.36. "Personal Property" Tax ~$1,000 (stoves, refrigerators, etc.). "Gross receipts" (not "profits") tax of about 0.25%; about $1,500 (I don't remember exactly). State liquor license $500.00. City "by the drink" weekday Liquor license; $750. City "by the drink" Sunday liquor license; $600. Restaurant license. Dance Hall license; ~$200 (now canceled – we used to have Tango and Square Dances [at which some Symphony fiddlers fiddled for free]). Mardi Gras fees (not gov't body) about $2,500. We also get charged if our burglar alarm goes off. No one can say that they are not creative. I have probably forgotten a few, too.

Do I believe that the "big boys" (e.g. InBev [ersatz, erstwhile Anheuser-Busch Breweries]; Monsanto; Ralston-Purina; Express Scripts; A. G. Edwards; Edward Jones Investments; Scottrade; Energizer; Solutia; University of Missouri–St. Louis; Hardee's; Enterprise Rent-A-Car; Emerson Electric; Charter Communications) pay anything like we do on an equivalent percentage basis? Ha! My sides ache and my mouth tastes bitter from the alkali laughing. No, no we, us little farts, are buying them ball parks and paying their taxes while they make grandiose gestures of charity and pretended largess, pretended giving to us pretended inferiors.

Taxpayers earning in the range of, say, $40,000 to $100,000 annual income usually are on payroll and have almost no chance to grab the tons of deductions to which the very rich have easy access. These taxpayers live in a world of weary worry; these are "The mass of men [who] lead lives of quiet desperation" of Thoreau. Things haven't changed much since 1854 or even 1854 B.C. Struggle though they may or might; it is only a few who hit the lottery of life who escape to island of the rich; and they do not reach back to pull anyone with them or to change the rules; no, they erect the walls and moats that Warren Buffett prescribes.

But, ho!, when one's income falls in the range of $500,000 to $1,000,000 the tax burden begins to fall away, the yoke becomes slightly padded and lighter. One can begin to accumulate wealth and the tax on wealth and purchases virtually disappears. The income tax is still healthy but the income is large enough that these taxpayers can keep most of it ("everything" is a deductable expense). And, as wealth is accumulated, the hooded tax collector is blindfolded; he cannot see wealth when it is stacked this high.

And, blessed are the saints, when the income soars above, say, $1,000,000; taxes, as a percentage, shrinks to virtually nothing. Lordy, lordy; ain't we got fun. The hooded tax collector has his hood on backwards. He don't see nutin, not even the sun. We's all got a barrel of money; they's all ragged and funny, we'll travel along singing a song side by side. Don't know what's coming tomorrow, we're certain our money will grow, we'll roll 'long the road, dumpin' our load far and wide. Thro' all kinds of weather, what if the sky should fall? Our load's light as a feather, it doesn't matter at all.

Beyond $1,000,000 to $10,000,000 and flying to even $1,000,000,000 the tax man seeth not. Lo! We have blinded the hooded beast. The money doth cometh but it goeth not! Lo! The Lord God seeth us and blessed us for we are mighty and God Fearing for we know that the Lord Above loveth us. Leona Mindy Roberts Helmsley; beloved of God, affirmed the universal truth: "We don't pay [no] taxes. Only the little people pay taxes." Drum roll, Maestro, please; thank you, thank you, thank you. Taxes? What taxes? We ain't got no God damn taxes!

What's taxes anyway? Ha ha ha ha ha. Fuck you all! You little pricks! You ain't paid yo' dues, you Little Fuck Offs. Buy you some god damn lawmakers then come an' see me, yaw little Dingleberry. Where da fuck is yo Senator? Where yo keep yo Congressman? He up yo asshole? Bring 'im out, lay 'im onna line; stretch 'im out; show me 'is vote, Dink! Fuck you asshole! Grow up!

****

There are several anomalies here:

1. Why do Al and Annie, and Bob and Betty, who have no (net) wealth, pay taxes on wealth while Frederick and Flame Flasher, Emmanuel and Elizabeth, and Donald and David, who have great wealth, pay tiny taxes on wealth?

2. Why do Emmanuel and Elizabeth who earn ten times what Donald and David do, pay less tax?

1. The answer as to why Al and Annie pay a greater percent of Taxes on their non-existent wealth than do Emmanuel and Elizabeth on their excessive wealth is that they, Al & Annie, have neglected two important things: one; they have not made wise purchases; they have not purchased any office holders or law grinders; none, whether city, county, state, or federal. Two; they and none of their friends have run for and been elected to lawmaking office. Oh! And I might as well add a third thing: Three; they have failed to purchase any media outlets. They have allowed their rich counterparts to own all of the newspapers, radio stations, T.V. stations, magazines, truth fountains, think tanks, lawyers, and lobbyists. You can hardly expect the Professional Liars in the Think Tanks to toot your horn if you do not pay the piper.

Al and Annie's taxes paid on wealth only include those real-estate taxes passed on down to them in some ordinary retail purchases. I have not included personal property taxes. If they owned an automobile, in most cities and states they would pay 'personal property taxes' on that too. Many cities also charge taxes on small business 'personal property' such as all of the furniture and fixtures, small ware, manufacturing equipment (ranges, freezers, refrigerators, computers, and the like), and in-process inventory. These taxes, too, are passed on to the retail consumer.

Oh, you say, the rich also pay taxes on those items and at the same rate as the poor. Ah! But there are two differences. For the rich, the tax on those items is an insignificantly tiny portion of their wealth. They pay no taxes on the vulture's share of their wealth; none whatsoever. Then too, the real-estate of the rich is almost universally appraised at a lower rate than that of the common man and/or woman for two reasons; first, they have great influence and strike fear in the neck of the appraisers who, therefore, slice value from the assessment of those castles which the rich call home (or second home); second, the rich often live in conclaves of one kind or another and, because of their clout, obtain reduced rates on public services such as water and sewage, police, fire protection, road maintenance and the like.

2. The answer as to why Emmanuel and Elizabeth pay less income tax than someone who earns one-tenth as much is because of expertise, know-how, and experience. Emmanuel and his ancestors have been at it for 200 years. Donald and David just stumbled in. Emmanuel and his ancestors have owned law grinders by the dozen for ten-score years. They have had hundreds of paragraphs slipped into defense budgets, farm programs, space programs, energy bills, and every other appropriations boondoggle written expressly to protect them and their "essential to national defense" businesses. They have, under extreme duress, even stooped to visit common congressmen. The congressmen, of course, curtsy to them; they don't bow to the congressmen although they do condescend to shake the hands of even ordinary grinders.

In the matter of taxes, I have a small personal story to tell which, I believe, is telling as to the difference in treatment of the son of the town drunk compared to someone wealthy, say, the President of the United States.

In about 1956, I was working my way through the University of Wisconsin, Madison (in those days you needn't add "Madison". Madison was it.) working meals in various restaurants for what was called a "meal-job" – work an hour, get paid with a meal – and at night in various bakeries. The State Auditor told me to haul my ass down to his office. I did. It turned out to have been mistaken identity as my Old Man's name was Theodore J. West and mine was Theodore V. West. The Old Man had just moved and somehow the State lost track. But, since I was there and was a nobody, they would have some fun sticking a few pins in this helpless and hapless bloke. (At the time, I was in top shape as a varsity boxer and could have kicked the shit out of this asshole in fifteen seconds [the count takes ten seconds]. I only mention that because it is disgusting to be talked down to and to be belittled by idiots who are also fat asses who are abusing their positions of petty power in their tiny Camelots.) He, the goddamned auditor, queried me. Yes, I had a meal job. No, I did not pay taxes on those meals. Well, he billed me, fined me, and had me pay interest. I was, of course, totally unable to argue. I paid. Had I been quick on my feet, I might have suggested that the tax on a meal should be no more than a biscuit. Some people enjoy killing a helpless robin. Those small things by small thugs, fines and interest, are tremendous blows when you have to hold the cost of your meals down to one dollar per day.

So it is instructive to compare the tax treatment of son of the town drunk to that of the son of privilege. But, alas, the sons of privilege do not release their tax returns. It is the I.R.S.'s sacred duty to keep all evidence of crime classified due to National Security. Oh! But wait a minute! Didn't I read that the President of the United States of America, the Bushy, had, in fact, released his tax return? Yes, I did read that very thing some dozen or so times; plus hear and saw it on the air. But it ain't so Joe. Find it on the internet! You can't. No, Joe! What was released was his adjusted gross income. They extolled his tax paid and all of the thousands of dollars given to charities in great and repetitive detail. And, plus, the advance his wife got for "writing" a children's book (isn't she just so special). There may have been more information released to a few Pro-Slavery Professional Liars but, if so, they are keeping it behind and under the counter along with their pornography.

But that can't stymie a gnawing engineer. I have designed whole machines (that worked) with less information than that. I found more information about the President's 2004 tax return. With that and the scanty information from 2007, I could fairly reconstruct the President's 2007 return. Reported facts: Adjusted gross income = $719,274. Income tax paid = $221,635. Deduced figures: Gross income = $910,000. Deductions = $190,726. Deductions as percent of gross income = 21%. Effective tax rate = 24.4%.

But, to be fair to the President, he actually earned much more than that. I mean, if he were the son of the town drunk and had a meal job – that is, if part of his pay was given to him in the form of meals – he would have had to pay taxes on them; that we know with absolute certainty. Also, if the son of the town drunk were allowed to drive the company delivery truck home some nights, that, too, must be counted as income and would be taxed as any ordinary income. And, in fact, anything that the son of the town drunk received from his employer, such as rent free use of an apartment or beach house, or any other housing, food, transportation, clothes, utilities, furniture, health care, or any other benefit would be counted as taxable income. That we know for sure. So, to be fair to the President, all of the room and board (and transportation, health care, utilities, furniture, etc.) that I gave him this past year (I needn't remind you that I am one of his employers) should be counted as ordinary income (unless you believe that some people should shirk their fair share of taxes because of a privileged position. But that would be too un-American to be countenanced, although all stock market listed companies do, in fact, supply privileged employees with all sorts of goodies which are 'cost free' and tax free).

I estimate that I gave the President about $2,000,000 worth of taxable tax 'free' value this past year in the form of room (including the use of two houses and the upkeep on a third) and board (free meals for the whole damn family plus all his beer drinking buddies), transportation (dozens of limos, two air force 1s), etc. (dozens of servants and Marine Corps statues) The items that I gave him actually should be valued at maybe $200,000,000 so $2,000,000 is a very generous discount from what I actually supplied. So the President's actual taxable income was about $1,110, 000. His actual effective tax rate was more like 7.6%; somewhat less than Al and Annie who made $10,000 and paid 21.8% total tax.

And that is what is wonderful about our tax system: it has been an instrument of social engineering (I hate it when writers use the word "engineer" or "engineering" where it clearly is not; so I chastise myself for falling in line here) reorganization for hundreds of years. It has been a marvelously constructed "moat with alligators" as I think Warren Buffett expressed it in another connotation to prevent the riffraff from presuming any of the privileges of the ffarffir born. It is absolutely breathtaking how the system has been engineered (there I go again; maybe I should switch to "orchestrated" or "doctored". [Can't use "lawyered", "bankered", "accountered" because they don't create anything.]) to make those who have little or no wealth pay huge taxes on that tiny or negative wealth whereas those with huge wealth pay little or no taxes on their wealth. It is brilliant, it is deliberate, it is highly successful. It has been adjusted so that it is easier for a dog to become wealthy (witness Leona Helmsley's dog who inherited $12-million) than it is for someone born with a lead spoon in his mouth to swim the alligator and water-moccasin lined moat preventing the poor from getting beyond subsistence.

Clearly the lemming economy is the American Way. "This great wealth producing machine" as the Professional Liars in the Think Tanks like to call it; wherein two thirds of the wealth is given to ten-percent of the people and the remaining 300-million of us are fighting over the dregs and the economy goes in great hoops as the over-rich chase one pie-in-the-sky after another so the economy is like a drunk drinking to puke. And the Professional Liars just see that we are all wealthy because on average

--- because if Bill Gates is in the room with 2,000 of us, on average, we are all millionaires. The king's dogs are fat and farting and their excess food is rotting in their sty and the peasants are starving but, on average, they are all getting enough food. Here's yesterdays paper, SL, P-D 7-6-8; B4, "*Esterline* [Economist, USC] *attributes the phenomenon of happiness levels' not keeping pace with economic gains to the fact that people's desires and expectations change along with material fortunes. Where an American in 1970 may have dreamed about owning a house, he or she might now dream of owning two. Where people once dreamed of buying a new car, they now dream of buying a luxury model."* It never snows in Camelot. L.S.D. is schizophrenic in Camelot. Esterline gets well paid for building castles in the air in Camelot. Esterline is party lying in Camelot. Everyone dreams of two houses while living in refrigerator boxes in Camelot. Everyone dreams of buying a luxury car while living in the wrecked auto down by the railroad tracks in Camelot. If your brain is as entwisted as Harry Lauder's Walking Stick, you can teach at USC in Camelot.

Here's another twisted brain three days later. Republican Presidential Nominee John McCain's super economic advisor, Lord Phil Gramm, says that we are only in a "mental recession" and that we are a "nation of whiners". He was Senator Lord Gramm a little bit ago, when and where he consistently voted for the Second Depression. Now we's agittin' it an' he calls it a "mental recession". You can call it that if you personally have a mental recession. But he's not awhinin' 'bout all the money he stole when he was a Senator, a U. S. Senator, an' then a lobbyist for the rich. Now he didn't legally steal no money; he just voted lots a money fer his friends. Wink, wink! Now you can't really be upset with him for being oblivious and obtuse about the poor; he doesn't know anything about the poor. He's never seen one up close and so he doesn't believe in them although he does believe in all kinds of angels, heavens, gods, and Valhallas thet he ain't never seen neither. Were he present here I could tell him about the poor who have no voice but then I would be advancing the cause of the dumb to the deaf.

John McCain also has no idea what a "recession" is. He has never done a productive day's work in his entire life. His wife has never done a productive day's work in her entire life. His parents never have done a productive day's work in their entire life. His children have never done a productive day's work in their entire lives. He has never known anyone who has done a productive day's work in their entire lives. Likewise, he and everyone around him have always had absolutely secure jobs working for the government so can have no appreciation of what it is like to "lose" your job. What is "work", what is "layoff", what is "recession", what is "depression", what is "black hole", what is "nanometer", what is "calculus", how could he know? Why should he care? He doesn't!

So, our employees, the law grinders, are searching with a magnifying glass and a metal detector for things to atax. They find the property of the poor, the personal property to tax because all except the very poorest among us is agonna have a car and so the law grinders manage to find the property of the poor, small though it is, and clamp a tax upon it. Good! Now we got the car ataxed how can we shove more tax up the ass o'th'poor. Oh! Damn! Thet Car is agonna use some oil and gas (and so's the bus if they's stupid enough to ride that), let us atax thet. Tax aliddle gas, call it an excise tax, blame the oil companies, nobody'll ever notice; everybody needs a little excise; maybe they'll lose weight (spechally if we make 'em walk ta work). What else the poor got? Well they gotta buy stuff; some ordinary stuff. Oh! I know! Let us aput a sales tax ona thet. Naw, theyda never let us git away with a National sales tax. Well let's put a heavy tax on corporate profits; it's the same damn thing. It's the same damn thing as a sales tax on the poor. Nobody'll ever figger thet out, they'll say it's ataxin' the rich. Theya dumb. And the Professional Liars in the think tanks'll lie it up real good like. They'll say that that corporate profits tax is a tax on capital; they'll say it's a tax on the rich. Theysa good liars. We pays 'em well!

Now, them law grinders is arunnin otta things to atax. They search high and low but can't fine nuttin. It's like a lumber jack searching for a tree in the Sequoia

National forest or in the dark redwood forest. The Sequoias is only about thirty feet around and the redwood is only about 300 feet tall. They's hard to see. So them law grinders/lumberjacks is acuttin down vine maples, tanbark firs, and huckleberry trees, en blades a grass cause they kent see them little sequoias (the worlds largest consolidated living things) or redwoods. So, hard as them law grinders is alookin they can't see the wealth of the rich. It's ahiddin better than them Sequoias is ahiddin from the lumberjack. It'd hafta fall on ya afor you cud see it. Well, it doesn't exactly fall on them; lots of it accidentally just slips into their pockets.

I'll give you one quick example here of how the law grinders tax the wealth of the poor. When my wife and I bought our first house we had to borrow the 20% down payment as well as mortgaging the 80%. I was just out of school for three years and we still had a bunch of college debt. So, our real-estate taxes were just $600.00 (annually) on a $15,000.00 house. Since we had no equity; no wealth in-other-words, our tax was infinite. But, hang on there, at the end of the first year we had paid off $50.00 per month on the principle. So our 'wealth' was $600.00 or, if you will notice, the same as the real-estate tax; or the tax on our wealth was 100%. (Of course that was just the "equity" in the house; we still had a mess of other debts, so our net worth was a sparkling negative.) Second year wealth was $1,200.00; tax $600.00; tax rate 50%. Third year, wealth $1,800.00; tax $600; tax rate 33%. Fourth year, wealth $2,400.00; tax $600.00; tax rate 24%. Fifth year, wealth $3,000.00; tax $600.00; tax rate 20%. Sixth year, wealth $3,600.00; tax $600.00; tax rate 17%. Of course, this was not REAL wealth as we had a very strong negative net worth. These taxes were just the rich making sure that we were never able to get a start; they made god-damn sure that we were tax-water-boarded.

Then, just as it was getting good; we had to sell the damn place and move. The best it got; the wealth-tax on the poor; was 17%.

Now, let's take a look at today with our restaurant. Real estate taxes: we may have equity in our building of maybe $200,000 with R.E. Taxes of about $7,000, tax rate on our wealth: about 3.5%. Personal Property taxes: about $2,000; value of Personal Property, maybe $20,000; tax rate on our wealth: about 10%. Taxes on Gross Receipts (not profits) of about 12%. (Idiots in the State Sales Tax Department say, "Well, you are just collecting that, you are not actually paying that!" If they weren't stupid and lazy, they wouldn't be working for the State.) If I suggested those kinds of taxes be applied to the rich, I would promptly be called a Communist. Anyone who suggested that the rich pay 10% on their wealth as I have to pay, would be stomped on by the Professional Liars at the Wall Street Journal, Forbes Magazine, the American Heritage Foundation, the Manhattan Institute, the Cato Institute, etc. "Oh, goodness gracious; you are an extreme socialist; you are a radical socialist; you just believe in that horrible "spreading-the-wealth-around"; oh, my, god, oh, my, god, oh, my, god, oh my god; you are a commie. Help! Help! Help! I'm being attacked by a commie."

Now, just for comparisons purposes lets see what the tax on the rich's wealth is. I don't need a specific example because we all know what the tax on the rich's wealth is: it is Zero. Zero. None. None. None at all. I'm not even going to listen to some stupid ass (Professional Liar) saying, "Well now; they own houses too!" They own oceans in untaxed stock (etc.) wealth and own drops in taxed real-estate wealth. Whereas all of our wealth was in that one little ole house (and our NET worth was very negative) we had NO wealth yet we had 100% tax on the APPEARANCE of wealth. This is the rich making damn sure that the son of the town drunk doesn't have a 'leg up'; "don't give someone who's not born rich an even break". Old slogan: "Never give a sucker an even break!"

We have spent a great deal of time and effort looking at taxes as they now exist; present reality; now, now, now. What have we learned?

What do we know for sure? What is certain?
The "wealth" of the poor is confiscated.
The poor never have a chance to get started.
The wealth of the rich is untouched.

We do have wealth redistribution. The 'wealth' of the poor is taken and given to the rich.

This is no accident. The rich rob the poor on purpose with malice and aforethought.

If there is such a thing as "evil"; the rich are it.

Then the Professional Liars (including the Corporate Press and the Moneyed Religions) who are bought and paid for by the rich, act terrified that the "liberals", the "socialists", the "communists", the "Marxists", etc. etc. etc. are going to start (or are already engaged in) a "Class War", "a Politics of Envy", etc. etc. and may, just may, try to "spread the wealth around". Egad, horrors. Horrors! Horrors! That would be terrible because now ALL the effort and effect is to concentrate ALL wealth in as few hands as possible. I am not making that up. That has always been the reality. The results prove it (one percent of the people control thirty-eight-percent of wealth).

Here is the real news; here is "the rest of the story": There has been a Class War since time began. The rich have always been warring against the poor very successfully. The Religion Industry (not Christ or Mohamed or other core ethics) have always been on the side of the rich in the Class War.

There, as shown, is the situation which I consider a problem. I cannot say what is "right" or "wrong"; or what is "good" or "evil"; that is not my area of expertise. I can, however say what works and what doesn't work. That IS my area of expertise.

The tax "system" that we have now is working. It is working to impoverish the poor and middle-class. It is working to force the poor and middle-class to labor for sub-subsistence wages. It is working to make it easy for the rich to get richer. It is working to make the economy become clogged with bubbles which burst into recessions and depressions. It is working to favor the rich. It is working as the rich want it to work. If that is working for you; then the tax system is working. But if you want fairness or justice; the system is a failed system and needs to be destroyed and rebuilt.

So I will lay out here what we ought to do. Then I will tell why we will not do it. Then I will say what we might do to move in the direction of "what works".

What we ought to do:

Let me start with the worst tax that I know of: the business (corporate) profits tax. This is a horrible tax.

A. It, the business profits tax, is monstrously regressive; that is, it falls most heavily on the poor and then the middle-class. It is regressive like a sales-tax or a value-added-tax (which the rich and their Professional Liars love). This tax, the business profits tax, is always included in the sales price (as it absolutely must be) and is paid for by the purchaser of the product. The Professional Liars claim that this tax is paid by the stock-holders (owners) of the companies (corporations); this is, of course, a dastardly lie. The only reason that corporate profits taxes are as high as they are is because the Professional Liars do, in fact, know that this tax is paid by the poor, otherwise they, the Professional Liars, would long ago have had their law-grinders kill it like a poisonous snake in their bed.

B. The business profits tax punishes the more efficient companies: The more profits, the more profits taxes.

C. The business profits tax encourages companies to lie and cheat. Though they will still charge the customers as though paid, they will keep "funny" books and make false charges to decrease the appearance of profits even though the profits actually exist. I won't take the time here to list the specific scams that I have observed (or committed) over the years, trust me, accountants (and CEOs) are very creative in this matter. (That is why most corporate bonuses are based on stock price, not on "profits"; profits are easily manipulated and, if allowed to rise [which would be wished if bonuses were based on profits], corporate profits taxes would have to be paid. If the stock price goes up, it does not require taxes to be paid; but bonuses are then paid).

D. The business profits tax skews the company's efforts from actually producing well-designed, functional, competitive, honest products to manipulating numbers and appearances until companies actually seem to forget what they are in business to do. (Witness the auto industry, the steel industry, the airlines, etc. etc. etc.) The score-keepers become more important than the coaches and the players (accountants become more important than engineers and managers, and the workers). The game becomes score-keeping and the action on the field is forgotten.

This tax, the business (corporate) profits tax, ought to be slain like the, dastardly, destructive, ancient dragon that it is. Kill it forthwith! Slaughter it before it does yet more damage. Please.

Another terrible tax is the excise tax. This tax too is monstrously regressive. In addition, this tax can never be fair. First, this tax is in reality a sales tax that is limited to a specific product such as whisky, tobacco, or gasoline. These taxes are generally enacted to alter or control someone's behavior; often to give one producer or user an unfair advantage over another producer or user.

Let me illustrate by using a ludicrous (made-up) example (then you can easily understand real examples which you can see everyday and are even more ridiculous). Illustrative Example: gasoline, as we all know, was commonly used to burn witches at the stake because it was cheap, effective, accessible, safe, and easy to use – the 'perfect' fuel for that ancient and honorable purpose. So naturally, the woodsmen who produced burning-logs went forthwith to their Representatives and Senators (through their agents sometimes called "lobbyists" [the constitution, after all, guarantees our right to petition our government]) and demanded that an excise tax be placed on gasoline so that it would no longer be competitive with burning-logs. (The woodsmen also explained to their Representatives and Senators that they, the woodsmen, were hardy outdoor types who lead a clean, Christian "way of life" which was, obviously, to be protected since, particularly, the gasoline producers were known to be communist sympathizers. [They, the woodsmen, were also able to make 'significant' contributions to the Representatives' and Senators' re-election campaign funds]). The Representatives and Senators, being enlightened and intelligent Christians, could immediately see the unassailable logic in the woodsmen's plea and promptly passed a law placing 'significant' excise tax on "gasoline". And, thus, the woodsmen lived happily ever after and, as we know, witches ever since have been blissfully burned at the stake using the less hot and, therefore, more effective (the witches died more slowly and, thus, had more time to repent) fire-logs.

If you will examine any and all excise taxes, you will note that all have some such anti-competitive, anti-free-enterprise, anti-efficiency, intended-compulsion, hopeful-behavior-altering purpose (counter-productive to the free functioning of the free market) as my little Illustrative Example. They are each and all stupid: heartily deserving to be matched with their lobbyists and Representatives and Senators.

All excise taxes should be repealed. They are all close relatives to the sales tax and thus warmly beloved of Professional Liars. The logic of excise taxes is the logic of Professional Liars. Said logic makes one cock one's head and ask, "Do they REALLY believe that shit?"

Finally we come to the sales tax itself. This tax also is monstrously regressive. Thus it is dearly beloved of the Aristocratic Class Terrorists such as the Wall Street Journal and Forbes and the like Professional Liars and the Professional Liar Guppies in the Think Tanks. This tax is a kin akin to the V.A.T. (the Value Added Tax) discussed next. (Why, one might ask, if one buys stock [a cow or a steer] one pays sales tax. However, if one buys stock [a piece of a company] one pays no sales tax. A puzzlement. Cow buyers must have forgotten to buy law-grinders.) As developed earlier in this chapter the sales tax paid by someone making $10,000 could be higher than 2.3% (of total income); the sales tax on $100,000, perhaps 1.9%; on $1,000,000, maybe 0.2%; on earnings above that, the percentage of sales tax paid is inconsiderable. Is that regressive enough for you? The reality is probably worse. If we had any religions in the United States which were followers of Christ, there would be no sales tax in the United States. It is just too ugly to be countenanced. This would be the dragon that St. George would slay. But, unfortunately, we just have religious businesses; we have religions which call themselves "Christian" but we have no religions which follow Christ by example. We love the money changers – as long as they tithe in the collection box.

The sales tax is disgusting and should be repealed.

The words "Value-Added-Tax" makes the Professional Liars drool like Pavlov's Dogs at the dinner bell. This tax also is wonderfully regressive and it has the political virtue of being stupid to boot. It is a screwy screw-you, confounding, complex, corrupting, convoluted tax. If you buy paints and a canvas for $25 and paint a picture that you sell for $65, you would pay tax on the $40 "Value-Added" that you created. Simple, eh? But what about the oils, the turpentine, the gesso, the brushes, the spatulas, your time, etc. etc.? O.K., so you have to hire an accountant to keep track of all that shit. And, guaranteed, the accountant will get it wrong. The accountant will need your help to keep track of all that shit. You will paint an hour and keep records for two hours. Your accountant, the score-keeper, will quickly become more essential to your little-'ole painting business than you, the painter. You will spend two hours making and keeping records or you will become a criminal. But instead of complaining, you should 'count your blessings' that you do not build houses, autos, or run a restaurant where it really gets complicated. We don't have a V.A.T, a Value-Added-Tax, here in the United States. Yet. But the Aristocratic-Class-Terrorists have not and will not give up. They want the poor and middle-class to be yet more heavily taxed.

Let us not have a V.A.T. in the good-'ole U.S. of A.

The personal property tax is a hilarious tax. It is an impossible, unequal, unjust, ludicrous tax. This tax too is marvelously regressive. Let me first mention its most usual manifestation. This is the tax on the autos, cars, automobiles of the poor and middle-class. Like the real-estate-tax, one may be certain that any wealth of the poor and middle-class will be found, discovered, licensed, deeded, tracked, magnified, and taxed. The rate varies from state to state but runs 3% to 6% but this, by no means, tells the story. Again, because the car 'owner' may only own 20% of the car, the rate is actually as much as five times the stated rate. So the actual rate may be 15% to 30%. This is confiscation. If the wealth of the rich were taxed at this rate, all of the Professional Liars would be screaming about "Property Rights". Communism! Socialism! Radical Socialism! Extreme Socialism! Creepy, Crawly Socialism! Sometimes they must have a difficult time to keep from laughing; if only they had a sense of humor.

At the restaurant we also have a "personal" property tax. We are supposed to pay this tax on everything. I think. It is so god-damned complicated; it is well neigh impossible what to make of it. It would take me forty hours to fill out the multi-page form; I don't have forty hours for such nonsense. I try and the functionary in City Hall just tells me what to pay. There is not a god-damned thing I can do about it. It is a ridiculous, asinine tax and I know god-damned well that the big companies are not required to pay anything near what I have to pay. This is an outrageous tax.

Anyone with a speck o'sense or a dab o'decency would agree to abolish slavery and the Personal Property Tax. (The only good thing about it is that it is proof positive that the government can, when motivated by ataxing the poor, keep track of every ten dollars worth of property of the poor. Don't claim, when we talk about taxing the wealth of the wealthy that, gosh, we can't possibly find and keep track of those millions of dollars.)

Can you believe that we finance our schools with the real estate tax? This is wrong, wrong, wrong. And stupid. Is it true that if you own a house, you benefit from schools and if you don't own a house, you don't benefit from schools? (I know; I showed earlier that if you rent, you also pay real-estate tax. That is true.) If you live in Chicago, you are not hurt by the poor schools in Mississippi? If you live in a poor neighborhood, you should go to a poorer school than if you live in a rich neighborhood? Not only is this wrong, it is as nutty as a hickory tree and as fruity as a pear tree. For years now, school standards have been taken over by the Federal Government. Even the most conservative administrations have been asserting their right and duty to "Take Over" the administration of the schools (have you heard of "No Child Left Behind"? I believe that that is the Feds. Someone told me that that is a right-wing program. Really!). And, I mean Primary and High School (in the current jargon, K through 12.) Tough shit, buddy, if you want to run the schools, you damn well better be prepared to pay for them too. So there! Ike sent the National Guard to Mississippi schools to demand that they accept certain students that the school-board did not want to accept; does this not mandate that he, Ike (the Federal Government) also pay for the cost of the schools? Isn't that an 'unfunded-mandate'? Taxation without representation. Where in the hell is our tea party?

Another bad thing about the Real-Estate-Tax is that it is unfair. House appraisals are very ragged. When we lived in Massachusetts, new houses were appraised at market value, plus; old houses not sold for forty years were not reappraised. New houses were paying ten or twenty times what old houses of equal value were paying. Don't move to Massachusetts (at least not back then). But even in towns which attempt to be fair (and Lunenburg did not), it is impossible to accurately and fairly appraise houses (or why then the housing market 2008 'meltdown'?).

Real-Estate-Taxes are wildly unfair. They are regressive. They highly tax the wealth of the poor and middle-class. The Real-Estate-Tax should be abandoned.

We do not have the "Flat-Tax" in the United States of America. Thank god! But, Professional Liars who wish to rake all of the money toward the rich are proposing it ever-so-too-often. The idea is that everyone would pay the same; exactly the same; percentage tax on their income. Except for thousands or millions of exceptions. The income of the rich is, of course, offset by lots and lots of expenses. And they get lots and lots of benefits and goodies that are not counted as income. The guy who gets a mill paycheck has, of course, no offsetting expenses. In fifteen minutes, the Flat-Tax would have more exceptions, exemptions, offsets, deductions, expenses, forms, asides, outsides, sidesides, etc. than the non-Flat-Tax. Only people who believe in the Flat-Earth believe in the Flat-Tax. Let us not have the Not-So-Very-Flat Flat-Tax unless we can prove that the earth is flat.

It is very difficult to get information on the Capital-Gains tax. There are 'short-term' and 'long-term' Capital-Gains tax rates. The short-term tax rate is higher. When I have paid Capital-Gains taxes, I had difficulty finding the "basis" for the tax. The "basis" being: when the asset was purchased and the price that was paid for the asset. A few years after you buy an asset and you (or at least I) say, "What the hell did I do with that paperwork?" If you can't find it and you guess wrong; you are a criminal. Maybe you won't get caught; maybe you will. I don't have a strong opinion as to the merits of the Capital-Gains tax. On the one ear, the Aristocrat-Class-War-Terrorists and their Professional Liars hate it; so it can't be all bad. On the other ear, it (the Capital-Gains tax) does interfere with the smooth and unfettered operation of the Markets; so it cannot be all good either. The capital-gains should be counted as simple Income and be taxed accordingly. If it is taxed as Income, then there should be no other tax levied on it.

We are running out of taxes on which to comment. Do I hold that all taxes are "bad"? I don't do "good" or "bad" but I do do "effective" or "ineffective". If government is necessary, it would seem that taxes are necessary. Someone must, after all, "pay the piper". We know, unless some among us shall be immortal (which has not yet occurred), that there will be taxes. We now come to the two taxes which I believe should be dominant, if not exclusive: the Income tax and the tax on Wealth (the wealth of the wealthy since we already have taxes galore on the 'wealth' of the poor and middle-class). The first, the Income tax, exists only imperfectly. The second, the tax on Wealth has never been born. The Professional Liars have planted and nourished huge and extensive briar patches of fictions around the Income tax which we will have to trim and burn. These same Professional Liars have hidden the second, the tax on Wealth, behind enormous moats, walls, barbed wire, false maps, etc. Then they, the Professional Liars, stand there, arms akimbo, rocking, whistling Dixie and trying to see their eyebrows; while the havoc that they have created does massive harm to mankind and the economy (the Life and Sex Island). They are dirty crud.

We have already talked at great – I hope not boring – length about the existing Income-tax situation. But I wish to summarize it just one more quick time. The poor pay far dearer Income-tax than the rich especially in the sense that they are impoverished after they are 'taxed' but the rich are still hundreds-of-thousands of times better off after taxes than the poor (after taxes). The rich are not "taxed" at all in the sense of "depleted". The poor are crushed. The poor have no escape. The tax is withheld before they see their pay. The rich have dozens of escape hatches, doors, tunnels, secret-panels, sky-hooks, and shutters and blinds.

The poor are bricks in a wall. Any one can replace any other. At the restaurant when someone quits (or is fired) we simply say, "NEXT"! We have a core of wonderful, "permanent" employees, but there are always applicants knocking at the door. The 'system' is arranged such that there is always a shortage of work and not workers. The workers have, in reality, no bargaining power.

The rich, too, are bricks in a wall (it is, to be sure, a slightly smaller wall); but they control the appearance of reality. "Oh! We are so rare!" (And their Professional Liars play the chorus, "Soooooo Rare, so very, very rare".) "We are so delicate that we simply could not, I say, COULD NOT; work if we weren't smothered in money to keep us warm and cozy." "We are such lazy bastards that we simply would not be motivated by mere progress, achievement, and uncommon results, or excellent effectiveness! Oh No, indeed, we wouldn't lift a goddamned finger if we weren't paid hundreds-and-thousands-of-times more than mere mortals." "My dick is bigger than your dick; I simply know it! Don't be presumptuous! You naughty little boy!" "I don't give a shit about this product (whatever it is), nor this company, nor this town, nor this state, nor this country; I give a shit about bloating my bonus. Got it! That is the one thing that I concentrate on; THIS MONTH; everything else can be fucked." (And the Corporate Press echoes whatever is said, "They EARNED their bonuses". [When the banks were laying-off hundreds of people, they were paying "retention" bonuses!]) Suppose G.M., for example, employs 100,000 people. If they are average people, then 2,000 of them are geniuses (by definition). The management of G.M., for at least the last 50-years, has not had the intellect of geniuses. Yet they are paid as though they are Supermen. They are men, they are not super. The simple truth is that they could be replaced (and could always have been) by better wo/men, at one one-thousandth of the cost, four-score years ago and every minute since by any of those 2,000 geniuses that are directly underfoot and fully trained. The existing bosses are lousy, arrogant, rotten managers. And scummy humans. ALL of the major corporations have been likewise ripped-off. By scummy humans. It is time for a sip of reality. Reality can be a heady wine.

What do we know for sure?

You can't, cannot "earn" a $Million (or more) (or even close) per year!

Someone who takes a $Million (or more) from their employer is stealing in one way or another (and is also guilty of murder).

The "wealth" of the son of the town drunk is confiscated to make sure that he can never get a start in life.

The Aristocratic-Class-War-Terrorists have been waging war against the poor and middle-class since pre-history (a long time). They have won.

What must we do about it?

We must make the income (and other) taxes fair.

I am going to suggest some rates that would be fairer. I am also opting for a modified "flat" tax; not in the sense that it would be non-progressive but in the sense that there would be few if any exemptions or deductions. (Few complications). I am going to talk of income any source (all income treated equally). (Capital gains are treated as ordinary income.)

Income	Tax rate
$0 to $10,000	5%

$10K to $20K	10%
$20K to $50K	15%
$50K to $100K	20%
$100K to $200K	25%
$200K to $500K	30%
$500K to $1M	35%
$1M to $1.5M	40%
$1.5M to $2M	45%
$2.5M to $3M	50%
$3M to $3.5M	55%
$3.5M to $4M	60%
$4M to $4.5M	65%
$4.5M to $5M	70%
$5M to $5.5M	75%
$5.5M to $6M	80%
$6M to $6.5M	85%
$7M to $7.5M	90%
$7.5M to $8M	95%
$8M to $8.5M	99%
$8.5M to $9M	99.9%
$9M to $9.5M	99.99%
$9.5M to $10M	99.999%
$10M to $10.5M	99.9999%
$10.5M to $11M	99.99999%

ETC. (add another "9" for each half-$million)

These rates assume that all of those taxes which are designed to confiscate the wealth of the poor have been eliminated. Those are the taxes discussed earlier: Corporate Profits Tax; the Excise Taxes; Sales Taxes; Value Added Tax; Personal Property Tax; Real Estate Tax. Eliminating all of those redundant taxes would be enormously cost-effective. (Excess Tax-Collectors could be recycled to plant trees. [If any of them are capable of actual work.]) Then the excess Federal Taxes (from Income and Wealth) would be paid to replace all of those unfair taxes. Also assumed is that all those numbers (the "suggested Income" primarily) are rigidly tied to the Cost of Living. (ALL of the touted [but unobtainable] benefits of the "Flat-Tax" could be obtained by eliminating ALL deductions.)

The suggested tax rates would raise far more

revenue than the current (2008) tax rates. (But not more than the eliminated taxes.) These tax rates would move far more of the income to the lower levels (it's gotta go somewhere; and executives would be paid more fairly [far less]) and the total income would rise significantly because of the greater productivity at the lower levels (slaves produce far less than free and fairly paid citizens [when Russian workers were way underpaid, the workers said, "They pretend to pay us and we pretend to work."]). (Almost ALL workers would endeavor to raise productivity when and if they shared in the benefits rather than [as now they] attempt to avoid work and have no interest in increasing productivity when they know that they DO NOT share in any progress; nor is their labor valued fairly compared to the CEOs.) (Why do the Professional Liars imagine that workers will work effectively for sub-subsistence wages but executives must be paid $Millions to get them off their asses? [A puzzlement!]) Since productivity would rise significantly; corporate profits would also rise significantly. Since we do not have Corporate-Profits-Taxes, the value of corporations would rise significantly. The greater value of corporations would significantly increase the revenue raised from the Wealth-Tax (discussed next).

Now let's talk about the fairest tax of all: The Tax on Wealth; the Wealth-Tax. If it has been fair, for all time, to confiscate the wealth of the poor to insure that they cannot get a start in life; certainly no one will object to a small tax (compared to the tax on the wealth of the middle-class) on the Wealth of the Wealthy (which now is not taxed at all).

The Taxable Wealth of the U.S.A. can only be estimated now. (Until 1976, the U.S. Government put out a Statistical Abstract which had all of that information in [or on] it. But the public was learning too much about their government so, of course, that could not be allowed [we CANNOT have an informed citizenry, heavens]). It is out there somewhere on the Great Internet and dwellers in statistics could probably quote it from memory and break it into its rainbow of components – IRAs, Stock,

Bonds, etc. The G.D.P. is $13- or $14-trillion. From this G.D.P., I figure that the Taxable Wealth must be about ten times that or $130- or $140-trillion. I have seen figures that would indicate that that was twice-too-high and others indicating that it is ten-times-too-high. Total Federal Tax Revenue is a little over $2.7-billion; of this, $1.25-billion comes from individual income taxes (Federal). Business net income was about $270-billion (reported on tax returns) (an order-of-magnitude estimate for the value of the assets that produced that $270-billion would be $3-trillion). Total State Revenue (Taxes, Licenses, & Fees) is about $750-billion. Municipalities in the U.S. also require about $750-billion to operate (my estimate). Using Bureau-of-Census numbers for median house-hold net-worth; the percent of that net-worth that was income producing; and the number of house-holds, one can estimate (calculate) that the Taxable-Wealth is about $4-trillion. Other approaches confirm that $4-trillion is a reasonable estimate for the FINANCIAL (Taxable-Wealth; Income-Earning-Wealth; NOT residences) in the United States of America. A one-percent tax on $4-trillion would yield revenue of $40-billion.

Total revenue required to be raised from the Wealth-Tax: ~$1.5-trillion. (The new income tax rates would raise about $2.7-billion.) This would be a suggested tax rate table for the Wealth-Tax:

Taxable-Wealth	Tax-Rate	Revenue Raised
$0 to $0.5M	1%	$4.5B
$0.5M to $1M	2%	$10.0B
$1M to $2M	3%	$28.6B
$2M to $3M	4%	$48.0B

$3M to $4M	5%	$34.0B
$4M to $5M	6%	$31.7B
$5M to $6M	7%	$22.7B
$6M to $7M	8%	$20.5B
$7M to $10M	9%	$14.4B
$10M to $100M	11%	$1,400.0B
$100M to $1B	13%	$20.2B
Over $1B	15%	$15.3B
Total		$1,700.0B

(Estimates from various sources including Forbes' Richest Americans.)

As an engineer who has made thousands of estimates of future costs and revenue, I am usually pretty good at it. However, this is a moving game (what ever strategy we try, the players and coaches can adjust and then the original assumptions are far afield.) Also, I had information, for example, on how many $Millionaires and $Deca-millionaires there were (2000) but no information on anything in between, e.g. how many $5-Millionaires there were. So I filled all that in by guess, by god. Also my data is a little dated; the info that I had claimed 51 $Billionaires; now, in 2008, Forbes 400-richest are all more than $Billionaires. So the actual revenue would likely be considerably larger than my estimate.

Let me give two examples of how these taxes might alter behavior as individuals react to the suggested changes.

Suppose you are a $3-Billionaire. Let us suppose that the above tax rates are enacted suddenly instead of being phased-in over, say, five years. Suppose you are running about a 20% Return-On-Investment (ROI) before the suggested tax rates. First, before the suggested tax rates, you will be paying very low Personal-Income-Taxes and you will be paying NO Wealth-Taxes. Your wealth will have been growing faster than a mushroom cloud. You could not spend all of your income much less all of your wealth. Meanwhile, the "wealth" of the poor will have been ataxed to death. The poor will be renters or homeless all of their lives because they simply cannot get ahead nor escape the tax collector. You, on the other ball can afford the best tax avoider that there is (say, an ex-senator). You'll be taxed at maybe one-half-of-one-percent while the poor will be ataxed at about twenty-percent or a rate forty times higher than you. You think that that is wonderful; I don't.

Your income would have been about $700-Million ($100-Million salary + bonuses plus $600-Million ROI. Your income taxes would jump from about $8-Million to about $697-Million; leaving you with "only" an income of about $2.7-Million (I'm not shedding any tears).

What happens if you are only moderately wealthy? Say you are a $3-Millionaire with a salary income of $300,000 and a wealth income of $600,000 = Total income of $900,000. Then your Income-Tax would be $600,000; leaving you with an after-tax-income of $300,000. Your Wealth-Tax would take $120,000 of that so that your wealth would grow by about $180,000 (less living expenses).

Maybe it would be interesting and instructive to look at our earlier examples: Al & Annie, Bob & Betty, Charles & Cherish, Don & David, Emmanuel & Elizabeth, and Fred & Flame. You will recall that their incomes went up by one-order-of-magnitude each. For example Al & Annie earned $10,000; Bob & Betty earned $100,000, Charles & Cherish earned $1,000,000, etc. Let's look at it in a table so it is more easily seen. Now, all these numbers are in thousands of dollars; so, for example Al and Annie's Income is $10,000 but we have expressed it as simply 10; Charles and Cherish's Suggested Income Tax is $306,000 but here we simply use 306. And we have rounded the numbers up or down to the next unit; for example, Al & Annie's Suggested Income Tax is $500 and we have rounded it up to 1; their Existing Income Tax is $1,500 and we have rounded it up to 2.

	Income	Suggested Income Tax	Existing Income Tax
A	10	1	2
B	100	16	17

C	1,000	306	552
D	10,000	7,000	3,200
E	100,000	97,350	1,700
F	1,000,000	997,350	4,700

Even the most Aristocratic Class Terrorists would probably not take credit for the nonsensical Existing Income Tax system (taking into consideration ALL taxes, including those cleverly hidden). Clearly, the Existing Income Tax system is not rationally designed. It has been shamefully tacked together like a poverty-shack out of pieces of litter as junk became available on the trash heap. There is no logic; there is no beauty; there is no intelligence; there is no grace. It does not perform the functions of keeping out the wind of injustice or the rain of dishonor. We should all hang our heads in embarrassment and disgrace. We atax the poor at rates twenty or thirty times the rates of the rich and then hire hundreds of Professional Liars to, yes, lie about it. "Oh, ya but." "Oh, ya but." "Oh, ya but." ("Oh, ya but 40% [or some asinine lying number {they speak blackwhite}] pay no taxes at all!" Surely, surely they know that this is a damnable, double damnable lie. "There ya go again!" Can they possibly be wearing three-piece-suits and be THAT stupid and misinformed?) The only logic, the sole purpose of the Existing Income Tax system is to prevent the poor and voiceless from getting a start in life. There are better ways to raise money than to punish the innocent.

Please note that, in the Suggested Income Tax system, even the most highly taxed individual is still left with $2,649,556 income remaining after tax. I'm not shedding any tears for such.

Let us look at the tax on wealth. Again, we are expressing the amounts in thousands of dollars. So, for example, Bob & Betty's wealth is $24,750; we express that simply as 25; and their Existing Wealth Tax is $9,800 which is listed simply as rounded to 10.

		Suggested	Existing

	Wealth	Wealth Tax	Wealth Tax
A	0	0	1
B	25	0	10
C	4,011	136	11
D	54,528	5,403	14
E	5,096,454	741,983	14
F	2,567,000	426,079	16

The Existing Wealth Tax is insultingly idiotic. It was obviously designed by the Aristocratic Class Terrorists to insure that the poor are endlessly carrying water in a bottomless bucket to quench their family's thirst while the rich are riding a Cigarette Race Boat riding over the poor out of control to ever greater wealth. The Professional Liars would have us believe that the rich are so clever that they never make a mistake when the truth is that the Existing Wealth Tax system insures that, whatever they do, the tax system will protect them. The rich pay a contemptuously tiny amount of taxes on their wealth while the poor pay well over 100% annually. Been there, done that. Don't tell me that it is not so. Take your Professional Lies to your Professional Liar Bosses. Certainly with your pathetic need for affirmation you must have something akin to the Clio and Mobius Awards?

Notice that the Suggested Wealth Tax never reaches 15% at the highest level. The Professional Liars will call this CONFISCATION or COMMUNISM but, strangely enough, the Professional Liars never call the Existing Wealth Tax of over 100% on the "wealth" of the poor anything but GOOD. I guess we po white trash don't pay them enough. Money can't buy me love but it sure can buy allegiance and obedience from the legions of Professional Liars.

We now look at the Income and the Wealth that one clings to AFTER he pays the Masked Ax-Man, the Tax-Collector. Anon, I remind thee, we express the numbers in thousands of dollars; thus A (Al & Annie) earn Income of $10,000; we express this as a simple 10; and Al and Annie's Income after Suggested Income Tax is $9,500 which we round and lop off three zeros to get the simple

10. Thank you. And F (Fred & Flame) are left with a mere $2.6-million Income after Suggested Income Tax which we note as 2,650 and their wealth after the Suggested Wealth Tax dwindles all the way down to $2.6-billion which we show as 2,564,472.

	Income	Income after Suggested Income Tax	Wealth after Suggested Wealth Tax
A	10	10	0
B	100	84	25
C	1,000	694	3,875
D	10,000	2,650	48,125
E	100,000	2,650	4,354,472
F	1,000,000	2,650	2,564,350

Remember Frederick and Flame keep 2-and-one-half BILLION dollars of ill-got wealth. Let us not weep for them. The Professional Liars will supply their own hankies.

So, now we're talkin'! Now we do have a tax that is fairer. We do have a tax that is more reasonable. We do have a tax that is honest.

So, yes, these suggested tax rates are like the Colt 45; a great leveler. They don't keep anyone from earning a very nice life style. They do prevent major economic disruptions and even revolutions. They also force thieves; present and past to give back some of the money that they stole! I am not going to talk about "Justice" or "Injustice"; that is not my area of expertise. But I will say that this will work goddamn well. It will function better than a Swiss watch.

Why 'what we ought to do' won't be done:

I am not such a fool as to think, for even a moment, that my recommendations will be adopted this side of heaven.

The chapter on "The Media" will discuss the structure of "information" dissemination in this country. Reality didn't stand a chance. The rich controlled all of the corporate media; ALL. The rich also bought and paid for all of the "Think" Tanks. The "Thinkers" ("Fellows" like "Senior" and "Executive Directors" [sounds good; don't it?]) those "Thinkers" apparently never stop to ask themselves, "What am I being paid to do here?" "Am I building cabinets for them?" "Am I cooking their meals?" "Am I taking care of their kids?" "Am I fucking their wives?" "What are they paying me for?" They didn't want to ask themselves that question. "What benefit are they getting from me?" They avoided that or those questions like shunning a dead, rotting body on the street. Their little minds crossed the road (now you know why the chicken crossed the road) to avoid those questions. They knew. They knew deep down that they were intellectual whores. They were the sweepers pushing all of the money to fewer and fewer people until, of course, there would be a collapse or maybe a revolution. They knew it. But the pay was good. Tainted, but good. Dirty, but easy. "Who gives a shit if people commit suicide? I am well paid." "Piss on everyone else! I am well paid." Even outlets like C-Span I and C-Span II concentrate the propaganda. They, the C-Spans, "put on" the Guppies from the Think Tanks and never, never, ever counterbalanced them. Never challenged the layers of propaganda. Never offered the truth. Never.

Now we have the internet. Now maybe there is a chance. A chance for the honest leveling of information. The Professional Liars may be losing their grip on the throat of truth. The rich are terrified. They do not want an open internet. They want control. They are attacking from many angles. "Let us control pornography. Pornography is bad. We must have control." "Let us control the blogs." "What horrors may befall us if we lose total control of the monologue?"

So how have the Professional Liars kept the taxes of the poor at a rate forty times higher than that of the rich?

They lie. They ignore the state and local taxes which are highly biased against the poor and they, the Liars, talk only about the federal taxes. A tax is a tax, goddamnit. They talk incessantly about the 40% (or so) who pay no federal tax. And do not mention that they are students and others who make almost no money and also those who are simply too unsophisticated to file a return and (not to be forgotten) the rich who are gaming the system and despite large incomes connive to pay no tax. They pretend that Business Profits Taxes are taxes on the rich. They are not. They claim that the taxes on dividend income and on Capital-Gains are really double taxed because that money has already been taxed as business profits. (They never suggest eliminating the Business-Profits-Tax.) They talk about the "Death Tax" as being gruesome and morbid. It is not a tax on death. It is a tax on wealth. (I would as soon eliminate it anyway and replace it with the suggested Wealth-Tax.)

To fight the suggested Wealth-Tax, they will also lie. They will say that the wealthy will move their wealth to some friendlier place. But, to the extent that this could be done, it is already done. You can't move Yellowstone or the Grand Canyon overseas. Nor can you move Restaurants, Theaters, Baseball Teams, Disney World, Farm Land, Wind Farms, or the like overseas. Nor can you move all of our workers and consumers yonder. Furthermore, the suggested tax code will give the middle-class and the poor a "piece of the action" this, in turn, will vastly increase the productivity in the United States of America and it will take other countries some time to dump their Aristocratic/ Monarchy tendencies so they will not catch on or catch up soon. (Back in the heyday of Sears, Sears had one of the most generous profit-sharing programs; ordinary employees retired rich; Sears was the marketing behemoth of the world. New management said, "I don't give a shit if it works and is making all of us rich. It is making the employees rich and I can't stand it. Stop it. Stop it now." Stop it they did. And Sears is now an also-ran, it went downhill almost immediately after profit-sharing stopped. That is what is taught in Business School, if it makes the employees rich; stop it. Employees are pieces of shit and must be kept in their place. They are less than human; don't let them put on airs.) Management, MBA Management, thinks of employees as an expense; not an asset. The fools.

What we might do to move in that direction (the directions of correcting the vast injustice and stupidity of our present economic [and, therefore, life] situation [brought on by our American-Aristocratic-class-warfare tax shysters]):

In the old days (before the Internet from, say, 3-million-BC to, maybe, 2000 AD) the rich controlled ALL means of mass communication and most efforts of local intercourse. There was little chance of any discussion of REAL economics. Anyone caught in such a discussion among friends or compatriots was removed from society (if not from the earth). So, it was only in exceptional cases such as the French and Russian Revolutions where the rights of the poor were asserted. But, when things get so tense that they explode, as in those two revolutions, the results are unpredictable and often, though not always, disastrous. Revolutions are often discussed among the poor but those discussions are never heard by the rich since it is their passion, the passion of the rich, to have no intercourse (excepting sexual) with the poor. Thus the first symptom of discontent, the earliest warning, that the rich receive that something is amiss is when their heads are being separated from their shoulders at the neck or when they are placed on a spit prior to roasting.

Now, with the advent - nay, explosion - of the internet there is the possibility, if not hope, that reasonable economic corrections can be discussed. That is my hope. Clearly this book will never receive wide circulation but the ideas contained herein may. Someone, cleverer than I, may see some light in these pages and find a way to shine that light in a wider arena.

My Old-Man used to say something like, "Only believe half of what you see, a quarter of what you hear and nothing of what you read". I'm afraid that I did not take most of his sage advice. I fell into error and studied engineering and came to believe a great deal of what I read. I am fairly fond, for example, of the three laws of thermodynamics. (It is entirely possible, even likely, that my Old-Man never knew of those "laws".) But those "laws" were never proven. They are empirical. (Maybe they should be called "the three theories of thermodynamics" to put them on the same footing as the "theory" of evolution.) Still they make a great deal of sense and I never heard of an exception to them outside of religion (and Paul Bunyan) – no one has yet come up with a perpetual-motion-machine; not for lack of trying – many have been patented although those patents are no longer allowed without a working model which, regrettably, hasn't happened (even Madoff's perpetual money-making-machine petered out finally).

But I cannot claim to know or be-aware-of everything that has been expounded. There are many streams of information that I deliberately keep myself ignorant of. I don't give a shit who is the current or any previous American Idol; I don't know who or what Prada is; I don't know or care which fashion designers are dead or alive (although I do have a passing interest in ladies thighs); I don't care who played in the Rose Bowl since I graduated from Wisconsin after Allen The Horse Ameche; same for the World Series; although I will watch a few minutes of a boxing match, a basketball game, a dance contest, a gymnasts or swimming match, or even a fashion slut strut if I come-across it when I am channel surfing.

So, since I am not and cannot be informed of everything, perhaps someone has expounded the ideas which I have laid out in this chapter and elsewhere in this book. But I have looked. I have read widely in economics and politics and have seen neither Hyde nor hare of any of these ideas. (Nor Jekyll nor tortoise either.)

It could be that my ideas are too wacky to be considered. But I was always pretty steady and on track solving engineering problems. If my wife's opinion is an indication of the general public's blessing, my ideas will fly when oinkers do. But, fool that I am, I am willing to toss my book unto the general idea fire and see if the smoke will burst into fire and light.

Chapter Six

The Life and Sex Island

O.K. I lied. This chapter is not about life and sex; it is about Economics; the "Dismal Science". But, if I had said that it was about Economics, you wouldn't have read even this far. And, well, Economics IS about 'life and sex' (I could have called it "Sex With Many Partners" and really gotten your interest so I wasn't as dishonest as I could have been; let's call that a virtue). I'll try not to be dismal even though my confirmation name is Dysmus. And, what the hell, there is an Island where there is Life and there must be Sex, so maybe I only thought I lied. And, "trust me" (Nixon), "read my lips" (Bush I), I'm going to cover in this one chapter everything important about economics that you need to know. To hell with 'diminishing returns' and 'elastic' and 'inelastic' demand; Satan take 'capital', 'labor', and 'property'; you already know all that bullshit. Henry George, Adam Smith and that bunch spend chapters just defining 'capital' 'til your eyes cross and your brain spins; and still they disagree with each other; they quibble 'til the stuff that you know from your Pappy and Mammy, you don't trust anymore. The important stuff you've been lied to about so long and so often that you probably believe the damnable lies. I already told you that I lied too, so read this chapter like a skeptic; don't let me get away with any bullshit.

I'm going to get into some heavy stuff down a little ways but I'm not going to dump all that manure on you all at once – I want you to get accustomed to the smell a little at a time so you won't notice the odor so much when you are in it. A little fairy tale first:

We are looking at a little island; here's Defoe's Robinson Crusoe or Golding's Lord of the Flies only more civilized; this is our Life and Sex Island. We've got two or three dozen little families living together peacefully here. They are each multi-talented but, still, they have become somewhat specialized so one family digs wild potatoes, another catches crabs, Joe's kids dig clams, someone else spears mahi mahi (they call that fish "hahoona"), there's Mike-the-coconut-man, and so on (don't forget taro, everybody loves poi). The island's bounty seems sustainable. Nothing is being over harvested so it does not appear that they will go the way of Easter Island anytime soon. The population increases by one or two every decade or so. They have their own means of discouraging large families that are too embarrassing to talk about. Let's just say that their methods work.

It was a very nice and peaceful tropical island, this Life and Sex Island. They had never discovered or invented fire which was just as well because there was very little to burn. So they ate the fish sushi style with the raw coconut and this, too, was just as well because they were very healthy. They slept in the open because there were no mosquitoes and no crime and no cold and, curiously, no rain; only a heavy mist every night that watered all of the plants perfectly. In the middle of the island was a very tall, extinct volcano with a snow covered caldera. The sides of the volcano were so steep that no one had ever attempted to climb it. The snow on the top of the volcano melted and ran into the caldera where it ran down a cave that had been formed by the lava. That water from the melted snow, fortunately, bubbled up through the sand in one spot very near the beach; free spring water. (Pay attention! There may be a test.)

Without fire and clay, they had never discovered (invented) pottery (there was no clay on the island anyway, only sandy soil of degraded lava [fortunately, plants eat air {for solids} and sunlight {for energy} to make themselves]); the islanders carried their water in clam and coconut shells; not much at a time and no storage either. But they had learned to weave baskets and bras from grasses, roots, rushes, bark, leaves, and fish skins. The girls all wore bras because they wanted their breasts to look as attractive as anyone else's; the bras formed them all into desirable, firm shapes. But they didn't wear anything down below (that's part of the secret of their birth control, when you can see what you are looking at, it don't look that good at first blush – it doesn't go down well with sushi.)

The people only had a few needs beyond food, water, and sex. They needed a few tools for digging, spearing, and weaving. They only had one real conceit; they all desperately wanted the tail feathers from the Malarkey Bird to admire and to decorate themselves with. Wondrous feathers they were too. In the dark, they glowed bright yellow; in the sun they glistened with all of the colors of the visible light spectrum (the poor devils had never seen a rainbow and, so, did not know about the pot of gold at the end thereof). In addition to the Malarkey feathers, boats were a desperate need. Everyone wanted a boat even if they didn't fish. It was one of the few ways "to get away from it all". All of the trees on the island were of the palm type; the wood of which was not very suitable for boat building. Some not-very-successful boats were made from rushes and bamboo but the very best boats were laboriously carved from the mother rock which was all light and foamy lava like strong, heavy Styrofoam (yeah, they didn't know what that was either!). Those lava boats were good boats (compared to woven rushes or bamboo) but very expensive. One had to gather a lot of coconuts or whatever to pay for one or spend a lot of time learning know-how and the making of one.

The barter system that they used sometimes caused problems. It was two-and-a-half clams for one coconut. One mahi mahi for four-and-three-quarters large potatoes. All kinds of different amounts for other things so, if they didn't have exactly the right things to trade, they had to memorize all the things that they owed or were owed. They tried writing it in the sand on the beach but the damn tide washed away all of their records. Sometimes clams were hard to find and Joe wanted slightly more of-what-you-had for each clam. Bartering and record keeping were becoming arduous, troubling, and troublesome. A couple of fist fights actually broke out! They needed a change.

Fortunately, one of Joe's Kids was a mathematical genius (they were of the Robinson family, Swiss, you know). This Joe's Kid noticed that all around the island in the sand were hard bright stones. Each stone was a single color: bright clear red; blue; yellow; etc. Most of these special stones were the size of a golf ball (they, of course, had no god damned idea what a golf ball was; I only use that comparison because the odds are quite good that you know what a god damn golf ball is). The most abundant, though still rare, were the red stones (you would probably know them as rubies and the green ones as emeralds, but, what the hell; a red stone is just a red stone; though formed in the Vulcan furnace of the volcano!). Some red stones were bigger and some smaller, certainly, but they could be reasonably estimated to have a specific relationship to each other by reasonable men (and the women who did most of the trading); so that was not a real problem. There were quite a few of the red stones but very seldom would new ones appear; there were not too many and not too few which means there was just about the right amount. Joe said, "Let us call these red stones 'Rocks' and use them as a medium of exchange instead of all this god damn bartering all the time. (You, of course, immediately recognize them as "money" but, fortunately for these islanders, the lucky bastards had never heard of money and, as such, had no root of all evil – yet. Everyone got along just fine.) (Ah, Joe! Joe! Joe! Joe! Always the god damned do-gooder; couldn't you just have left well-enough alone? No Jo! Lev dem go. Ledit lone. Tymes iss guut. No need tousan trubles ina ro.) (Invention is the mother of necessity – or do I have that wrong.)

So, with Joe's Kid's direction and encouragement, "the people" gathered up all of the Rocks (the hard, clear red stones) in their baskets and dumped them in a pile on a barren stretch of hard, cold lava. They divided them equally among the families. (They had some trouble at first; some lighter colored guy wanted to give one darker colored family only three-fifths as much as the lighter colored folks; but it all worked out with justice after a while.)

Very quickly, they worked out an exchange rate. So many rocks for a mahi mahi; so many coconuts for so many rocks. It worked so well, that there is no record of the exchange rate; anyway it was not fixed; it fluctuated according to the availability of this or that; it was quite marvelous; almost like an "invisible hand" guiding and controlling the market; everything found its own balance. If a family's pile started to go down, they either charged more for their specialty (if they could) or switched some of their efforts to a better "paying" specialty. There wasn't perfect equality, of course, some families and individuals were better at this new gambit than others. New specialties arose; one of Joe's older brothers, Mac, did nothing but trade one thing for another; "buying" one thing and "selling" it for more Rocks, making sure he kept a little of everything for himself.

Slowly, some people impregnated the Rocks with meaning and value that they didn't have when they were just lying freely on the beach. It was almost as if the Rocks had life and inherent value in and of themselves (and, what the hell, they were just red stones not inherently worth a taro root)! Some people seemed to almost worship the Rocks; so much so that they would sneak some from neighbors when they weren't watching as though the Rocks were more important than the friendship of the neighbors...

Then, omigod, then a very odd, strange, weird, wacky, thing happened!

Mac the trader - Trader Mac everyone called him - took control of the water fountain - the free spring water! Like it was his! And not Mother Nature's. Like it was all his. He charged everyone a Rock for a half-coconut-shell full of water and a Small (half) Rock for a clam-shell full of water, the free spring water. He, Trader Mac, was just gathering stones like crazy (from other islanders who had to buy his water or die of thirst)! Some very wise man said, "There's a time to gather Rocks and there's a time to cast away Rocks." Now if that ain't brilliant; what the hell is! It was Mac's time to gather Rocks. Well, let me tell you, there were some hot-heads who weren't going to put up with that shit so they came after Mac – bunch of Hooligans just wanting to take by fighting what they could not get honestly. But Mac, you guessed it, had more Rocks then they did and, so, he "hired" some of the big, dumb, lazy guys to protect him and to watch 'his' water, the free spring water, when he wasn't there. That wasn't the end of it. The hot-heads were not finished; not by a long shot. No siree! I could write a book about their envy, like class envy; it was pretty sickening. Just because they didn't think of it first! It was clearly intellectual property. Trader Mac's intellectual property.

Trader Mac realized that some people just didn't understand how things worked so he started Truth Fountains; the first he called Really Analytical; Not Dumb! Coming On Right Policies! Or the acronym; RAND CORP. Their job was to tell the truth. They, of course, had the infallible guidance of Trader Mac to enlighten them to the right course; the course of truth. But they were absolutely free to make up their own minds on any subject just as a Catholic novice priest is free to make up his own mind regarding faith and morals.

With all of this envy, Trader Mac had a lot of expenses. He had to hire the people mentioned before of course, water merchants and water police; but he also had to fight that terrible green-eyed-monster ENVY. So he hired Truth Fountain Poets to sing his praises; enforcers to punish anyone who doubted his rights, his water rights to the free spring water. He was a genius. Obviously a genius. Listen to the Truth Fountain Poets, they all agree, Trader Mac is a genius. Everyone says so.

Trader Mac is a genius,
He's got a super penius.
If you want his water
You gotta sell yer dauter.

Another Truth Fountain Poet wrote:

Trader Mac fills all our needs
He makes all the plants and seeds
We know he's so god damn smart
It goes way beyond an art.

The cycle: expenses up: collect more Rocks: more

expenses: more products to collect more rocks. You wanna be safe at night now; you gotta pay Trader Mac for the Night Enforcers. You wanna feed your family if you die: you gotta pay Trader Mac for "Life Insurance" (but if you die and you can't pay; you, obviously, can't collect! No pay; no collect; simple; same with accident, storm, health, and 'act-of-god' insurance).

But now fewer people were actually digging potatoes and digging clams. And the people who weren't digging had just as many Rocks (working for Trader Mac) as the people who were digging; they had more even; they were more even.

Some people became discouraged; Mike, for example, spent the whole day gathering coconuts and at the end of the day he was thirsty; he sold all his coconuts for twenty Rocks – that was more than he usually got; he bought two half shells of water and only had ten Rocks remaining – the price of water had gone up. For those ten rocks he only got half a mahi mahi to feed his whole family; mahi mahi had gone up too. He tried to get a job with Trader Mac but he had no experience guarding or selling water, the free spring water. He had to buy water, the free spring water, every day; he had to feed his family; he was desperate! He had an old woven-rush boat and so he decided he and his oldest son would try fishing. The boat was so slow that it took most of the day to go forth and back to the fishing reef; and, one day, his basket of fish tipped and he lost most of his harvest. He needed one of the better, faster carved-lava boats. Wow! The price of those had sure gone up! How could he buy one when he could not accumulate many Rocks?

He went to Trader Mac and begged for a pile of Rocks to buy a boat. Trader Mac said, "Sure! I will give you a pile of rocks big enough for you to buy a carved-lava boat." Then he revealed the catch; catch #1: "When the sun has risen 300 times, you give back a pile and a tenth." Mike was pretty sure he could do it; besides, what choice did he have? None! He went to buy the boat and the price had gone up again, but with the pile he had gotten from Trader Mac and a few Rocks he begged from his old uncle, he was able to buy the boat. He fished successfully for a few days and then, to his surprise, his neighbor offered to give him a pile and a half of Rocks plus three Malarkey Bird tail feathers for his boat. He took the deal. The next day he went and bought another boat but it cost him a pile and a half – the price of boats had gone up again! Mike was still ahead by three Malarkey Bird tail feathers. The next day he didn't fish or gather coconuts. He went all over the island looking for boats. He made deal after deal. He would strike an agreement with someone then run to Trader Mac for the necessary pile of Rocks to pay. Busy sunrise! Then a busy ten-sunrises. Then a busy twenty-sunrises. And he wasn't the only one.

Trader Mac was an easy lender; he had baskets and baskets of Rocks (as a result, most everyone else had fewer Rocks) and he was eager to loan them out at a profit. But even all those baskets were not enough. Trader Mac had his guys (employees) gather up ALL the colored stones from ALL the beaches (they thought it was dumb – just stones after all). When he had secured all the colored stones, Trader Mac announced that a Black Rock would equal ten of the Red Rocks; and a Blue Rock would equal ten of the Black Rocks, etc.; so suddenly the island (that is, Trader Mac) had thousands and thousands of times more Red Rocks!

But Mike, by frantic trading and borrowing, had been able to keep ahead of the game and was able – just able – to feed his family, buy water (the free spring water) and pay Trader Mac. But it was making him crazy. He could hardly keep up with the price increases and still keep some Rocks for himself and family. And Trader Mac was frantic to loan out all of his excess Rocks; so Trader Mac was making more and more loans to people who would have a problem paying them back. But most people who were actually digging, spearing, and gathering were "in the same boat" struggling to buy water, the free spring water, and food for themselves and their families. Many people were actually borrowing from Trader Mac just for food and water without any real idea as to how they were going to pay him back. But they were desperate enough that they would do anything to put food on the table today and the "devil take tomorrow".

Everyone (except Trader Mac and the Truth Fountain Poets) was having trouble "making it". Everyone worked harder and harder but Trader Mac just raised the price of the water and no one could catch up much less get ahead. Even with Joe's Kid showing everyone how to use leverage and other tricks to produce more, it did no good because Trader Mac was always one step ahead raising prices so that they could never catch up.

Trader Mac didn't want any Rocks in his baskets; he wanted them all loaned out fetching even more Rocks. If people were stupid enough to borrow money, excuse me, Rocks which would effectively reduce them to slavery, that was certainly not Trader Mac's concern nor his responsibility; his concern was to make sure that they paid him back at any cost to them. They borrowed the Rocks; they had to pay it back with interest. Right is right; fair is fair after all.

So many things were happening that it was hard to keep them all straight. Maybe we should follow what happened to one "thing" while holding all other "things" constant. (Just kidding!) There developed groups, interest groups, divisions, levels of people. At the 'bottom' were the people actually getting the food; next, in the 'middle' were people like Mike exchanging one thing for another, at each exchange keeping enough to make it worth their while; next, at an upper level, were people helping Trader Mac at several intermediate levels (trading rocks and charging for the favor); the "fellows" and "senior fellows" who were the truth fountain poets; then, of course there was Trader Mac himself.

Another "thing" that happened was that many different people (including some of the people at the food supply level who needed boats) 'tried their hand' at making a Rock by trading boats. So the value of boats just went wild until some of the fishermen, who needed a boat every day, actually sold their boats just to feed their families. And the boats used for actual fishing went down. So the actual supply of actual fish actually went down.

Remember Mike had three Malarkey Bird tail feathers? Well, he sold one for more Rocks so that he could buy more boats. He sold that Malarkey Bird tail feather for so many Rocks that he decided to go and buy as many Malarkey Bird tail feathers as he could before people realized how valuable THEY were. Well, you guessed it; pretty soon what happened to the price of boats also happened to the price of Malarkey Bird tail feathers. What happened to the price of potatoes? Well, you know what happened to the price of potatoes. The price of potatoes went up too. Not, of course, as far or as fast as the price of Malarkey Bird tail feathers; but WAY up. Remember now, there were far fewer people getting food but just as many eating it. And Trader Mac could charge as much as he wanted for his water, the free spring water, because you HAD to have it (there was, of course, no coercion; you were free NOT to buy his water, the free spring water, no one MADE you buy it; you HAD free will). The people getting food worked round the clock but still had only enough money to buy water (the free spring water) and little food. The people getting the food fell into misery, despair, desperation, poverty, illness, hunger, and, sometimes, into effective slavery.

Some people went mad because they drank sea water when they couldn't afford to drink from Trader Mac's well, the free spring water. But, fortunately, this ugliness was kept hidden from Trader Mac.

The price of boats went so high that only Trader Mac could afford one and he didn't want more than he already had. Poor Mike was left owing Trader Mac dozens of Rocks of multi-colors. Mike's yard was filled with boats that no one could afford. He couldn't give them away for even one Red Rock; no one had any Rocks to spare. He tried insuring them with Trader Mac for more than their book value with an eye of persuading a tree to fall on them but Trader Mac saw through him and just laughed at him. Trader Mac had all of Mike's Rocks and all of the Rocks that Mike would earn for many years. The Malarkey Bird tail feathers became nearly worthless too. Mike went back to fishing (even though he had a problem with selling his fish because everyone used all their Rocks to buy water, the free spring water); at least he could eat the fish. He also loaned one or two boats out to people who would fish; in return he got a small part of their catch.

The Truth Fountain Poets explained everything:

You went and sold your dauter,
For a little drink of water.
Now that you made the gods madder,
They broke the rungs on your ladder.

That was clear enough. This Truth Fountain Poet gives you the basics:

If you were more fervent
Then you could pay your rent.
Give to God to plant some seeds
Then I'll have him fill your needs.

The Supreme Court Truth Fountain Poets stuck to time-honored principles.

The Hooligans in their fights
Want to take Mac's water rights,
His interests to his heirs
Is just the same as theirs.

And another economist Truth Fountain Poet:

It's a good thing that Trader Mac
Knows that some things are out of whack,
He's working hard to make things right,
You can trust him to fight your fight.

Still another economist Truth Fountain Poet:

The enforcers are spending,
And the lenders are lending,
Without those heroes mending,
All our hopes would be ending.

This op-ed Truth Fountain Poet tells it like it is!

Just Trader Mac has the dough
To make the job market grow.
Without the rich to invest
You'd walk the streets like the rest.

This conservative economist tells it like it is:

Trader Mac is your lovin' pal
He's way too big to let him fail.
That there puts on us the onus
To make sure he's paid his bonus.

More truth from the editorial Truth Fountain Poets:

Times're gooder than yesterday,
Then you had far lesser pay,

And now you can rest your back,
Get a loan from Trader Mac!

This Truth Fountain Poet is tough!

I'm sick of your damn crying,
I think you're just not trying,
I have had it up to here,
Shut your mouth and kiss my rear.

This RAND CORP Truth Fountain Poet has no sympathy for your laziness.

You're jealous of their success,
Instead you should honor and bless,
They worked hard to get that far,
Why are you stuck where you are?

The Op-Ed Truth Fountain Poets always discussed weighty matters:

Are Trader Mac's toenails too long?
It's a matter of right or wrong;
The conservatives have it one way,
But the liberals too want their say.

And finally the neo-con Truth Fountain Poets:

That other island is bad,
Your freedom just makes them mad.
Mac's job is to protect you
From the Arab and the Jew.

Some people didn't believe anything that the Truth Fountain Poets said. Some believed some. And others believed everything that the Truth Fountain Poets said. These last were the same people who were captivated by the reflected sparkling colors of the Malarkey Bird's tail feathers in the bright light and enchanted by the false-golden glow of the Malarkey Bird's tail feathers in the darkness.

Looking at a picture, it's easy to get lost in the palette and brush strokes, beautiful though they are, so let's pull back and look at the painted naked saint from across the room, shocking though she is.

I have to admit that I don't understand anything that happened on my little Life and Sex Island. But, if you understand what happened on that little Life and Sex Island, then you understand what happened in the Panics of 1797, 1807, 1819, 1837, 1857, 1860, 1861,

1873, 1884, 1890, 1893, and 1907; you understand what really happened in the crash of '29 and the continuing panics through 1933, the Savings and Loan crisis of 1987 to 1990, the dot com bubble of 2000, the Sub-prime Mortgage crisis of 2008, and all of the little recessions along the way (1953, 1957, 1973, 1980).

If you can understand how two birds can, together, make three more which makes a total of five; then you can understand the simple arithmetic of 1+1=5. But, if I just gave you the numbers, then you would find the understanding hard to come by. So, now that you have understanding, allow me to present the numbers which simplifies the understanding. Are you getting used to the smell yet?

One of the major problems corporations have is to reduce the cost of labor; and then reduce it some more. There is no bottom that is too low. But this is an ancient problem. The best solution is to work people without paying or feeding them. Hitler is definitely not the first or last to do so. Most corporate executives wish that they could (but would feign outrage at the suggestion that they might like the idea.) Some people call it "slavery". We've been doing it forever. Slavery was an ancient institution at the time of Hammurabi about 1760 BC. In 1452, Pope Nicholas V allowed any pagans and other nonbelievers to be made slaves which made slavery legal for Catholics (Christians). There's a lot of history between 1492 and 1776; 284 years; that is more than between 1776 and 2008; 232 years. Columbus crammed as many Taino Indians onto his ships as he could and sold them as slaves in Spain in 1495. Other Indians he put to work as slaves in mines and plantations throughout the Caribbean. Slavery was the norm from the Old Testament to the Emancipation Proclamation in 1863; not just in the U.S. South, everywhere in the world. Massachusetts became the first colony to legalize slavery in 1642. New York and New Jersey legalized slavery in 1664. Tsar Alexander II freed 23 million Russian slaves in 1861 (even a Tsar beat us to the punch bowl). On July 1, 1863 the Netherlands abolished slavery freeing an estimated 45,000 slaves, most in Surinam. We could list every country and find that most trended toward officially ending official slavery in that century. Although, as recently as the 1950s, our good friend by way of the Bushies, Saudi Arabia, had an estimated 450,000 slaves. There are still millions of slaves in the world; many are "white" or sex slaves. And, in case you are interested, Lincoln's Emancipation Proclamation "freed the slaves" but no laws were passed against slavery so slavery continued until 1942 when the first slavery conviction finally actually was successful. Until then it was "oh yeah, the slaves are freed". But they weren't in fact free.

I find it interesting that your and my ancestors were and had slaves; were slaves and were slave owners; yup. The history is so long, deep, and dignified that it is ridiculous to think that it is anathema to religion or to man; to think that we would not be slavers and our ancestors were not slavers and slaves is ridiculous. A king just had to lose a battle and he and all his supporters were slaves if they were lucky (if not lucky they were tortured to death). It is pretty undeniable that, if you or I had a chance to have slaves, we would. Not, of course, under today's conditions, under today's "enlightenment". People would look down on us; even George W. Bush doesn't openly advocate actually "slavery"; he and his buddies just push conditions toward slavery. But, if you and/or I and/or Lincoln lived in a situation where slavery was acceptable and if our lives could be made easier and 'richer', we would have slaves. If we could absolutely, confidently get away with it, we would have slaves. We are all Trader Macs given the opportunity.

I am just trying to get rid of the idea of good or evil regarding slavery or pro- or anti-slavery sentiments. All of the moneyed religions in the Antebellum South were pro-slavery and proved that slavery was approved in the Bible. We all try to 'better' ourselves and to 'better' our children's prospects. That sounds so much better than saying, "We all want to be rich" or, at least "richer" and, indeed, if we are rich we want to be still richer (there is no acceptable top and I have never heard of an exception [though, I am sure there are some]).

Now I am almost three-quarters-of-a-century-old and, so, I am pretty sure that I am not going to be rich. Therefore, I am anti-slavery. (I want to be clear: this is not 'good' or 'evil' this is simply my own self interest; what works for me, god damnit.) If I were Trader Mac or one of his Truth Fountain Poets, I would be pro-slavery. The vast majority of us are never going to be Trader Macs or, likely, one of his Truth Fountain Poets. Therefore we should start a conspiracy to limit Trader Macs wealth and power knowing, of course, that Trader Mac's Truth Fountain Poets will damn us with all sorts of damnableness. Knowing, also, that it is not a limitless pie that may be shared with everyone to everyone's benefit. Knowing, also, that if only a few are sharing in the pie (as is the case now) most of the pie will rot and benefit no one. Knowing, yet again, that if a fair share of the pie is given to everyone there will be far more pie to share; even the rich will benefit.

I am against the vast-wealth-differential that developed on our little Life and Sex Island for five reasons: One: I am not one of the 'lucky' rich and, thus I am envious and wish to 'fix' the "problem"; the problem that others do not see as a problem. Two: Some of us are in "desperation mode" because of the systematic, vast, unrelenting, terrible lies that were told for the last sixty years and these lies and liars ought not to be rewarded. Three: While I would agree that "the harder you work the luckier you get", I would also say that the fact that only a tiny tiny percent get 'lucky' enough to be among the super-rich (virtually all the super-rich began life rich) while at least two-percent (by definition) of the remainder of us are geniuses and a much higher percent work very hard and very smart and, in fact, the super-rich are not usually smart, dedicated, or hard-working that it is a matter of a lucky break that a few, by luck, become super-rich and it is, therefore, unfair. Four: Because the rich can and do buy the lawmakers and the 'newsmakers', the system is biased in favor of the rich and is, therefore, unfair (the homeless own very few newspapers, foundations, think tanks, or politicians). Five: The vast-wealth-differential doesn't work; as on the Life and Sex Island, the economy collapses because the vast poor don't have enough wealth to provide the necessities of life; the super-rich are desperate to earn more money on their wealth and cannot stand to see any of their wealth sitting idle and they begin to chase one or another scheme to increase their return and the system spirals up and collapses because there is no base; thus, the vast-wealth-differential doesn't work.

I hope that, at sometime in your life, you were or will be a serious poker player just as I hope that at sometime you had a really good chocolate ice-cream-cone. I have been in poker games where the 'host' 'dragged' the pot. That is, the 'host' took a fixed amount of money out of every pot "to pay for the beer" or some such thing. It is amazing how much more difficult it is to go home a winner when someone is 'dragging' the pot then when no one is 'dragging' the pot. Well, in today's economy, folks, the rich and super-rich are dragging two-thirds of every pot. That's ten percent of us is/are taking two-thirds of the money. It is hard to win, folks. The game becomes pretty senseless and nigh impossible. It simply doesn't work. Lots of people simply give up (in various ways: alcohol, suicide, drugs, abandonment, etc. No question that the rich are monsters and murderers. They can be as "charitable" and "philanthropic" and found as many "foundations" as they wish; it changes nothing: they are monsters and murderers. [But remember, you and I would be there if we could!])

I say 'it', the system of vast-wealth-differential, doesn't work but that is from an engineering system viewpoint. Obviously, the super-rich prefer the present system which collapses into slowdowns, crises, panics, recessions, and depressions periodically and demands that most people become servile and forces them into thralldom to the super-rich. But, from an engineering standpoint, a ship that is slow, impossible to steer, leaks water so bad that half the crew spends their time bailing, and, despite valiant efforts on the part of the crew, the ship sinks or partially sinks ten to twenty-five percent of the time is not a successful or properly functioning ship. From an engineering standpoint, it is time to trade ships or put this one in dry-dock for major repairs. The super-rich will "pull out all stops" (including sinking the ship) to prevent any repairs. All of Trader Mac's Truth Fountain Poets will begin a cacophony of objections.

This is an aside to punch home a point: A few years ago, maybe as much as twenty, there was a documentary on T.V. that followed four fantastically successful entrepreneurs while they were starting a new, second business. I only remember who two of the examples were: one was Steve Jobs, co-founder of Apple Computer after he had been fired by the guy from Pepsi who he had hired. He, Steve Jobs, was starting a new company that he called Next! (S. Jobs later went back to Apple.) I'm pretty sure the second example was Frederick Wallace Smith the founder of Federal Express. I don't remember what second business he was starting. There were also the two other founders of extremely successful companies who were each founding a new, second company. The point of the documentary was to show us tyro wannabes just how simple it was in the hands of pros. Well, it didn't work out that way. All four new businesses failed. Despite an infinite amount of money poured into them and experts crawling all over them; all four new businesses failed. The lesson that I learned was that you can be very smart and very rich and still fail in a new venture because you are missing one key ingredient: luck. Without Lady Luck holding your balls, you will fail.

On with the story of American economics. I'm not going to give you Digest Biographies. There are many books about America's Robber Barons or, if you prefer, America's Industrial Giants who founded America's super successful free enterprise system and benefited the rest of us. I'll try not to take sides. Had I been born in their shoes with their luck, I would be, or would have been, one of them and not be apologetic. So would you. Don't lie about it. But I want to show how we got into the pickle that we are in. I will scan about 100 years from about 1908 to 2008. I have to set it up with: J. D. Rockefeller who really belongs to an earlier period and is one of the prototypes for the new-nibs-super-rich (and Trader Mac).

I promised no Digest Biographies, nevertheless, I have to mention John D. Rockefeller the Much Maligned, the Master. At his peak in about 1908 he was worth about a billion dollars, today that might be $25- or $250-billion but you probably won't find the Rockefeller name on any list of "The Rich". In 1895 he paid taxes of a little less than $15,000 on income of about $1.25-million taxed at two-percent – he had some deductions, expenses, etc. (a coal miner then earned about $300 a year). He was pretty clumsy then yet; he got better and it was our own fault. Judge Landis ordered Standard Oil broken up in 1911. That may be what started J.D.R. on the road to even greater success. He, J.D.R., did not want Standard Oil broken any more than you or I would want our kid cut in two. You or I might ask a lawyer, "What can I do?" The rich don't think that way; they say, "Make what I am doing legal." J.D.R. started a bunch of trusts; he oiled a little here and he oiled a little there. Pretty soon Standard Oil was all broken up. And all (or most) of the pieces were still in J.D.R.'s hands. Today there are so many Rockefeller trusts and other paper entities that no government has any idea how much the Rockefellers are worth or how much they own. The people on the "The Rich" lists are the new kids on the block who haven't learned anything yet.

Oh! I almost forgot two things: how did J.D. Rockefeller earn his money? And, why do the rich put so much money into trusts and other, often do-gooder, entities?

Did J.D.R. invent oil? Was J.D.R. the first to discover oil? Did J.D.R. develop oil like someone develops a new variety of tomato? No, he didn't invent oil; if you are religiously inclined, God invented oil and put it in the ground for free; anyway it was in the ground for free. And, no or yes, oil had been discovered by others long before; and J.D.R. was not an inventor or developer. As Trader Mac controlled the free spring water, John D. Rockefeller controlled the oil; as Trader Mac sold free spring water, John D. Rockefeller sold oil. John D. Rockefeller made his money selling free spring water.

(Note: In those days it probably cost about two-bits-a-barrel to get the oil out of the ground. Nowadays it may cost a couple-a-bucks-per-barrel ta git da oil otta da ground. [Don't listen to the oil economists, or to the Guppies from the think tanks, or to the Truth Fountain Poets. They lie. They get paid very well to lie.] So, whether the Modern Trader Macs are selling it for fifty-bucks or five-hundred-bucks-a-barrel, the cost at the pump is almost entirely the cost of the Free-Spring-Water.)

Why do the rich found so damn many trusts and foundations and the like? I can list a few reasons but there are probably many that I don't know about. Trusts, like the Rockefeller trusts can be used to launder money and ownership. They can go back and fourth with so many owners and names and countries and secret accounts that they can befuddle any tax collector. They can hide income and estate taxes in a number of ways. E.g., if the largest non-taxable gift is $1000 and Junior gets a $1000 gift from multiple trusts every year for forty years, a very sizable fortune can be transferred tax free. Since trusts are not traded in a free market they can be worth anything that the trustees say they are worth. If the trusts are worth a hidden billion-dollars and accumulating a hidden hundred-million-dollars in earnings every year; they are still only worth a dollar if the trustees say that they are only worth a dollar. And they can be transferred to Junior for a tax-free-dollar. Trusts can be used to concentrate control and to hide ownership. If all of the stock with voting rights is put in a trust that the Family controls, the general public can be sold large amounts of stock with no voting rights whatsoever. Or the public can be sold stock with apparent (advisory) but not real voting rights.

Trusts and foundations can also be used to launder the family name. When the public found out some of the tricks that J. D. Rockefeller had used to amass his fortune, his approval rating was lower than congress's in 2008, J.D.R. hired a public relations genius, Ivy Lee

("Poison Ivy"), to make him (J.D.R.) seem lovable (giving shiny new dimes to people of some small merit [the Corporate Press had the munchies; they ran with that story over and over; "J.D.R. is really a pleasant, harmless old coot."]). Today, his descendents can be elected to public office without changing their names and without anyone remembering the scandals.

National Public Radio (N.P.R.) repeatedly sings the praises of one after another of the Rich wonder boys and girls and how they are using their trusts and foundations to better mankind in every conceivable way. It works. Hear it often enough and you know it as well as you know that Coke Refreshes (and, in the old days, that Chesterfields are good for you [and taste good, too]).

Trusts and foundations are also used to hire Think Tank Guppies to prove that the world works better if the rich are made richer and the poor are made poorer. These are the equivalent of Trader Mac's Truth Fountains and the Truth Fountain Poets. The Guppies also prove that the poor are really not poor and, with no hint of irony, that the poor are really happier being poor than if they were miserable like the rich. The Guppies also make magical studies that prove that you miraculously collect more taxes by taxing the rich less. Plus; envy is a vice; greed is a virtue.

Finally, it is psychologically impossible for the rich to collect less money from whatever their source was or to simply give the money back to the people from whom they took it in the first place. If they collect less, they might slip in the ratings and that would dent their ego; also they see no reason that they shouldn't continue their god-given quest to be ever richer (thus proving the equivalence between money, intelligence, and holiness). That is unthinkable! Not getting richer, when you have the chance, is un-American (after all, didn't Louis the XVI continue to get rich until he lost his head?). If the rich gave it back to the people from whom they took it in the first place, that might cast doubt upon their business ethics. That is unthinkable! Any bishop will tell you that, if you are rich, you are going straight to heaven (after all, didn't they canonize Louis the IX?). If they gave it back, someone might think that maybe, just maybe, they should not have taken it in the first place.

Enough of this bullshit! Before I give you the numbers, let me present an overview of the economy from about 1908 to 2008 for your consideration.

The First World War (then just called the Great War; they didn't suspect that we would need a numbering system for World Wars) ended in 1918. We came out of the First World War with a huge debt (laughable by today's standards). The world's economies were in shambles (war kills not only people; it also kills economies; more or as many people starve from the war as are killed in the war). After the Great War there was no warm and cuddly trend toward economic equality or justice and there was no Truman-Marshall Plan to rebuild the world (which would have stimulated our economy).

The distance between the rich and the poor was vast. The Roaring Twenties did not roar for most, they Growled. The Aughts, Tens, and Twenties were periods of enormous engineering and inventive progress but little or no wage progress; productivity soared, wages sagged, wealth rocketed; humanity reeled. Union membership (percent of non-farm labor) was about 6% in 1900 and rose to about 10% in 1910 and again to about 19% in 1920 then, after the Great War, the super-rich began a war on unions and membership declined to about 11% in 1930 and this was part of the cause of the First Great Depression (yes, we need a numbering system). Most of the farmers were already in poverty (farmers were about a third of the population then; farm mortgage foreclosures rose from about 0.4% in 1920 to about 1.8% in 1927, about one out of ten every seven years (that's like, if you lived on a block with ten houses, one would be sold for back-taxes every seven years); about 4-millon people quit farming ['lost' their farms] in the ten years before the Depression). All regular workers had trouble feeding their families. Unions were attacked by chattel legislators, cops, and armies (police, the U.S. Army, and private armies such as Pinkerton murdered workers like cars kill possums; or more like Tyson kills chickens). The rich were impoverishing the economy by taking all the loose cash. The people who were doing the work were not getting a fair share of the fruits of their labor. Warren G. Harding (president from 1921 to 1923; generally conceded to be the worst President until that time) and his super-rich Treasury Secretary, Andrew Mellon, and the chattel legislature gave super-tax-cuts to the super-rich (top rate cut from 77% to 24%, a tax reduction of almost 69%). Calvin Coolidge (the second worst President until that time) continued with Mellon and the tax cuts. But there were still Lincoln-progressives in the Republican Party until about 1932. And the Democrats were split between the pro-slavery-states-rights-Dixiecrats in the South and the Progressives in the North.

Having already built multi-million-dollar mansions, the rich (like Trader Mac) were desperate for a place to put their money, most of which was excess. In 1920 the average stock carried a P/E of about five (5). (P/E, Price-Earnings Ratio, can be looked at as the number of years it will take to double your money if earnings stay the same and you don't invest the gains as you get them.) Ten years later, in 1930, the average P/E was thirty-two (32); more than 6 times higher. A stock that you could buy for ten bucks in 1920 would cost you sixty bucks in 1930, and its value had not gone up (it was the same damn carved lava boat); people were paying way too much. The stock market acted as a huge money-sponge to soak up all the surplus money but not to create more value. (Something like what happened to the lava boats and the Malarkey Bird tail feathers on the Life and Sex Island.)

Many people, having watched the price of stock rising forever (ten years) thought it would never stop and they borrowed money to buy stock. When the market dipped, they were forced to sell to stop their losses (or the broker sold automatically when their investment was gone). Soon everyone was selling. (Someone wrote that there were no buyers but, of course, there can be no selling unless there is buying and buyers; some people were getting bargains.) The stock market crash released huge amounts of cash but it was in the hands of people who did not need it. The people who were starving had no cash and no jobs and the rich were protected by private armies which they could buy cheap (Henry Ford had machine gun emplacements installed on his lawn.) one of the super-rich said that he could hire half the workers to kill the other half. (Compassion flowed like crystallized honey.)

It is important to remember that the stock market crash of '29 was a symptom of the economic unbalance not the cause of it. Let me restate that: the vast money or wealth inequality caused the stock market crash and the Depression. (The idea that monetary policy had something to do with it is just part of the Truth Fountain Poets [Think Tank Guppies] truth syrup. Here's one now, WSJ A23 6-11-8, "the Great Depression – which was caused by the new Fed, trade protectionism and tax rate increases". Those very valuable Professional Liars are insufficiently paid; some are paid less than Pro Baseball Players. It might be noted that the Wall Street Journal is one of the great leaders in the war against the poor. They will never rest until every member of the middle-class is securely locked in debtors' prison. This highly respected newspaper is on the desk of virtually every captain of every terrorist fighting organization in the world; they are determined to destroy every terrorist cell that is attempting to move industrial workers and engineers above the sub-subsistence level.) The start of the Depression is usually set at the Crash of '29. But is that accurate from an engineering standpoint? If I don't put oil in my car in '20 and it continues to run until '29 when the pistons finally freeze up, when did the failure begin? I propose that some of the engineers among us might consider that the failure began in '20 not '29! I think that the Depression began in '20. Once the economy froze up the Depression Death March lasted about twenty years and caused unimaginable suffering and millions of deaths. It is important to remember that this human misery, suffering, and death was deliberately, callously, and selfishly caused by the rich and the super-rich and their chattel allies in the Legislature and the Presidency. The death, pain, and misery that the rich and the super-rich caused was a hidden, unpunished crime against humanity.

I was born in '35 so I can't claim that I remember much of the Depression. Still I was marked by it (partially because ours lasted at least until I graduated from college). And I was close enough to it that I am aware of how it marked everyone who lived through it (not the rich and the super-rich – or their Truth Fountain Poets – who deliberately didn't and don't 'get it'). George Burns, after he had become ancient and a multi-millionaire, said that he still could not leave a room without turning out the lights. And he probably still stooped to pick up a penny from the sidewalk. Marked for life. "A stitch in time saves nine." Yes, all wives darned socks until the socks were nothing but darning; and when the washcloths became worn through in the middle and less on the corners, they were cut into quarters and sewn together with the outside corners in the middle. When clothes could no longer be patched or mended, all the buttons and zippers were cut off and saved and the clothes were torn into strips and made into braided-rugs. Patchwork quilts were made from worn-out clothes; necessity was made into an art. Sow bellies were rendered: the cracklings mixed with buckwheat flour to make balkenbrij; the lard mixed with wood ash to make soap. Hobo jungles were populated by lost men who could no longer stand to see their children starve around an empty dinner table – and maybe the children could get welfare if their father was no longer present. Read Steinbeck's 'The Grapes of Wrath'. Humans stood in a crowd by the mill gates in the morning hoping to be the one out of five-hundred to be picked for a day's miserable, killing work (with four-hundred-ninety-nine going home to a more miserable day). And the rich and the super-rich had a grand ball with debutants who were, fortunately kept ignorant of the horror predicated by their parents.

> "My Lords, you are loftily placed. It is well. We must believe that God has his reasons for this. You have power, opulence, joy, the sun always motionless at your zenith, unbounded authority, undivided enjoyment, an immense oblivion of all others. So be it. But there is something beneath you. Above you, too, perhaps. My Lords, I come to tell you news. The human race exists. … I am he who comes from the depths. My Lords, you are the great and the rich. That is perilous. You take advantage of darkness. But take care, there is a great power, dawn. Daybreak cannot be conquered. It will come. It is coming. The irresistible ray of daylight is within it. And who will hinder that sling from hurling the sun into the sky? The sun, is Man's Right. You – you are Privilege. You may well be afraid. The real master of the house is going to knock at the door. Who is the father of privilege? Chance. And who is his son? Abuse. Neither Chance nor Abuse are firm or enduring. Both of them have an evil morrow. I come to warn you. I come to denounce your own happiness to you. It is made of the misery of others. My Lords, I am the hopeless advocate, and I plead a lost cause. God Himself will gain this cause. I am nothing but a voice. The human race is a mouth, and I am its cry. You shall hear me." – Gwynplaine, The Laughing Man, set. 1690; pub. 1869 by Victor Hugo.

A French-Revolution-like was imminent in the United States. Roosevelt's alphabet soup (WPA, TVA, etc.) saved democracy, the 'free' world, the "free" market, and "free" enterprise. Mobilization for THE war ended the Depression. THE war did have several salutary effects. The universal draft seemed fair. True, the rich and super-rich did become officers and spent the war on the home front but, then, so did some of the poor (my brother Jim furnished ships and never left the States though my brother Al, as a navigator, flew missions over the Pacific, was shot down, and was one of but three crewmen who survived to be picked off the wide wet waves by a seaplane within gunshot of the Japs; three miles off Formosa). Some of the mill owner's sons were in the same foxholes as the mill worker's sons. It's hard to be an arrogant son-of-a-bitch when you are fourth on a "three to a match" rule. Some of the mill owner's sons became G.I.s and almost human. Some of them learned to understand and to smile at SNAFU. Many said to Bob Hope "thanks for the mammaries". And G.I.s who fought the Japs in the jungle and learned to be shot at, to use a gun, and to organize would never, ever put-up with "standing in a crowd by the mill gates in the morning hoping to be the one out of five-hundred to be picked for a day's miserable, killing work". Never. Never. Never. Never. Never. The Truman-Marshall Plan helped to prevent a return to the Depression. This accidental President turned out to be one of the best. The G.I. Bill substantially raised the education level in the United States and spread-out the crush of men stripping off their uniforms and demanding jobs.

These years after THE war were some of the best in United States history. There were forces in action driving a trend toward equality. A laborer could support his family (a one income family); and own a house and a car. Union membership rose to about 33% in 1953. Education was free or cheap. (My tuition was under $100 in '54.) The top income tax rate was raised to 94% in 1944. Unions were strong. The top income tax rate bounced but in 1963 it was still at 91%; it fell under L. B. Johnson and ended at 77% in 1969. (Now it's about 35%, but there are so damn many deductions for the rich it is effectively much, much lower.)

There is probably not a single melting point to the economy but the first signs of the good times starting to soften (heading in the wrong direction) was probably in the mid 50s. The civil rights movement giving blacks more equality, brought blacks into the real economy bringing downward pressure on wages.

The top marginal tax rate plummeted steadily to 35% under Bush II; its lowest value since, surprise, just in the Depression slide in 1931. Women came into the labor market in strength in the mid 60s onward, putting further downward pressure on wages. Membership in labor unions fell to about 27% in 1962; there was a slight up-tick to about 29% in 1967 then a continuous slide to about 12% in 2008; about where it was (surprise) at the start of the previous Depression (we'll need a numbering system like we did with World Wars – let's call this one The Second Major Depression [should be "The Second Major U.S.A. Depression" because there were other depressions such as the one in France before the French Revolution and the one in Russia before the Russian Revolution]).

This was in today's paper (SL P-D 5-8-08, C2, Bloomberg News): *CONSUMER CREDIT RISES AT FASTEST PACE IN 4 MONTHS... The increase in consumer debt totaled $15.3-billion at an annual rate in March... Economists said consumers were being forced to use their credit cards during hard economic times when they are being battered by job losses, soaring gas prices and higher food costs. ... The Fed's measure of consumer borrowing, which does not include any debt secured by real estate such as mortgages or home equity loans, stood at a record $2.558-trillion in March. ... U.S. worker productivity unexpectedly accelerated in the first quarter and helped curb inflation as companies showed no loss of output with fewer employees. ...the total number of jobs lost this year [4 months] ... 260,000.*

This was in the same damn paper; the same damn day, the same dame page (Associated Press): WORST OF NATIONS CREDIT CRISES MAY BE OVER, [TREASURY SECRETARY] PAULSON SAYS. *...rising gas prices will blunt the effect of 130-million economic stimulus checks. ... "I think we're closer to the end of this"* than to the beginning. So deliberately stupid. He's not blindsided if he has no vision.

Compare this to the above: *"I see nothing in the present situation that is either menacing or warrants pessimism... I have every confidence that there will be a revival of activity in the spring and that during this coming year the country will make steady progress."*
- Andrew W. Mellon, U.S. Secretary of the Treasury December 31, 1929 An echo of stupidity. Blindsided by a hoard of locusts.

You can't BE Secretary of the Treasury if you have been known to ever have touched anyone making less than a million dollars per year.

The P/E ratio of stocks went from a local low of about nine (9) in 1980 to a high of about 43 in 2000 (43 is well past the stupid level [the highest in history] and indicates super desperation; Trader Mac's Truth Fountain Poets were busily inventing new "financial investment instruments" which we can liken to economic I.E.D.s, Improvised Explosive Devices; handle with care). Too much money chasing too little value. Good money put to bad use. (Demand for Carved Lava Boats Hits New High! Malarkey Bird Tail Feathers Soar! Hedge Fund Manager Earns 5-Billion-Dollars! Leona Helmsley's Dog Earns 12-Million! Fifth Largest Bank Rescued From Collapse! G.E.'s Earnings Unexpectedly Topple! Oops, Wachovia Too! Oops, Citigroup too! Lehman Bros., $3-billion loss, oh well, chump change. Major Companies Renege on Pension Benefits! One-Third of Homeowners Have Negative Equity! Banks to Homeowners: "Fuck You"! Homeowners To Banks: "Fuck You, Too; Twice"! Congress Changes Bankruptcy Law to Make Slaves of Four-flushers! Airlines Seek Government Bailout! Fed Chairman Declares, "B of A Too Big To Fail"! Pension Benefit Guarantee Corporation Turns Pockets Inside-Out! U.S. Officials Boycott Chinese Olympics to Protest Human Rights Violations! (U.S. has 525% more prisoners than China, proportionally!)

The Democrats had control of both houses of congress from 1959 to 1995 but, with the pro-slavery

Dixicrats (Is it cruel to call them "pro-slavery" when all they did was to fight every humanitarian effort that came in sight and that they were under the same sheet as the Ku Klux Klan passing out ax handles to all able-bodied white men?) making up about 30% of the Democratic Party; the pro-slavery chattel conservatives had actual control. With Nixon's Southern Strategy in 1968, the Dixicrats became Republicans and the Republicans (pro-slavery conservatives) took total control and completed driving the country into the dirt.

Finally, at long last, we had everything in place: the spread between the rich and the poor had never been greater; executives were paid hundreds-of-millions-of-dollars (sometimes Billions) for doing demonstrably negative jobs (unless destroying the company [and the country] is positive); a great victory was evident in the war against workers; unions were in a fetal-position on the mat, melting into the sub-basement; about a third of the working class had negative net worth; almost everyone that I knew had two or three jobs and terror in their eyes; no matter how hard nor how smart people worked, they fell behind; the banks and investment houses had put much of their money in Derivatives ("investment instruments" or "economic I.E.D.s, Improvised Explosive Devices"; "investment instruments" was the Very Smart, Very Modern, Up-To-Date name for Malarkey Bird tail feathers); we (the government) poured our last money that we borrowed from China into preventing the moneyed houses from facing failure, they could still keep taking hundreds-of-millions from us; we had segued nicely from one made-up-enemy to another-made-up-enemy without anyone noticing (Communism to Terrorism [We're at war! – Bush II's favorite sentence as he gives his gap-brained smile]); there was no fear that we would run out of dire enemies; because of National Security, everything that our hired idiots did was kept secret from us; we had soldiers stationed in something like 700 countries "US operates and/or controls between 700 and 800 military bases Worldwide" and some 400 domestic bases; "In total, there are 255,065 US military personnel deployed Worldwide." we had an active war that promised to utterly destroy us with a death-of-a-thousand-cuts lasting over a hundred years; we had sold our children and grandchildren into slavery to the Chinese; the "Stimulus Package allowed us to borrow money from the Chinese to buy products produced in China"; Bush II did a little tap dance at the doorway (like Nero fiddled while Rome burned); debutant balls were more lavish then ever; had we forgotten anything? I don't think so. Bush II's personal tax rate on "adjusted" gross income of almost a million-dollars was 24% (after free room, board, and transportation; if you include his perquisites [as you would if he were the son of the town drunk], his effective "adjusted" gross income was probably about twenty-million and his effective tax rate was closer to 1.2%).

That was just too much fun. Now for the full manure load. Numbers here I come; ready or not.

I would like to make a big wall chart where I could tie everything together, but I can't. We will just have to make do with these little, tiny pages. (Hey! Maybe I should include a big fold-out wall chart like the Playboy Bunny 'chart'! Naaaw. Darnn.)

Seventeen Presidents? That's doable. I, one time, drew (designed – it looked like it was going to rain) a whole factory building on letter-size-paper – in a day (and it went up without a flaw or a hitch, 'going up' took a little longer than a day). Analyzing 17 or 18 Presidents? No problem! Only about 100 years; I'm damn near that old. First the list:

26 Theodore Roosevelt, 1901-09 (Republican)

27 William Howard Taft, 1909-13 (Republican)

28 Woodrow Wilson, 1913-21 (Democrat)

29 Warren Gamaliel Harding, 1921-23 (Republican)

30 Calvin Coolidge, 1923-29 (Republican)

31 Herbert Clark Hoover, 1929-33 (Republican)

32 Franklin Delano Roosevelt, 1933-45 (Democrat)

33 Harry S Truman, 1945-53 (Democrat)

34 Dwight David Eisenhower, 1953-61 (Republican)

35 John Fitzgerald Kennedy, 1961-63 (Democrat)

36 Lyndon Baines Johnson, 1963-69 (Democrat)

37 Richard Milhous Nixon, 1969-74 (Republican)

38 Gerald Rudolph Ford Jr., 1974-77 (Republican)

39 James Earl Carter, 1977-81 (Democrat)

40 Ronald Wilson Reagan, 1981-89 (Republican)

41 George Herbert Walker Bush, 1989-1993 (Republican)

42 William Jefferson Clinton, 1993- 2001(Democrat)

43 George W. Bush, 2001- (Republican)

Let's look at what those Presidents did. No bullshit, just numbers; numbers that I am not making up; just reporting. Here're the Presidents again: Column letters are as follows: **N**, Number of President; **INT**, Initials of P.; **YE**, Year End of P's. term; **P**, Party of P. (R=Republican, D=Democrat); **TX**, Highest marginal income tax rate at end of P.'s term, % (all of the following are at the end-of-term, All from the Urban Institute); **UM**, non-farm union membership, % (figures kept by unions 'til '80, by census bureau after '83, some figures approx.); **GDP** (Gross Domestic Product) per capita (constant yr. 2000 dollars [adj. for inflation], thousands of dollars). **G** The Gini Index indicates the income disparity, 1 being perfect inequality (you got a million and I got nuthin) 0 being perfect equality (we each got fifty bucks) for more information about Gini you'll have to look it up, I pulled the numbers off a chart so they are all approximate. We multiply by 100 to get rid of the decimal. (I'm writing this 4-14-08 so I have to estimate GWB based on trend lines and reasonable expectations; the CIA Gini is at .45 in 2004. As I proof read this 7-16-8, it is clear that GWB's performance is far worse than it appeared just three months ago (now, final proof, 5-19-9; wow! What a disaster!) – but I am not going to rework this section. Now 5-4-9; we have a better idea of the major disaster was H.W.Bush and "supply-side- stupidity" Jack Kemp fortunately died to a wave of praise and no mention of his contribution to the Second Great Depression caused by "Supply-side-stupidity"; **1%** share of income by top 1% of earners. **PD**, Public Debt as % of GDP. **SCR**, Score as calculated below. **R**, Rating from the SCR**.**

N	**INT**	**YE**	**P**	**TX**	**UM**	**GDP**	**G**	**1%**	**PD**	**SCR**	**R**
26	TR	09	R	7.0	11.3		56		9		
27	WHT	13	R	7.0	11.5		58	18	8	0.80	11
28	WW	21	D	73.0	19.6	5.5	60	15	32	6.89	17
29	WGH	23	R	56.0	9.7	6.3	62	17	29	-11.55	1
30	CC	29	R	24.0	10.0	7.1	63	21	17	-3.65	3
31	HCH	33	R	63.0	13.0	5.1	42	16	30	2.75	16
32	FDR	45	D	94.0	30.0	13.5	38	11	70	1.45	13
33	HST	53	D	92.0	32.7	13.1	36	10	71	-0.30	7
34	DDE	61	R	91.0	28.0	14.1	37	9	54	1.88	15
35	JFK	63	D	91.0	27.0	15.0	36	9	50	1.45	14
36	LBJ	69	D	77.0	28.5	18.7	35	10	36	0.53	10
37	RMN	74	R	70.0	21.0	20.2	36	8	33	-1.40	5
38	GRF	77	R	70.0	18.0	21.6	37	7	32	0.47	9

39	JEC	81	D	69.1	15.5	23.1	37	8	33	-0.98	6
40	RWR	89	R	28.0	16.5	28.1	40	14	52	-7.14	2
41	GHB	93	R	39.6	15.0	29.0	42	14	65	0.00	8
42	WJC	01	D	38.6	13.0	34.7	43	17	57	1.09	12
43	GWB	08	R	35.0	11.0	34.6	49	22	70	-2.53	4

Wow! I don't know what to say! Four things: Objectivity; Accuracy, Relevance, and Significant Results.

Objectivity: Engineers are trained to go with the facts. Do we have prejudices? Of course: I say to the cabbie, "Take me to the airport." I am prejudiced (pre-judge) that he will do so. You can't survive one day without prejudices. We are all prejudiced; there is no soap or facial cream named "Pigeon"; "Dove" yes. No army has a "vulture" as its standard it always seems to be his cousin the "eagle". And, if you want to get ahead in any hierarchical organization (or even to survive), you must ignore the facts and give the boss what he wants. But in problem solving and analysis, we engineers strive to stick to objective reality. I have chosen the factors that I have analyzed here for three reasons: 1. They were available; someone else had already done the hard work of digging them out or calculating them and recording them; I only had to find them. I did NOT "massage" them or "tweak" them or "finagle" them or "factor" them, I did not just pick the pretty girls, they are as found except that the 'GINI Coefficient' and the 'Gross Domestic Product per capita' have been brought into the size range of the other numbers (falling between zero and one-hundred) so that they do not dominate or disappear. 2. These factors are real; they have a significant relationship to the economy of the United States and, thus, to the welfare of the citizens of the United States; either as causes or effects of prosperity or 'hard times'. 3. Since the bulk of the information that we get is passed through the eyes and ears of a legion of Professional Liars (Resident Scholars and the like whose job is to prove the agenda and prejudices of the organization that they pays them),

I had to look for myself. Clearly, some 'scholars' believe that inequity is a good thing and would disagree with my judgment of making an increase in inequity a 'negative' for scoring a President. E.g., I say that an increase in the Gini Coefficient is a 'negative' on the President's record. Likewise, I believe that increasing the public debt is a 'negative' reflection on the President's Administration. Some Learned Scholars propound the idea that public debt is good (Just see all the Professional Liars who adore Reagan; the biggest spender in history until George W. Bush went and spoiled his record).

Accuracy: All of these factors are taken from reputable sources. (I have chosen to not give sources in some cases. In olden days, before the internet, to be considered a serious student or researcher, I would have had to give reams of references and resources so that any other student could check my work. Today, anyone can check my work in minutes on the internet! The world has changed. Since I am running an active retail business; open ten hours per day, seven days per week; and can only work on this book an hour a day plus one half day per week, I would not have been able to write this book before the internet.) Feel free to check my work; I encourage you to do so. In several cases, I found two or more sources for the data which did not agree in every respect and I was forced to choose or average. In no cases were the discrepancies significant.

Relevance: I saw in a cartoon the other day a woman, upon seeing that the economy was crashing, bemoaned that she "would rather vote her conscience". The last time that people like her voted their 'conscience' they voted for a Presidential candidate who, upon winning, brought a major portion of the apocalypse to a large part of the world. What is her conscience telling her? Poverty for most is wonderful? I wonder if there is anything more important than the "economy" – the success or failure thereof – that has greater bearing on the happiness and well-being of the greatest number of people. I believe that the factors that I have chosen represent or summarize the cause and/or effect of the economy as well as any such group of data. Though each factor that I have chosen could be argued endlessly from ten sides as to significance, they are, as a group, pretty damn good. But one must settle on something sometime. (In engineering they used to say, "Shoot the designer and build the god damn machine". Most of us designers always wanted to make 'just one more' improvement.)

Significant Results: We are only dealing with the last hundred years approximately. After I had gathered all of the numbers, it dawned on me that I would have to analyze them and make some sense out of a spaghetti bowl of wet noodles. I needed a "score" for each President's Administration. It turned out to be a rather easy job. I simply took the numerical improvement for each factor during the period of that particular President's Administration divided by the number of years that he served and totaled the results. (Doing this in a spread sheet – Excel in this case – was quite simple.) The "scores" and "ratings" that resulted from this straightforward arithmetic supports and is supported by what we know to be true of history (reality). For example the grouping of the better Administrations is in the period after the Second World War which we know to be the "fat" years of American economics. The worst Administrations brought on "hard times" Notice that Warren Harding has both "War" and "Hard" in his name.

Some results:

The nine "worst" Presidents (the ones with the lowest 'scores") were, in order: 1. Warren G. Harding; 2. Ronald W. Reagan; 3. Calvin Coolidge; 4. George W. Bush; 5. Richard M. Nixon; 6. James E. Carter; 7. Harry S Truman; 8. George H. W. Bush; 9. Gerald R. Ford Jr.

The nine "best" Presidents: 17. Woodrow Wilson; 16. Herbert C. Hoover; 15. Dwight D. Eisenhower; 14. John F. Kennedy; 13. Franklin D. Roosevelt; 12. William J. Clinton; 11. William H. Taft; 10. Lyndon B. Johnson; 9. Gerald R. Ford Jr.

What did I start out to do here? Keep focus, Old Man! I wanted to find out; to determine; what economic policies "worked". Not which were 'good' or 'bad' but what worked (without starting from some ideological assumption so that I would prove the assumptions with which I started – I am not happy going in circles); which policies were successful from an engineering standpoint! I am going to define "success" as those policies which allow the economy to grow at a steady pace and bring the greatest happiness to the greatest number of Americans (well, U. S. citizens anyway, at this point I cannot worry about other Banana Republics). I did start with one assumption; I have lived about three quarters of a century; the best, most prosperous times were those times just after WW II. What were the puppeteers doing then that made the show work?

Just a note about what the columns are: the first four (**N, INT, YE, P)** identify and define the President and his Administration. The next three (**TX, UM, GDP)** are factors which, if they increase, create success. The next three (**G, 1%, PD)**, if they decrease, they indicate success. The next column (**SCR)** is the arithmetic "score" for that President and his policies. Last (**R)** is the "rating" of the President and his administration – number one (1) being the worst. Note too that **TX, UM, 1%,** and **PD** are controllable, directly or indirectly, by the President (and Congress) and that **GDP** and **G** are the direct result of those actions or policies.

So far I have done absolutely the minimal "touching" of the numbers; they are almost exactly as found in the wild. But the variation in one column (Maximum Differential Tax Rate) is almost seven-and-a-half times as large as that in another column (Gini Coefficient) so I stretched the shorter ones so that they would be as tall as the longer ones. But it is still just straight arithmetic; I don't believe that I am fondling here; I am just making all the numbers comparable; what I do to one, I do to all. With these new 'score's and 'rating's I am just going to list the presidents in order of worst to best.

29 Warren G. Harding, 1921-23	-33.45
40 Ronald W. Reagan, 1981-89	-11.68
43 George W. Bush, 2001-09	-11.07
30 Calvin Coolidge, 1923-29	-6.34
41 George H. W. Bush, 1989-93	-4.01
37 Richard M. Nixon, 1969-74	-3.84
39 James E. Carter, 1977-81	-3.38
38 Gerald R. Ford Jr., 1974-77	-1.18
27 William H. Taft, 1909-13	-1.01
42 William J. Clinton, 1993-01	-0.20
26 Theodore Roosevelt, 1901-09	0.00
34 Dwight D. Eisenhower, 1953-61	1.60
33 Harry S. Truman, 1945-53	1.91
36 Lyndon B. Johnson, 1963-69	3.25
35 John F. Kennedy, 1961-63	3.70
32 Franklin D. Roosevelt, 1933-45	8.92
28 Woodrow Wilson, 1913-21	9.40
31 Herbert C. Hoover, 1929-33	30.20

There's the famous story of Hoover asking Andrew Mellon for a nickel to call a friend and Mellon says, "Here's a dime. Call them both." The pop-history umpire gives Hoover a really, really, really bad call; that was no 'strike' that was a 'homerun'. He comes into office and there is already a tower of people with no money and standing on top of them are a few guys with hundreds-of-$Millions and the tower is starting to fall; and it does fall shortly (less than nine months) after he takes the oath. If you look at the numbers, he is doing almost everything that he can to rebuild the tower on a solid base; but he cannot quickly undue the ruinous iniquities of his immediate predecessors, Warren G. Harding, Calvin Coolidge, and, indeed, especially Andrew Mellon. Poor Herbie; the Pop-Pop-History has "thrown him under the bus". He tries to stop the avalanches but he is inundated putting up snow-fences. Pop-Pop-History has snowed him under.

With Wilson, we are coming out of the Great War and the economy is returning to 'normal'. He does things right to get the economy back on a strong peace-time footing.

F.D.R benefits from some of the things that Hoover has already done. And he does continue along the path of economic enlightenment.

The next four in rank, J.F.K., L.B.J., H.S.T., and D.D.E (in historical order H.S.T., D.D.E., J.F.K., L.B.J.), hold pretty much to the path following from F.D.R. and we have a great period of steady growth and prosperity from say 1945 to 1969 (24 years with some little bumps in 1953, 1957, and 1973) but, if you look at charts of the various factors, we are slowly but steadily heading in the wrong direction to the point where we are today (4-24-08) with a very sick economy and millions of Americans in financial trouble and vast inequality with the money-tower top-heavy and teetering. (To show that I am letting the numbers speak [it is not me speaking] I can let you in on a little secret: I never liked J. F. Kennedy any better than R. W. Reagan but I am not trying to knead him out of his "fourth best" position."

Coleridge and Reagan are both in danger of being canonized by pro-slavery groups. Reagan already has the nimbus glow; they may be moving Coleridge's remains to St. Peter's Square and selling his bone shards as miracle-creating-relics. Twenty years or so ago, I went through the Reagan Library with a couple of my granddaughters (I think that they called it a library even though he was not a reader [except astrological charts]; the building is located in California, I believe in Semi or Seamy Valley). He was credited with everything good in history and he put up an heroic fight against the Tsars and Mullahs or something like that, anyway he single-handedly defeated all of the evil forces in the world; Ronnie always confused his acting roles with real life and, apparently, his pro-slavery biographers are also confused. Oh yes, in case you hadn't noticed, he gave us great prosperity, a Reich that would last a thousand years; except, of course, for the Death March to get there.

So what do we know for sure? Slavery is not a good economic system. Not because it is good or bad (all of the moneyed religions have almost always supported it) but because, from an engineering standpoint, it doesn't work. We know for sure that there are mighty forces moving us in that direction (toward a slave economy) in the hands of people who will 'prove' that it is far, far better than fairness and equality. They no doubt know that they are wrong and don't give a damn – the pay is good.

Here's a little aside: Imagine that I'm a college professor (you can do it, you can do it; close your eyes); in my lecture class I have exactly 100 students. Naturally, this lecture hall has tiered seating like the Hollywood Bowl. My wife bakes a cherry pie; her cherry pies are so good that they can make your knees buckle. I cut the pie into three pieces. I'm not a great cutter so the pieces are almost but not exactly even. I decide to distribute the three pieces to my 100 students. I bring my wife's pie to class in 2004. There is one very pretty girl who sits on the aisle to my left slightly above eye level. She never wears panties; she does wear short dresses and no bra (and her blouse always seems to become unbuttoned); she squiggles around in her seat a lot and, well, I am looking at her pussy much more than half the time and her boobs frequently – and they are nicely, nicely boobs. I call her up first and give her the second largest "third". There are nine other girls whose pussies I have seen at least a dozen times. I call them up next; I give them the largest "third" to split among the nine of them. The other

90 students have not been nearly so co-operative; they don't deserve much. I leave the last smallest "third" for them, the ninety, to divvy up. That is how the quantities of wealth in this country are distributed in 2004, but the reasoning is not nearly so sensible and logical nor the merits so clear and compelling. Yes, it was worse in '29; then I would have had a thousand students and given one of them about one and a quarter pieces.

Oh, but that wealth (the wealth considered in the previous paragraph) includes homes and autos. If we just include FINANCIAL wealth (wealth that earns an income) then things are more fair (more fair if you listened to the Guppies in the Think Tanks). Then the pretty girl who winks at me with her pussy gets almost half of the pie; the next nine who have shown vagina respect get almost all of the other half. The next ninety kids (the kids who either don't have or don't show me their cunts) get the pits. Fair is fair after all.

Ooops! Damn! I almost forgot about our friends on the Life and Sex Island! Remember them? I wonder what is happening there. Let's look.

Oh, that's right: The bottom fell out of the boat market. Poor Mike was left owing Trader Mac dozens of Rocks of multi-colors. Mike's yard was filled with boats that no one could afford. He couldn't give them away for even one Red Rock; no one had any Rocks to spare. Trader Mac had all of Mike's Rocks and all of the Rocks that Mike would earn for many years. The Malarkey Bird tail feathers became nearly worthless too. Mike went back to fishing (even though he had a problem with selling his fish because everyone used all their Rocks to buy water, the free spring water); at least he could eat the fish. He also loaned one or two boats to people who would fish; in return he got a small part of their catch.

Gosh! Isn't that what happened to the Stock Market in '29? Yes it is. Inequality was putting too much money in the wrong hands, desperately searching for value where value is already stretched to transparency and, as a result, removing money from the hands that earned it.

Ooooh! Wow! That's almost like our Savings and Loan debacle under Ronnie Reagan; remember the Gipper "get the government off our back; get rid of regulations"; cost us (taxpayers, you and me) several billion dollars. (If you get rid of regulations – which I am for – you should make stealing a crime even if it – the stealing – is done by the rich! But that is not the American Way.)

Oh! And it also smells of the Dot Com Bubble under Clinton-Bush II. Too much good money in the wrong hands chasing bad money in the same wrong hands, desperate to find an investment for excess wrongfully gained funds (earned by selling free spring water).

Holy Cow! There again is our housing bubble under "the Decider". One third of the pie going to one-percent of the people and one third going to ninety-percent of the people. It can't work, Folks. It ain't agonna never ever work. Not fur long, it ain't agonna. Don't listen to the Professional Liars at The Heritage Foundation, the Lugwig von Mises Institute, The American Enterprise Institute, The Hudson Institute, etc. We're forever blowing bubbles; pretty bubbles in the air. And, in 2007 – 8, we are blowing an oil bubble (the most colorful), who cares if it destroys the economy; certainly not the rich who can only benefit from greater poverty and misery.

Aren't those bubbles colorful? The '29 Stock Market Bubble, the Savings and Loan bubble, the Dot Com bubble, the Housing Bubble, the current Stock Market Bubble, and the Oil Bubble. All different; all the same. They are really boils on the body economic caused by too much money in the hands of too few chasing more greed with too little value. We know how to prevent them but we won't; it is un-American! It is Radical-Robin-Hood-Socialism!

Well, on the Life and Sex Island things just kept getting worse. Soon, no one except Trader Mac had any

Rocks to speak of. Soon, almost no one could even buy water. (Joe's Kid had figured out a way of shaking the leaves in the morning to get a few drops of water, but it consumed a lota, lota time.) Since few were buying water and almost no one had any rocks, Trader Mac didn't need as many guards and marketers nor even so many Truth Poets; so, naturally, he let them go (nice way of saying he fired them). Besides, Trader Mac had people "working-off" their debts so that he got his labor for "free" (the poor nuts had to keep borrowing money to live on so, darn, they may never get over being "free" – sort of like the workers at the Pullman Palace Car Company; or half the people in 2009). Potato diggers could not sell their potatoes (except a few to Trader Mac who paid what ever he wanted because everyone was so desperate for Rocks they took whatever he offered). Still, according to the few Truth Poets who remained working, people weren't so bad off, they weren't starving although their diets were drastically restricted because the mahi mahi fishers were only eating mahi mahi and the potato diggers were only eating potatoes. And they managed to squeeze enough liquid from their foods to survive the man-made drought. Well, let's leave it there for now.

You've heard of the Roaring Twenties; well, hold still, they are a close kin to the Booming Nineties (and Early Aughts).

First, the Republicans were in power both times. Don't hang up on me, Please! I'm not saying one party is good and another is bad (remember, damnit, I don't do good or bad). It's the people who wear the feathers that make the difference. And the people who wear the head-dresses are not branded. They can change costume at the first sign of Trader Mac paying more. As Lincoln said, "These two guys fought so long and hard that they ended up in each others' clothes." (Please don't look up that quote; I'm doing it from memory.)

Yet, the Party of Lincoln was not the party of the '20s or of the '90s. But the party of the '20s was the party of the '90s.

In the twenties and in the nineties (and early aughts):

Business had won the battle. Unions and workers were defeated absolutely. Business had total control of the boardroom, the office, the factory floor, the media, public monolog, congress, the Presidency, and the Supreme Court with no input or interference from workers, blue or white collar or from the 'people' (who the hell ever they think they are). And there were and are grand sports teams, clever entertainers, and powerful moneyed religions to keep the public's mind off what was going on.

This is an aside: in about the year 1970, while I was working for them, du Pont decided to survey their employees concerning management-worker communications. Yes, I was one of the 'lucky' ones of the ten-percent who received a questioneer. The cover-letter promised me that my response was absolutely confidential; there was no way that they could tell who answered and who did not. I read the questioneer carefully. It was about communications; it was **not** about dialogue. Every question bored into how upper-management could better inform and influence the low and stupid workers; 'Get Their Message Out'. There was no sign that they had any interest whatsoever in anything that we poor slobs had to say or what we thought. I was so disgusted that I just threw the questioneer away, oh, what an egomaniac I was. I soon received a follow-up letter: why had I not returned the questioneer? So much for their promise of confidentiality! They sent me a new questioneer in case I had lost the old one. I did fill it in and out but I wrote across the top of it that they had to be smart before they could convince us that they were smart. Bad! Bad attitude. That is the worst thing you can have in a hierarchical organization. Bad attitude. It was downhill from thereon. ("You have no idea how fucking miserable we can make you! Do you? You dumb little shit.")

Back to the twenties and the nineties (and early aughts).

The Roaring Twenties were roaring only for the upper classes.

The Booming Nineties were booming only for the upper classes.

At the end of the nineties, about 29% under the age of 35 had a negative net worth; almost 37% of renters also had a negative net worth.

(It would soon get worse, anon about a third of home"owners" would have a negative net worth.)

From about 1923 to 1929, corporate profits increased by about 62%. This was slipped into the pockets of the upper classes. Almost two-thirds of families were below the poverty level. Lending to consumers for consumption grew to be one of the ten largest businesses in this country; from virtually non-existent in '20 to $3-billion in '29. In the '90's (and early aughts), credit cards were a major, major industry (and got meaner and crookeder by the minute with the chattel congress's help) (consumer debt is now about $3-trillion [a thousand times worse than '29 {not counting inflation}]) (Corporate debt is about $4.5-trillion) (Fannie Mae and Freddie Mac combined have about $5 trillion in debt outstanding.) (Federal debt is about $6.6-trillion; that's you and me, Friend). (That's the highest of any debt in the known universe for all eternity.) (I hope you are ready for a major fall; I am not!) (At least the Professional Liars have shut-up for a minute about putting all of Social Security into the Stock Market! They hid their trumpets and pied pipes.)

Like on the Life and Sex Island, worker earnings fell below minimum needs. No matter how hard and/or how smart a family worked and saved, they could not meet essential needs. All workers lived in terror of being "laid off" while the rich had more money than they knew what to do with. The Truth Poets were telling everyone that the rich earned a million-times what the poor earned because they worked harder and were smarter. At the beginning of the Depression, almost half of all farmers did not own the land they farmed. Farmers and workers borrowed money to buy essentials. Tens-of-billions-of-dollars of new stock was issued and sold. Four-fifths of Americans had no savings.

In '29, Henry Ford pocketed $14-million (that he reported) when Joe Average was earning $750. Here's a two inch article from today's Post-Dispatch (wire services 4-26-08): "GENERAL MOTORS; Wagoner's pay jumps; General Motors Corp. raised Chief Executive Rick Wagoner's total compensation for last year by 41 percent to $14.4-million as the largest U.S. automaker reported a record loss." That $14.4-million is 1082.7 times as much as a Missouri minimum-wage-worker would earn in a good year, $13,300. Of course, if a minimum-wage worker screwed up everything as Mr. Wagoner did, he would be fired the first day on the job not be given a bonus. And Mr. Wagoner almost certainly has a far greater income from other sources.

Should I shut up now? Did you ever go in to buy something and the salesman starts giving you his pitch, interesting for a minute, then you feel like saying shut up already and let me buy? And, if he doesn't shut up, you might actually walk across the street and buy? Because this line of thought, in this chapter, was mostly obvious to me before I started (although I have learned a great deal) and I am not looking you in the eye, I can not tell if you are nodding in agreement, nodding to keep me going, nodding off, or shaking in anger.

I've got a lot more data to back up this line of argument but, perhaps, if you are still in doubt, you can find it for yourself on the internet. This stuff (to find information on the internet) is just so wonderful these days (I remember weeks of library research). It is no huge difficulty for you to do a little research if you are still interested.

Before I began to write this chapter I thought that this line of thought was original with me. It is not. I don't know who the original thinker was. But I have now read other's who think similarly. But I hope my mode of expression is original.

And the tiresome repetition of our situation in the United States is not original or unique. The economic struggle of the rich trying to take everything and reduce everyone else to slavery or thralldom is hardly new (creating the periodic economic collapses). The tension created by the economic struggle played a major if not starring role in the French and Russian Revolutions, it was certainly a factor in the American Revolution; it was significant in the fall of the Roman Empire, and in the collapse of the English, Spanish, Dutch, Mongolian, and French Empires. Our question is: "Do we want to continue doing the same idiotic 'things' and finding the same horrifying results (or expecting some new results from the same inputs and thus to be considered, by Einstein's rule, to be crazy) or do we want to modify our economic behavior to the benefit of the vast majority of our population and, actually, to the benefit of everyone.

What do we know for sure? What could we do or can we do to fix the problem (I hope that I have convinced you that there is a problem).

Let us observe what our little Life and Sex Islanders do:

The problem (inequality leading to massive economic – and thereby governmental – failures) has been solved many times in several different ways. Let us begin with the more ancient and progress to the newer and then into the future.

The First Solution: Our little Life and Sex Island has neither a potent guillotine nor poison or a pistol as the French and the Russians did to 'fix' their problems but (in this version) what they did was to form a committee among the outsiders – those not in communion with Trader Mac – to select a time and place to "ides of March them". Things had been calm for a week or two and Trader Mac and his guards had become careless. They slept. The "committee" "stormed the Bastille" that is they pounced on Trader Mac and the insiders as they slept and tied them up. There was no need for a trial; everyone knew who was at fault for the collective misery of the times. The only question then to be settled – without a guillotine, poison, or pistol – was how to eliminate the problem permanently. They did have spears and stones but they decided on a more merciful method. (It was actually less merciful but since "they could leave it to nature or the Gods" they temporarily fooled themselves into thinking that their souls could claim innocence.)

The committee placed the tied-up men in rush boats – one each day – and towed them to the leeward side of the island where the waves were moving away from the island and the rush boats would ride the waves to distant sea. Everyone knew from experience that, within ten or twenty sunrises, the rush boats would disintegrate and the men would become seafood. By releasing the condemned men one per day, it was made highly unlikely that they could regroup and return. In fact none of the men were ever heard from again. Only I survived to be washed up on distant shores and write this book. (I was almost drowned but washed up exhausted on the beach in Malibu where I was discovered and nursed back to health by a bevy of starlets who took me in and made me pay them back with sex. Maybe. You can't be sure.)

But, every time the wind whispered though the palm trees or the volcano rumbled, the islanders lay awake staring at the stars and thought of what they had done.

I have no record how "the solution" evolved the future on the Life and Sex Island. Did the people go back to bartering? Did the excess Rocks cause dreadful inflation? Did they go back to using just the Red Rocks? How were the Rocks distributed? Did they next have a Washington, or a Lenin, or a Napoleon; or did they go back to no-one-in-charge? It is not written. What did they deserve? And, did what they deserve have any play on what they got? The results of this method of solution are unpredictable and the method is not recommended (though, sometimes, it is the only non-choice; how many methods are there to get rid of a dictator (or a dictating oligarchy)?).

Consider The Second Solution: Now I have to back track. This solution is to emulate the 'solution' to panics in the United States before the Great Depression. Consider, before and during those earlier panics, there was little or no consumer credit; only real estate loans (with massive down payments). So the "panics" were not really depressions or, even, recessions. They primarily involved bank (sudden) closures due to fraud, embezzlement, or mismanagement (in a word "greed"). The common people were usually involved only to the extent that they had money in savings accounts (savings accounts were not government insured). The 'Hard Times' would simply be continuous though they might waver a little. There was never a cure until 'things' got so bad as to be unbearable and there would be an upheaval of one sort or another.

So, with the Second Solution on our little Life and Sex Island, things (the economy) had not gotten so far out of hand. Mike, or anyone else, had not speculated in carved lava boats because they could not have borrowed the Rocks to do so, nor had anyone hoarded the Malarkey Bird tail feathers. None of the Islanders had borrowed Rocks to purchase necessities. So, though the breaking point would have come much sooner, it would not have dug so deep or been as severe. There would be hard times. People would go mad from drinking sea water. The people who were spearing the fish would never have enough to eat because they had to "share" with Trader Mac's minions. In short, nothing would change unless Trader Mac had an epiphany, moral insight, or death. Other than death, nothing would change Trader Mac (nothing ever changed Tsars, Princes, Kings, Popes, Mullahs, Despots, Rockefellers, Mellons, Carnegies, Gateses, Buffetts or anyone else like them. They, like the U.S. of A. rich, just kept getting worse and worse, more and more decadent until there is a final reckoning; revolution or surrender to an outside power.). So the Second Solution is no solution; just continuous hard times for years, decades, centuries, and millennia; the rich and super rich taking, taking, and taking.

Consider The Third Solution: Moral Outrage Resulting in Some Social Justice. On our Life and Sex Island, things (the economy) had degenerated to such a catastrophe that it became apparent to a few that either they would all perish or 'something' had to be done. Certainly Trader Mac wasn't going to do anything. Why should he. Life is good. He has as many servants and obsequious 'friends' as he desires. The girls are so desperate just to survive that they will do 'anything' for a trinket which is absolutely meaningless to Trader Mac but is extremely valuable to someone whose family is starving. Many girls will "be throwing themselves" at him; he can simply take his pick – everyday. It would not even occur to Trader Mac that anything is wrong. Dozens of Truth Fountain Poets and Poet Wannabes will sing his praises and extol his wisdom. The only change that Trader Mac would consider would be more and yet more inequality.

The Third Solution is the actual solution that was taken in the United States during the Depression. It was not very effective in ending the Depression but was effective in preventing another for a while until it was slowly undermined.

So the people who understood that 'something' had to be done formed a committee. The committee became such a majority that it was able to cow Trader Mac and his Truth Fountain Poets. Trader Mac huffed and he puffed and he bellowed and howled but in the end he had to agree to the changes. Trader Mac and all of the Truth Fountain Poets had to pay more for their food. Trader Mac also had to pay for training, all of the people who desired to learn, how to more efficiently produce food. Trader Mac had to pay anyone who was too sick or too old to work. Trader Mac also had to lower the price of his water, the free spring water. It was further agreed that, when Trader Mac died, his Rocks would be equally divided among all the people.

So the symptoms of the inequality problem were somewhat relieved. People stopped going mad from drinking sea water. People, most of them, didn't go to bed quite so hungry. People no longer died when they were too sick to work. They didn't die of starvation in their old age. So, thus, the immediate difficulty was ameliorated.

But Trader Mac and the Truth Fountain Poets were furious. The Truth Fountain poets hammered at this attack on the free market. They whittled at the "death tax". They expounded the merits of the "fair tax", the "flat tax" where everyone would pay the same as Trader Mac, "it's only fair" (but Trader Mac could deduct all of his "expenses" of which the producers had none). They wept that the "free market" was corrupted by forcing Trader Mac and the Truth Fountain Poets to pay the same as everyone else for their food. They said that soon, if the "free market" was not reestablished, the sky would fall and they would all be crushed. They rebranded the committee "the Flatheads" (they didn't have a word for "Socialist").

So slowly, ever so slowly, Trader Mac and the Truth Fountain poets got the old system back and everything went to hell again. The explanation, according to the Truth Fountain Poets was that they hadn't gone far enough fast enough. But 'things" (the economy) did go to hell again all too soon and all too predictably.

Consider the Fourth Solution: 2008. Again, the people formed a committee. This time there were not as many committee members who understood the problem. But, the committee that was went to Trader Mac and begged for a pittance. He gave everyone one Red Rock and told them to get lost. Everyone was so grateful, they took their one Red Rock and for a few sunrises things were better. No attempt was made to 'fix the problem'. Even better, no attempt was made to discuss the 'the problem' or even to figure out what the problem was (goodness, we might upset one of the big donors). And 'things' (the economy) went right back to where they were. "Equal opportunity not equal results!"

Consider the Fifth Solution: The Future. Joe's Kid, remember Joe's Kid, the mathematical genius who started this whole thing back when? Well Joe's Kid has been dispassionately observing the results of the introduction of his Rocks as a medium of exchange. Sometimes he laughs; sometimes he cries. Very seldom is he favorably impressed. He views the whole Rock mess as a reflection of the human condition. His Rocks – he tries to convince himself – HIS Rocks did not cause all of the chronic problems; humans caused all of the problems; no, no, no, not his Rocks. It started so well, the use of his Rocks, the utility of his Rocks; what went wrong? This wasn't how he planned it. Well, he thought, as long as people were just using the Rocks as a substitute for the actual thing that they were exchanging, everything went well; it was when the Rocks were imbued with other properties and became a 'thing' in themselves, the Rocks became a "them", a "THEM" that people began to love or respect – "them" being the Rocks, just the damn Rocks – that Rocks became more important than human relations.

Damn, he thought, ("damn" he thought, not "god damn" because, although Joe's Kid had been foolish enough to invent Rocks, he had not been so foolish as to invent god and really cause problems, money, he did not know, was not the root of ALL evil); so damn, he thought, if it wasn't for Rocks, would Trader Mac have started to sell free spring water? He could not have collected mahi mahi? NO! Mahi mahi are only good for a day; two at most (Joe's Kid himself had made a little bamboo pen at the edge of the sea where he could keep mahi mahi for a few days but that is neither here nor there.) Trader Mac might have collected potatoes or coconuts or something like that but think how foolish he, Trader Mac, would look with a pile of potatoes that would rot before he could use them up. No, Joe's Kid reasoned to himself, Trader Mac probably would never have grabbed the free spring if he, Joe's Kid, hadn't invented Rocks. The same with using another person's time (labor): You could use a person to help you move some stones or something but you would have to pay him in potatoes or something before Rocks were invented. You couldn't store up something as ephemeral as "labor".

But Joe's Kid, having invented Rocks, was not willing to blame Rocks, his invention, for all of the troubles which had invaded the Life and Sex Island. No, no, it wasn't the Rocks themselves, which after all, had no feelings or intelligence, which caused the problem. No, Joe's Kid reasoned it was somehow the way that they were being used that caused the problems. No, people were starving and going mad from drinking sea water but how on earth could you blame Rocks, mere stones, which, after all, had always been there doing no harm? What would happen, he thought, if you limited Rocks to their original, intended use? Just a medium of exchange. Go back to just using Red Rocks so that there would be only enough to facilitate commerce but not so many that huge numbers of Rocks could be stored for future use.

Don't let anyone get too far ahead of anyone else collecting and storing Rocks.

Joe's Kid was careful not to mention it; but, what the hell, he was as smart as anyone else on the Life and Sex Island, he worked as hard as anyone else, he worked as smart as anyone else (as his bamboo pen for storing mahi mahi demonstrated). Why, he thought, should someone who was no "better" than he in any way, be able to accumulate so damn many Rocks?

The truth is that Joe's Kid didn't have to work as hard as anyone else; he knew how to fish better, he could spot potato patches better than others, he knew how to use leverage to dig potatoes, he could knock coconuts down with a stick while others were still climbing the coconut palms, and he knew how to use leverage to move large stones. But those were natural advantages that he was lucky enough to have. He didn't have to stoop to selling free spring water to have advantages over others. No, he thought, "unnatural" advantages had to be neutralized. Joe's Kid decided that it wasn't his damn Rocks that were causing the problem; it was cheating. Just plain cheating. (He didn't have a word for "cheating"; he said "doing that which was not natural"; it sort of got the idea but not quite.

After Joe's Kid had thought about it for many sunrises, he had an epiphany, it was a paradigm shift, it was a sea change in his thoughts; it was an ocean of revelation. It startled him to suddenly realize that the whole structure, the whole edifice, the whole damn mountain of lies was supported entirely by cheating, that which was not natural. None of the Truth Fountain Poets was smarter than him; none worked harder; none produced more; none thought more; none was better looking; none could run faster; he could swim faster and further; and, in fact, none could write better poetry! Joe's Kid had had many chats with Trader Mac; Trader Mac was a simpleton. He, Joe's Kid, hadn't noticed the incongruity because of the Truth Fountain Poets constant haranguing lies about how Trader Mac was a damn genius (and that mahi mahi shit about his penius). It was all lies and cheating. Selling free spring water! Selling free spring water? All of Trader Mac's advantages; all of the huge inequality; all of the misery that that had caused;

all of the madness; all of the deaths; was caused by lies and cheating. It suddenly amazed him that he could have been so busy fishing and gathering that he let the constant buzz of the Truth Fountain Poets' lies enter his head uncritically. Wow! Mahi mahi shit.

But it was one thing to peel the skin back on a fish and find it was full of worms and quite another to make the fish well.

Joe's Kid knew several things: he would need to form a committee; a committee of a large majority of the Life and Sex Islanders; he would have to do it in absolute secrecy because if any of the Truth Fountain Poets (or any of Trader Mac's intimate companions) found out about it, he, Joe's Kid would be ostracized, or far, far worse. But now that he was absolutely certain of the cause and cure, he had to chance it and he had to begin. He knew speed was of essence because the longer he took, the more likely he was to be found out.

Joe's Kid's quest went well. Early one dawn, the committee held court and forced Trader Mac and all of his intimates and co-conspirators to attend. Oh! They, Mac's crew, were not quiet. They howled. They quoted every ancient hoary hair horror story (twisted to turn their tale and to tar Joe's Kid's tail). But the committee prevailed.

The new rules of the life and sex game on the Life and Sex Island were to be simple. 1. Trader Mac continued to own the water from the free spring. 2. Trader Mac could charge anything that he wanted for the free spring water. 3. Whenever anyone's pile of rocks became five times more than the smallest pile of rocks, the owner of the largest pile had to distribute from his pile until it was no more than five times larger than the smallest pile.

Things (the economy) never again became unbalance and collapsed. Never again. How could they? How could it? It was physically and economically impossible.

Time is a wonderful thing. I don't know if this is part of the Relativity that Professor Albert talked about or not. "Never" maybe becomes maybe.

Things never became unbalanced as long as things didn't change back. But, as we know, change happens. The Truth Fountain Poets could observe, like everyone else, that the new system didn't let things (the economy) become unbalanced, top-heavy and tip over. But the Truth Fountain Poets could observe but chose not to observe. They could but they didn't! As Yogi might have said, it is amazing what you can see if you look; but it is more interesting that you don't have to see if you don't want to. They did not observe or did not see, or did not care. Who knows? Maybe they just didn't like working like everyone else.

But day and night they attacked equality. It was unfair. It was inhuman. It was sure to cause some major problem if allowed to continue. "Equal opportunity, not equal results!", they shouted. It was unjust. Who was going to create the jobs if Trader Mac couldn't accumulate piles of Rocks? Who was going to make investments in the future? Would they all just stagnate? Why should Trader Mac be deprived of his intellectual property? Why shouldn't they maximize the return on the free spring water? Look at all the jobs that were created. If Trader Mac had money; he could spend and everyone would benefit. "Trickle down" they called it.

Little by little, like pigeons pooping on a figure of Justice or Knowledge, they obscured reality and created doubts. Here a little doubt, there a little doubt, soon, everywhere a little doubt. Yes, the Life and Sex Islanders were like us in that they would rather believe a good story (or even a bad story) rather than believe their eyes, ears, and fingers. Yup! The Truth Fountain Poets made converts. Here a convert, there a convert, soon, everywhere a convert.

Yes, then Joe's Kid, Mac's own brother, had a little accident. He fell off something or something fell on him, or – well, no one actually saw it. Just a little unfortunate accident; everyone grieved and sang his praises, The Truth Fountain Poets composed an elegy; it was wonderful. Joe's Kid was out of the way like Paul Wellstone and Mel Carnahan.

Little by little but amazingly quickly, they went back to the old system. Back to Trader Mac having ten times as much, then twenty, then a hundred, then a thousand. Back to people going mad drinking sea water. Back to people starving. Back to the old system. Back to that old time religion. The Truth Fountain Poets were very happy and had themselves a big ball. They sang of the good times that were now upon them. Had they had religion it is a near certainty that they would have canonized Good Ole Trader Mac; the Wonderful, the Holy, the Wise, the Saintly, the Man for all Seasons even when they only had one. Back to amazing unearned inequality.

It's the American Way.

We will never accept an obvious answer to an obvious problem; fairness works; equality works; we ain't agonna do it if'n it kills us. (Which it will.)

But there are good reasons for not solving an obvious problem with an obvious solution; here are a few; pick your favorite:

It's a communist plot.
It's a conservative plot.
It's an elitist plot.
It's a fascist plot.
It's a Catholic plot.
It's a Jewish plot.
It's a Muslim plot.
It's a Mormon plot.
It's a liberal plot.
It's an anarchist plot.
It's an Islamo-fascist plot.
It's a terrorist plot.
It's a Democratic plot.
It's a Republican plot.
It's an Independent plot.
It's a creeping Socialism plot.
It's a leaning left plot.
It's a hob-nail-booted rightist plot.
It's a Buddhist plot.

Do Buddhist's plot?

You must have heard one of those before if you listen at all? Two more plots and I'd have enough plots to bury the all the Truth Fountain Poets!

Or is that 'plats'? No 'plat' is what a moose turd says when it hits the ground; 'plot' is what the bull stuff says when it alights.

That's the end of the chapter but here's a little throw away:

So after the Savings and Loan Crisis when the Feds bailed out the banks, the Gov assured us that this could never happen again. Which brings us to the Sub-prime Mortgage Crisis.

"They" fixed it so that the banks would never have a problem again. They, the bank, can give you any deal (contract) and sell you (your contract) to someone else:

It's a slick deal. It beats old fashioned slavery; they have no responsibility for your welfare; they don't have to feed you or provide housing. Like this:

Hello, Mr. Banker. Thanks for meeting with us. We received a notification that our loan is up for renewal. Um, can we just refinance at the same rate. Yeah, I know that there is a balloon payment due but we don't have $200,000.00 in our account just now. Can we just refinance? You hold the mortgage. You don't hold the mortgage? You sold it for a hefty profit to a loan servicer in Kastelorrizon? Where is that? You don't know! If you did, it would be classified? You made $25,000 on my loan within five minutes after I left your office? So I'm not dealing with you on the loan? You're not involved? It is not your concern? Yes, I suppose that they have serviced the loan to your satisfaction. I mean, I could never reach them when they screwed up, but I suppose... English, you know, it's a difficult language.

But, yes, as you say we would like to put that all behind us. Yes, no sense beating a dead horse. Do you do loans anymore? Oh, you heard that we have gone elsewhere, but it is against the Bankers' Code of Ethics to prey on another banker's customer. Well, yes, they did refuse to talk to us. That's according to your code? I didn't know that bankers had a code of ethics. Oh! It's not a code of ethics; it's a banker's code. That's different.

Well, can we get a new loan? Yes, from you. We've paid $100,000.00 on this loan and paid off $10,000.00; we've never been late. You will? Great! Yes, I appreciate that interest rates have gone up. Sure, there'll be a balloon payment in five years. Yes, I understand that I can choose to be certainly destroyed today or probably destroyed five years from now. No, it isn't that difficult to choose. You need a new real estate appraisal? Can't you use the old one? If anything, the value has gone up. We've done a lot of upgrading. Oh! We shouldn't have upgraded? It's not in the contract? Not without written permission. O.K. But, you will call for an appraisal and, if that holds up, you will give us a new loan? The appraisal is 4,000 bucks up front. It's our responsibility, our cost? But we don't need the appraisal, you do. No, I'm not trying to be a smart ass. O.K. we'll give you a check. You have to wait two weeks for the check to clear? But it's drawn on your bank; can't you just check your computer to see that the check is covered? No. So, and we just need to sign this agreement? If we read it and there is something that we don't like, can we change it? No! But we should read it and sign it anyway. O.K. $4,000.00 for the appraisal. $2,000.00 title search. $2,000.00 title insurance. $2,500.00 legal fees. $500.00 copying costs. $300.00 editing fees. $500.00 for lunch. What's the $500.00 for lunch? You're going to eat at our restaurant? Terrific! But our lunches only run about $10.00. Oh, I see, the Appraiser, the Lawyer, the Bank President, the President's Secretary, your Secretary, your girlfriend, and You. Oh, and the $10.00 tip.

Hi, Mr. Banker. Thanks for coming to our restaurant to eat. And thanks for the loan. Our server will take care of you.

Yes, I'm back; your server said you wanted to talk to me. What! It's been an hour and you haven't received your food? Oh, yes; we sold your order to a processor in Yakutsk for a 50% profit. I'm sure that they will take care of you to my satisfaction.

Life and sex: it's fun. Try it sometime.

Chapter 6-1/2

You're Almost Done

O.K. A non-fairy tale this time. Now we are at June 3, 2009; just before we go to press. I'm too rough on you humans so far. You are not as bad as I say in my cynical way. At least, maybe some of you. Some of you do help others for no apparent gain. There is altruism. It is too easy to focus on selfishness as an explanation of Man's behavior (Man's inhumanity to man.) Yes, it is there. But so is kindness. I recall reading The Outline of History by H.G. Wells wherein he spends many pages, if not chapters, explicating the horrors that religion has brought about. Then, it is as though he catches himself (like he fears being criticized for anti-religion sentiments) and spends a few paragraphs saying, ya but; ya but there were many people, religious or no, who did do much unselfish good.

The explanation of altruism in evolutionary biology and evolutionary psychology has been a hot topic of the last several years. How do you explain social insects (e.g. ants and bees) if we all act selfishly to pass on our own genes (DNA) when the worker bees pass on none of their genes? Why do they work themselves to death for the benefit of their "cousins" when none of their own genes will be passed on as a result? Huh? "I will lay down my life for three brothers or eight cousins."

That was the intellectual gauntlet or glove-in-the-face. The quandary of the social insect has been satisfactorily answered. (I think the answer is something like: the relationship is so close that the worker bees do effectively pass on their genes.) But that does not answer the question which I would ask: Why are some humans almost completely altruistic and others almost completely selfish?

First, MRI studies (the brain readings) have shown that most of us get reptile (from the primitive brain area) pleasure when performing an altruistic act and a similar pleasure when performing a selfish act. Which shall I be? Helpful or selfish? It's an evolutionary tug of war. Second, game theory has shown that, in some situations, it is wiser to cooperate with others than to betray your fellows. BUT, once betrayed, it is wisest to crush the one who betrayed you. Those game theory studies were done with players who were on a sustained, relatively equal footing. That may represent your neighborhood. And, I would guess, most neighborhoods operate that way – with most of the neighbors trying to help each other in small ways. But most of the neighbors have a secret goal: to move to a better neighborhood.

Studies and observations made in a hierarchical setting (and I have fifty years of careful, non-prejudicial, scientific observations) show that the most ruthless and heartless are the most successful. "Most successful" meaning the most promoted. It is no accident that the current Pope is an ex-Nazi. And, in a hierarchical setting, superior performance is a hindrance to promotion (If you are supervising five or fifty people, promoting your best worker out of your group has the same stupid, damaging effect as firing your best worker [it is easier to promote a loud-mouthed; bossy nincompoop out of your jurisdiction than it is to fire her/him {and maybe, just maybe, s/he will remember you kindly}]). I have known many, many engineers who fully agreed with this assessment (please note Dilbert who is too kind to the system) and it was NOT as a result of sour grapes, most of these people did not give up and most were incapable of doing a poor job.

It is my observation that as we mature we go more and more in one direction or the other – more and more altruistic (and performance motivated) or more and more ruthless, sly, clever, selfish, trivial and worldly wealthier. We either go for the good feelings of service, helpfulness, performance and accomplishment or we go for the gold and the damn-the-torpedoes sent by our fellows (fuck you; I've got more money than you have).

The January 2009 Scientific American has a small article which shed some light on the matter for me. (What's Good for the Group) Does Natural Selection drive us to ruthless selfishness (betrayal of competitors ['kissin' up and pissin' down']) or can those with higher values (kindness, altruism) survive and prosper? (That last sentence was not a quote but it is a paraphrase.) Is making OUR group (family, tribe, neighborhood, village, city, country, and race) more healthy and fit, making it better and stronger, a good survival strategy? Or should we just take care of ourselves and our progeny? It is now generally conceded that evolution doesn't take place just at the organism unit or cellular level. Evolution takes place at every level. Survival of the fittest. Every unit whether virus, cell, organ, organism, family, neighborhood, village, city, country, continent, and, in fact, the whole earth struggles to survive. And the fit (on a species level) (and the lucky [on an individual level]) survive. Every unit cooperates when cooperation aids survival and betrays when betrayal makes survival more likely. We sentient beings can *choose* our path. I believe that that path becomes rutted at an early age. Probably no sane individual human is totally Selfish or entirely Altruistic. The world is too complicated for one to prosper (or even survive) if one were completely one or the other; either entirely Selfish or totally Altruistic. There is too much happenstance in life to claim that this characteristic or that habit will determine when you will die, how happy you will be before you die, or how much worldly acclaim or earthly possessions one shall have at the end or, even, on the way.

On an individual level you flip a coin and you die rich or you die poor. But, as a society, those who die with money, acclaim, and/or power tend to be of a certain type. In probability theory there is a Law of Large Numbers. It has been fifty years since I studied Probability but I think that the Law of Large Numbers is something like, "when an operation is performed many times, the average result will tend toward the probability of that result". Flip a nickel to see which one of you two pays for lunch and one and only one of you pays for lunch, the nickel comes up heads or tails not half-heads and half-tails. But go out to lunch every day for three years with the same guy and pay according to a flip and you will come out damn even. Flip an honest nickel 1000 times and you will get damn close to 500 heads and 500 tails; the probability of a head at each flip is 0.5 (0.5 X 1000 = 500).

What is life? Chance or Plan? The flip of a coin or the Law of Large Numbers? I'm a lucky sonuvabitch or 'the harder I work the luckier I get'? God damn; it is all of both! All predestination; all free-will. All luck and all hard work! The conflict and swing between luck and pluck is the stuff and twist of every story, every novel, every movie, every T.V. show. It is so extensive that it is difficult to illustrate by example. But I am not black, I am not gay, I am not blind, not deaf, not handicapped, not lame, not illiterate, not stupid, not superstitious, not an Einstein, not a Mozart, not a Dickens, not a Sampson; even my intellect is not my doing, it is the chance of the chance of the chance: my parents DNA, the particular egg of thousands dropped by my mother the particular sperm of hundreds-of-thousands released by my father; the particular sperm that won the race. The food that I was fed, my position as the youngest of thirteen, the religion given to me, the medical attention I received, the neighborhood in which I happened to be, the neighborhood kids that I played with, my schoolmates, etc. Beyond the beyond before that; the particular black man who wandered from Africa, his particular chance mating with an aboriginal female or Neanderthal. The direction that my next ancestor wandered or paddled; north, south, east, or west – by chance; his escape from a bear, a flood, a volcano, a tornado, a battle wound, a brush-fire, the flu, small pox, and religious fanatics. Fifty-thousand chance matings. One-hundred-thousand droughts. Two-hundred-thousand wars. Five-hundred-million lineages ended. Not mine. By chance.

My life has been all chance. My life has been all pre-ordained. My life has been all free-will decisions and pluck. All three statements true. When chance is dissected; deep in its belly is hard-work and plucky, intelligent effort (or some trend toward the opposite – laziness, stupidity). When the acclaim that I have earned is turned over; under its belly is luck. My position, which I could only obtain by persistent struggle, was pre-ordained for all of eternity.

Everything about us is the direct result of a random mutation. The fact that you have free-will is the result of a random mutation. Everything about us is luck, chance, happenstance. We like to kid ourselves that we are little gods in charge of our destiny. "We choose to be nice." "We decide to 'outsmart' (cheat) our neighbor".

Those "decisions" (luck, predestination) do make a difference. One by one they build a character, a personality, a reputation, an M.O. (modus operandi). One by one they create a birth; a situation, a track, a career, a result. "Choose" altruism; you may be happy but you almost certainly will not rule. "Choose" ruthlessness; you may gain acclaim, you may gain jail, but you have a chance of being President of Something. The Law-of-Large-Numbers dictates that, to be "President", you must be ruthless.

Your life is in your hands. Don't forget Your Life and Sex Island. It can be fun. It should be fun. Make it fun. Is the choice between happiness and acclaim really that difficult? Seems to be!

The End.

No, really, I mean it this time. The stuff that didn't fit here, I put in the next book: Your Lively and Sexy Island! Join us again. Please.

LaVergne, TN USA
21 August 2009
155535LV00002B/5/P

9 780982 496602